Jacques Derrida: Live Theory

GW00758968

Also available from Continuum:

Jean Baudrillard: Live Theory, Paul Hegarty
Hélène Cixous: Live Theory, Susan Sellers and Ian Blyth
Julia Kristeva: Live Theory, John Lechte and Maria Margaroni
Slavoj Žižek: Live Theory, Rex Butler

Jacques Derrida: Live Theory

James K. A. Smith

continuum
NEW YORK • LONDON

Continuum
The Tower Building, 11 York Road, London SE1 7NX
15 East 26th Street, New York, NY 10010

www.continuumbooks.com

British Library Cataloguing-in-Publication Data
A catalogue record for this book is available from the British Library.

ISBN 0–8264–6280–4 (hardback)
    0–8264–6281–2 (paperback)

Library of Congress Cataloging-in-Publication Data
Smith, K. A., 1970–
    Jacques Derrida: live theory/James Smith.
        p.cm.
    Includes bibliographical references and index.
    ISBN 0–8264–6280–4—ISBN 0–8264–6281–2 (pbk.)
        1. Derrida, Jacques. I. Title.
B2430.D484S54 2005
194—dc22   2005 048474

Typeset by RefineCatch Limited, Bungay, Suffolk
Printed and bound in Great Britain by
MPG Books Ltd., Bodmin

For Jim Olthuis and Jack Caputo:
teachers, mentors, friends,
and deconstructors *par excellence*

Deconstruction as such is reducible to neither a method nor an analysis . . . .
*That is why it is not negative, even though it has often been interpreted as such despite
all sorts of warning. For me, it always accompanies an affirmative exigency. I would
even say that is never proceeds without love.*
—Jacques Derrida, 1982

Contents

Preface   x

Abbreviations   xiv

Exergue: A Work of Mourning   xv

Introduction   Derrida's Other/An Other Derrida   1
   0.1   Demythologizing 'Derrida': On Myths and Monsters   1
       0.1.1   The Cambridge Affair   4
       0.1.2   The *New York Review of Books* Affair   7
   0.2   Demythologizing 'Deconstruction'   8
   0.3   The Lens of Alterity: Deconstruction and the Other   13

1   Words and Things: Phenomenology's Other   16
   1.1   In the Beginning was the Word   16
   1.2   Writing: The Very Idea   18
       1.2.1   'Away with the Body': Why Socrates Didn't Write   18
       1.2.2   Husserl's Archaeology of Geometry   19
       1.2.3   Deconstructing Euclid   23
          1.2.3.1   Language, Incarnation, and Objectivity   23
          1.2.3.2   And the Word was made Flesh: Writing and Incarnation   25
   1.3   Talking to Oneself: The Critique of Husserl   27
       1.3.1   Husserl's Theory of Signs   27
       1.3.2   The Sounds of Absence: Speech and Transcendence   30
          1.3.2.1   'Phonocentrism' and 'The Metaphysics of Presence'   31

| | 1.3.2.2 | Speech, Thought, and Community: The Semiotic Conditioning of Consciousness | 34 |

1.4   Writing Speech: On Language, Violence and the Other as Other   38
     1.4.1   Lévi-Strauss: Structuralism as Ethnocentrism   40
     1.4.2   Rousseau: The Other as Necessary Supplement   42
     1.4.3   *Arche*-writing and *Différance*: Why 'There is Nothing Outside of the Text'   43

2   The Other (as) Literature: Critical Literary Theory   46
   2.1   Philosophy's Others: Literature, for example   47
     2.1.1   Making Room: Literature and the Future of Philosophy   47
     2.1.2   The Secret Politics of Literature   51
   2.2   Post Cards from the Edge: A Metaphor for Metaphoricity   54
     2.2.1   The Irreducibility of Metaphor: or Why Plato Never Gets out of his Truck   54
     2.2.2   Post Cards: Performing the Metaphor   57
   2.3   Reference to the Other: Interpretation, Context and Community   61
     2.3.1   Reference and the Ethics of Interpretation   61
     2.3.2   Context and Community as Interpretive Guardrails   62

3   Welcoming the Other: Ethics, Hospitality, Religion   65
   3.1   Deconstruction *as* Justice: A Legal Hauntology   66
     3.1.1   Opening Borders: Asylum, Immigration and Cities of Refuge   68
     3.1.2   Opening Ourselves (to Offence): Forgiveness Without Condition   71
     3.1.3   Opening Europe to Its Other   72
     3.1.4   Opening the Academy: The University to Come   73
   3.2   Religion *as* Hospitality: Levinas and Kierkegaard as Proto-Deconstructors   75
     3.2.1   'The relation to the other, that is to say, *justice*': Levinas   76
     3.2.2   Every Other is Wholly Other: Kierkegaard's Abraham   80

3.3 The Politics of Deconstruction: The New
     International and the Democracy to Come   84
     3.3.1 Conjuring the Spirit of Marx   85
     3.3.2 What Are We Waiting For?: The
            Enlightenment to Come   88

4 Derrida on Others: Others on Derrida   92
   4.1 Feeding on Others: Derrida and the History of
        Philosophy   94
        4.1.1 Plato   94
        4.1.2 Nietzsche   96
        4.1.3 Heidegger   97
        4.1.4 Freud   98
        4.1.5 Other Others   98
   4.2 Others on Derrida: Responses to Deconstruction 99
        4.2.1 American Reception: The Yale School   99
        4.2.2 German Reception: Habermas and Gadamer 99
        4.2.3 Anglo-American Responses: Analytic
               Philosophy   102
        4.2.4 After 'Postmodernism': Eagleton, Žižek,
               Badiou   103

5 Authorship, Sovereignty and the Axiomatics of the Interview:
   Derrida 'Live'   104

Epilogue   118
   After Derrida   118

Bibliography   120
   Works by Jacques Derrida   120
   Select Books and Articles on Jacques Derrida in English 125

Notes   130

Name Index   151
Subject Index   154
Index of Derrida's work   157

Preface

Some stage-setting might help to specify (but not absolutely determine) what Derrida would call a 'horizon of reception' for *Jacques Derrida: Live Theory*. First, a word about audience: I have tried to produce a text that is, as we often hope, 'accessible' to the fabled 'general reader'. But perhaps more specifically, I have tried to write toward an engaged undergraduate – even if I hope it will find collateral targets as well. Much of the work on these texts was first broached in the context of undergraduate seminars (at Loyola Marymount University and Calvin College) and this pedagogical context surely marks (and hopefully has improved) the book. Given my targets, scholars of Derrida will inevitably be disappointed with aspects of this book (though I hope they might also find some elements of illumination); on almost every page one could object: 'Yes, but it's much more complicated than that.' Or conversely, those already familiar with Derrida will find here what seem to be many statements of the obvious. Such are the risks of a project such as this. Derrida perhaps more than anyone was attentive to the way in which context governs the reading and reception of a work. Undoubtedly I make some moves here that are 'too fast', as scholars sometimes say, or that call for 'unpacking' (another favourite in the lexicon of scholarese). To be sure: but this book is an invitation into a corpus and a project, not an exhaustive, critical account. Indeed, I have for the most part bracketed a forthrightly critical voice, inviting the reader to first, charitably and sympathetically, try to inhabit Derrida's world. Those scholars or more advanced readers who are looking for more exhaustive analyses and critical engagements could consult my other work.

With this in mind, I have made two methodological decisions that govern the book and should be noted: First, growing out of the practices of my own pedagogy, and a conviction that much misunderstanding of Derrida has stemmed from a simple failure to *read* him first-hand, I have given a certain pride of place to expositions of important, classic texts in Derrida's corpus. Core aspects of each chapter involve a fairly close, though necessarily brief, exposition of texts that have either been important in the reception of Derrida across the disciplines or that I think deserve a wider appreciation in order to read Derrida well. The selection of texts that receive such attention is necessarily limited and is not at all meant to carve out a 'canon within the canon' of Derrida's corpus. While I hope the selections are representative, they are by no means exhaustive. Indeed, there are many important texts that receive little attention here, particularly the works on art (*Truth in Painting*, *Artaud*, *Memoirs of the Blind*), some of the important works on literary figures (Joyce, Mallarmé, etc.), and some of the more intentional engagements with psychoanalysis. I can only plead the conditions of finitude. However, I do hope the expositions in this book would provide a platform for further exploration of these other, rich fields in Derrida's corpus. Second, working in the spirit of the 'Live Theory' series – even if deconstruction will call its animating impetus into question – I have also given a certain privilege, or at least edge, to the vast corpus of Derrida's interviews as portals into his texts. Drawing on the interviews is not meant to be a *substitute* for engaging his published works, but rather as a catalyst for such reading. But the interviews also have a pedagogical value as points of entry.

The result is that the genre of this book hovers somewhere between commentary, anthology, and critical analysis. This stems partly from the nature of its task, but also partly from a desire to provide a 'performative' introduction to Derrida, whose works cross the same boundaries. One might suggest there is a 'midrashic' element to it, with my voice glossing in and around Derrida's texts, strung together here in view of certain themes. I have tried, as much as possible, to let Derrida's voice come through, seeing myself as something of a conduit of deconstruction's energy and passion (as Derrida says, 'We are all mediators, translators' [*Points*, 116]) without the naïvete of claiming to speak 'for' Derrida.

With these concerns about audience and fidelity in mind, I have also foregone extensive engagements with secondary literature (one can find that in my other writings on Derrida, including a forthcoming monograph) and tried to keep footnotes to a minimum. This is simply a pedagogical strategy and is not tainted by any naïve notion of presenting the 'real' Derrida or 'pure' Derrida. My reading and interpretation of Derrida is deeply layered and owes much to commentators and critics. But for the sake of a first encounter with Derrida, I have tried to keep the reader focused on his corpus; the suggestions for further reading and the bibliographies at the end of the volume will point the interested reader to a wealth of secondary literature.

Completion of this project was made possible by a sabbatical leave granted by Calvin College – a community to which I am deeply indebted. A grant from the Calvin Alumni Association made it possible for me to take up residence as a Visiting Fellow in the Faculty of Divinity at the University of Cambridge in the Michaelmas term of 2004, during which this manuscript was completed. This seemed fitting, as Derrida – despite a nasty 'affair' that he occasioned there – praised Cambridge because it 'chose not to close its doors to what is coming'. Indeed, he notes that 'Cambridge is for me always exemplary' and 'I am glad to remain, *honoris causa*, a proud and grateful Doctor of the University of Cambridge' (*Points*, 418). My sincere thanks to the Alumni Association for their support of faculty research, and to the faculty at Cambridge for their hospitality. During our time in Cambridge we also enjoyed the hospitality of the Christian community at Tyndale House, for which I extend my gratitude.

When I accepted Tristan Palmer's kind invitation to write this book, I was still young and foolish enough to have the hubris it would take to venture such a project. I have found the experience deeply humbling, and coupled with the death of Jacques Derrida in the closing months of my work on the book (see the 'Exergue' below), I must confess to a nagging sense of not being able to measure up to the task. But such is the very nature of responsibility, Derrida would remind us. My thanks to Hywel Evans, Sarah Douglas, Anya Wilson, Rebecca Simmonds and the folks at Continuum for their patience in bringing the project to completion. Special thanks also to Nathan Sytsma, one of my students from Calvin on sojourn in Oxford while I was in Cambridge. Nathan read the manuscript with care and interest, providing helpful feedback and comments that have undoubtedly improved the book.

Coming back to Derrida in this way, for this kind of project, has been both disconcerting and reinvigorating. Perhaps most of all, after having spent the past few years launching criticisms of Derrida (criticisms which I think are warranted, and which I will continue to develop), I found myself re-affirming much – like returning to a first love. So I would like to dedicate the book to those who have taught me the most about Derrida: Jim Olthuis, my graduate advisor at the Institute for Christian Studies in Toronto, and Jack Caputo, my *Doktorvater* at Villanova University (now at Syracuse). Jim and Jack have been not only outstanding teachers, but continue as mentors and are cherished as friends. It was they who taught me that deconstruction, above all, is a work of love – and I love them for that.

Cambridge
Advent 2004

Abbreviations

In order to facilitate reference to Derrida's corpus, I have adopted a system of abbreviations of Derrida's texts that are most often cited in the book. Here I have simply listed the title and date of publication (in French/English); full bibliographical information for each title is included in the bibliography.

Ad	*Adieu to Emmanuel Levinas* (1997/1999)
FL	' "Force of Law": The Mystical Foundation of Authority' (1992)
GD	*The Gift of Death* (1992/1995)
IHOG	*Introduction to Husserl's* Origin of Geometry (1962/1978)
Linc	*Limited Inc* (1988/1990)
MP	*Margins of Philosophy* (1972/1982)
OCF	*On Cosmopolitanism and Forgiveness* (1997/2001)
OG	*Of Grammatology* (1967/1976)
PC	*The Post Card* (1980/1987)
Points	*Points . . . : Interviews, 1974–1994* (1992/1995)
SM	*Specters of Marx* (1993/1994)
SP	*Speech and Phenomena* (1967/1972)
Taste	*A Taste for the Secret* (1997/2001)
WD	*Writing and Difference* (1967/1978)

Exergue: A Work of Mourning

Jacques Derrida took up with vigour the Socratic vocation of philosophy as a kind of dying. Notoriously linked to discourses on 'the death of the author' (and almost universally misunderstood on this score), Derrida's work was regularly haunted by ghosts. In the closing months of my work on this book, Jacques Derrida died of pancreatic cancer (in the early hours of 9 October 2004). Death, which inscribed itself in his corpus, has now left its mark on his body, and we are left to mourn. But that is only to say that we are left with the task of deconstruction: what Derrida described as the work of mourning. It is not without reason that some of his most powerful meditations – on Levinas, de Man, Deleuze, Lyotard and others – come to us in the form of eulogies and memorials.

It has been the mistake of his critics – both in the academy and media – to conclude from Derrida's complicity with death that deconstruction is simply the next nihilism. And so Derrida has been vilified as the enemy of truth, justice, the university, and many more of our cherished institutions and values. The myths and lies – yes, lies – about Derrida persist even in his death, evidenced by the obituaries in major newspapers such as the *New York Times* or journals such as the *New Criterion*. But this is a picture of Derrida and deconstruction that one could only have by failing to read him – and the restatement of these caricatures after Derrida's death seemed to justify a strategy I had already adopted for the book: seeking to demythologize the 'Derrida myth' that circulated in both the academy and the media. For in the end – or better, from the beginning – deconstruction is a work of love. Far from being a mere 'method' for critique, Derrida was at pains to demonstrate the essentially productive aspect of deconstruction. 'It is not negative', he once commented, 'for me, it always accompanies an affirmative exigency. I would even say that it never proceeds without love . . .'.

The news of Derrida's death came as a surprise, though we've known of his illness for over a year now. Most surprising is how sad it has made me. I received the news here in Cambridge (site of an infamous 'Derrida affair'), at work on a book whose title now seems ironic, perhaps even perverse, maybe secretly wishful: how could we continue to speak of Derrida's as a 'Live Theory'?

I initially took up this project as an invitation to return to texts I read a decade ago, though many I've never stopped reading. Just days before Derrida's death, *Of Grammatology* was on my desk and its tattered pages (and my sophomoric marginalia) were like a song that brought me back to a time, a place. Having spent the last few years launching criticisms of Derrida, after working *through* Derrida, this project brought me back to a deep appreciation for how much I owe to his work. In the week before his death, I had shared with a friend my excitement about sending a copy to Prof. Derrida as a small token of appreciation. The news of his death came to interrupt those plans. All of a sudden I found myself with a package – a care package with a little love note inside – but no address, no recipient (a scenario that would have interested the author of *The Post Card*).

Hidden in my sadness, I suspect, is an element of guilt, for I had also hoped that the book could be a token of apology. When I last saw Derrida, I was presenting a paper at the American Academy of Religion – a fairly blistering critique of his notion of hope, and Prof. Derrida was in the audience. We didn't have a chance to discuss the paper because Derrida had to hurry off to a book-signing (he was such a rock star). While I stand by the critique, I'm disappointed we didn't have that conversation, and more disappointed by the asymmetry of my brash-ness and Derrida's graciousness. For what I always found most disarm-ing about this intellectual giant was his personal humility – a kenotic humility that could put his critics to shame. I had been hoping that *Jacques Derrida: Live Theory* could correct the picture a bit, and be a sign of my profound debts to Derrida and respect for his labours. This reminds us of something that Derrida persistently emphasizes (emphasized, I guess – will I ever get used to the past tense when think-ing of Jacques?): remaining faithful to a thinker will require a certain break; being an authentic 'follower' will require that one part ways at some point, in the name of fidelity. While I make no claim to be a follower or 'acolyte' of Derrida, I owe him much. And if I must at times depart from the direction of his thinking, this is often in the name of following Jacques Derrida. It will be strange and lonely not being able to find new tracks.

In one of the treasures of his corpus, 'Circumfession', Derrida gives us a hint of his hopes in death:

when I am not dreaming of making love, or being a resistance fighter in the last war blowing up bridges or trains, I want one thing only, and that is to lose myself in the orchestra I would form with my sons, heal, bless and seduce the whole world by playing divinely with my sons, produce with them the world's ecstasy, *their* creation. I will accept dying if dying is to sink slowly, yes, into the bottom of this beloved music.

The viability of deconstruction as a 'live theory' – a live option in theory – might be understood as a question of survival. The Italian philosopher Gianni Vattimo once put a question to Derrida about death and the thought of survival: 'do you think about a "survival" [afterlife] or not?' 'I think about nothing *but* death,' was Derrida's reply. 'I think about it all the time, ten seconds don't go by without the imminence of the thing being there. I never stop analyzing the phenomenon of "survival" as the structure of surviving, it's really the only thing that interests me, but precisely insofar as I do not believe that one lives on post mortem' (*Taste*, 88). If *Jacques Derrida: Live Theory* has an apologetic function, beyond exposition, then it might be taken as a sign that Derrida 'lives on' (*survivre*), making a case for the survival of deconstruction as a live option in theory and cultural critique, even after Derrida.

Introduction

Derrida's Other / An Other Derrida

0.1 Demythologizing 'Derrida': On Myths and Monsters

Not very many philosophers have made it to the ranks of the notorious. Usually toiling away in abstraction, and having little impact on the university as a whole – let alone culture or politics – philosophers generally escape such villainizations. In other words, they tend to be too irrelevant to ever be notorious. The demonization of Jacques Derrida, then, could be taken as a sign of his impact and relevance beyond the narrow corridors of professional philosophy, spilling over onto the university as a whole – and beyond that to the worlds of art and design, politics, institutional life, and even popular culture. Beyond the influence of 'deconstruction' (that we'll employ, for now, as a shorthand for Derrida's work) on diverse disciplines such as literary theory, architecture, education, and theology, the lexicon of deconstruction has permeated popular discourse and practices – from music[1] to cuisine.[2] But it is precisely the ubiquity of deconstruction in popular and academic discourse which has posed a problem for Derrida's work, in two ways: first, almost all of the popular appropriations of the lexicon of deconstruction (the term itself, but also related themes such as binary oppositions, margins, *pharmakon*, etc.) are *mis*-appropriations, enlisting both the terms of deconstruction and the name of Jacques Derrida for some of the most silly – or, conversely, most traditional and hegemonic – cultural projects. Unfortunately, this is also the case even for many academic appropriations of deconstruction. The way in which Derrida's work is adopted, and then touted so pervasively in both academic and popular culture, fosters a widespread but deeply mistaken perception of both the man and his 'project'. Second, it is just this diffusion of Derrida's work which seems to provoke the ire of the guardians of the status quo who draft Derrida into the armies of the 'culture wars' – a surely unique instance in which one is drafted by the enemy, into the army the enemy opposes, in order to be set up as a target. First mis-understanding Derrida (often by failing to read him), then taking the popular and academic misappropriations of deconstruction as vicarious presentations of Derrida's own project, these culture war critics of deconstruction see it as a kind of virus whose infected hosts are 'spreading' deconstruction as a cultural disease. Thus, deconstruction has been demonized as the enemy of truth, justice, and yes, the American way – along with being an enemy of a host of other ideals and institutions, including the university, morality, reason, and more.[3] And because such critics of deconstruction often command powerful portals of cultural influence – the op-ed pages of international newspapers, for instance – their status quo rejection of what they take to be deconstruction has a pervasive inoculating effect, furthering the strategies of avoidance – avoiding, above all, the hard work of actually *reading* Derrida[4] – that these same critics have practised.

The result of both exuberant (mis)appropriations and aggressive dismissals has been the Frankenstein-ish creation of a kind of Derrida-monster: a mythic creature that either inspires rapture or pro-vokes terror. Derrida himself provides us with a conceptual apparatus to consider the creation of this Derrida-monster. First, the monster is often a kind of hybrid, 'a composite figure of heterogeneous organisms that are grafted onto each other. This graft, this hybridization, this com-position that puts heterogeneous bodies together might be a monster' (*Points*, 385). Second, the monster is 'that which appears for the first time and, consequently, is not yet recognized. A monster is a species for which we do not yet have a name' (*Points*, 386). Characterized by both novelty and strangeness, the monster emerges from the lagoon of familiarity, shows itself (*elle se montre*), but because we lack the categories to consti-tute it – and often because its very strangeness frightens us – we invest it with monstrosity.[5] Third, at the moment the monster is named as a monster, it is tamed: 'as soon as one perceives a monster in a monster, one begins to domesticate it, one begins, because of the "as such" – it is a monster *as* monster – to compare it to the norms, to analyze it, con-sequently to master whatever could be terrifying in this figure of the monster' (*Points*, 386). As an example, consider one of the final scenes from Disney's *Beauty and the Beast*: the anonymous Beast has made a sort of 'gift without return,' releasing Belle even though it means accepting his monstrous state forever. Gaston, who is both the quintessential male of the village and villain of the narrative, seizes upon the magic mirror which gives him a glimpse into the Beast's castle. Confronted by a creature which appears to him for the first time – a creature that seems to be a hideous and dangerous hybrid of man (walking upright, speaking) and beast (covered in fur, with paws and fangs), Gaston names the Beast as *monster* precisely in order to incite the wrath of the village, demonizing the beast, and thereby domesticating it like all of the other animals that hang on the wall of Gaston's lodge: it is simply an object to be hunted like the rest.[6]

Has not Derrida, unwittingly, just provided us with a framework to understand his own reception? If deconstruction has been perceived as a kind of monster slouching toward Gomorrah, could deconstruction itself provide the tools to deconstruct this reception?

Or, to put it otherwise, we might say that the diffusion of deconstruction across culture and the academy has generated the myth of 'Derrida', whose narrative repeats and disseminates so many misunderstandings of deconstruction – sometimes 'in the name of' deconstruction, sometimes as a target or enemy to be guarded against.

And so there is a great deal of haunting associated with Derrida. On the one hand, his work haunts us and our institutions; on the other hand, deconstruction has for a long time been haunted by the Derrida-monsters created by others. I have here invoked this scene of haunting in order to stage our task. Against the horizon of these monsters and myths – the Derrida-monster that ranges across the academy, or the 'Derrida'[7] myth that is told and retold in papers and journals – the primary task of this book is to stage a first-hand, albeit mediated, encounter with Derrida in order to 'demythologize' this pervasive myth of 'Derrida'. Or, to run with the monster metaphor, our goal is not to *domesticate* deconstruction or to eliminate its monstrosity, but rather to properly understand its monstrosity: it is not the kind of monster we think it is (though monster it be).[8] By undertaking this opening strategy, I don't mean to privilege Derrida's critics; rather, as Derrida himself emphasizes, we must begin 'from where we are'. Any fresh engagement with Derrida finds itself surrounded by these myths and monsters; it would be naïve to imagine otherwise.[9] Furthermore, Derrida himself often tries to explain deconstruction by indicating what it is *not*, and in doing so, explicitly responds to misreadings. But the challenge here is unique, for the 'Derrida' myth is something that has been promulgated by both friends and foes – by exuberant acolytes and virulent detractors. So if our opening task is to demythologize Derrida, this will require rescuing him, as it were, from both his admirers and his enemies. If I am interested in guarding Derrida from the unfounded attacks of his enemies, I am equally interested in saving Derrida from those assistant professors of English and cultural theory who tend to read Derrida as if he dropped from the sky, ignoring the phenomenological milieu out of which his work arose. We will need to be attentive, then, to the history of Derrida's reception (what Gadamer would call 'the history of effect'), particularly in the United States. By situating Derrida in the 'theory wars' (*New Criterion* vs. *Critical Inquiry*), I hope to sketch something of a third way in understanding Derrida and deconstruction. At the same time, one of my goals is to write an introduction to Derrida that both the *New Criterion* and *Critical Inquiry* camps would at least consider 'fair'.

This *via negativa* and demythologizing, however, will only be an opening gambit; we will then move to a more constructive and affirmative account of Derrida and deconstruction. In order to carry out this demythologizing, I want to first unpack the elements of this 'Derrida' myth, or what we might also describe as the 'received' Derrida. The mythic 'Derrida' is crystallized in two famous 'Derrida Affairs', which are symptomatic and indicative of broader sentiments. Each of them highlights a side of the 'Derrida' myth: on the one hand, Derrida is said to be intentionally obscurantist and difficult precisely in order to create something of a cultic following, thereby undermining the procedures of rational discourse which govern the space of the university. On the other hand, deconstruction is taken to mean, given the supposed 'death of the author', that 'anything goes' – that interpretation is cut loose from any criteria, detached from any concern with authorial intention, and thus gives rise to a hermeneutical nihilism.

0.1.1 The Cambridge Affair

The stakes of reading Derrida, in both the academy and broader culture, were intensely and publicly brought to the surface in 1992 when a proposal was made at Cambridge University to award Derrida an honorary degree (doctorate *honoris causa*). Almost immediately after the proposal was made, opposition manifested itself, calling for an almost unprecedented vote by the faculty of the university: a vote of *placet* to support the award, *non-placet* in opposition. Each of the camps, *placet* and *non-placet*, circulated 'flysheets' which made their case, and faculty of the university were invited to lend their signatures in support.[10] The picture of Derrida that emerges from the *non-placet* flysheets is a classic formulation of the Derrida myth and the supposed threat of the Derrida-monster. They charge Derrida with undermining the very task of scholarship: 'despite occasional disclaimers, the major preoccupation and effect of his voluminous work has been to deny and to dissolve those standards of evidence and argument on which all academic disciplines are based'.[11] Among Derrida's 'doctrines' – a term which, as Christopher Norris points out, surely indicates they've failed to really understand Derrida – they include the assertion that 'all texts, and all interpretations of texts, are on a par' and the related 'doctrine' concerning 'the irrelevance of an author's views and the impossibility of distinguishing correct from incorrect interpretations'.[12] But, in a move that we will see is common, what generates such ferocious response to the Derrida-monster is the *threat* it poses. 'What determines us to oppose this award', they conclude, 'is not just the absurdity of these doctrines, but their dismaying implications for all serious academic subjects. . . . By denying the distinctions between fact and fiction, observation and imagination, evidence and prejudice, they make complete nonsense of science, technology, and medicine. In politics, they deprive the mind of its defences against dangerously irrational ideologies and regimes.'[13] The Derrida-monster is seen as a threat that has crossed the Channel and, quite beyond dismantling the university as such, would also brainwash us into passively accepting the ideologies of tyrannical political regimes. Dangerous indeed.

As an illustration of the way the provocation of Derrida spills over the boundaries of the academy into a more public culture, the international media quickly became involved. Derrida's critics then seized upon the media as a venue to launch a critique (without evidence), most famously in a letter written to *The Times* of London (9 May 1992). Led by Barry Smith, the signatories of the letter included (mainly analytic) philosophers from a number of countries – but notably, not a single signatory from Cambridge.[14] The letter in *The Times* charges Derrida above all with failing to meet 'accepted standards of clarity and rigour': 'M. Derrida's voluminous writings in our view stretch the normal forms of academic scholarship beyond recognition. Above all – as every reader can establish for himself (and for this purpose any page will do[15]) – his work employs a written style that defies comprehension' (*Points*, 420). 'When the effort is made to penetrate it,' they continue, 'it becomes clear, to us at least, that, where coherent assertions are being made at all, these are either false or trivial' (*Points*, 420).

The same sorts of charges were repeated, after the vote was decided in Derrida's favour, from *within* Cambridge.[16] In a post-affair document, Brian Hebblethwaite amped up the rhetoric: 'One has only to read a little of Derrida's writing to become aware that one is dealing with a thoroughly decadent strand in modern philosophy.'[17] Then his vitriolic rhetoric gets on a roll: 'Derrida's work is particularly degenerate in its contempt for argumentative rigour and clarity of expression, and in its predilection for barbarous neologisms and idiotic word-play in the interests of relentless "deconstruction" ' (*Points*, 109). He then moves beyond mere questions of a barbarous style to what he sees as the content and effects of deconstruction, *viz*., 'Derrida's deliberate attempt to undermine all stable meaning and reference, and to "deconstruct" all identifiable authorial intention' (*Points*, 109); 'he deliberately sets himself to destroy the conditions of sensible discussion' (*Points*, 109); and his work 'is pernicious just because it attacks the very basic values of philosophy as such and of the university as such,[18] namely, disinterested search for truth, commitment to rational enquiry, respect for great minds, their insights and their power to illuminate reality' (*Points*, 110). Derrida is, quite simply one of 'the enemies of reason, truth, and objectivity' (*Points*, 111).[19] What a monster.

This kind of rhetoric repeated the criticisms of Derrida that had already been aired in the States by Alan Bloom, John Searle and others. This was particularly true of the *New Criterion*, a conservative journal of criticism and the arts which never missed an opportunity to demonstrate its disdain for all things deconstructive. Indeed, in an early article, René Wellek charged Derrida (and others) with nothing less than 'destroying literary studies'.[20] Mistakenly taking it that the 'new theory' (i.e., deconstruction) 'asserts that man lives in a prison house of language that has no relation to reality', Wellek teases out the effects of its most 'extreme formulation' (and Jacques Derrida is 'the philosopher who, for American students, has formulated this view most impressively'): it 'looks for the abolition of man, denies the self, and sees language as a free-floating system of signs, the theory leads to total skepticism and ultimately to nihilism'.[21] Thus he charges Derrida with propounding 'the preposterous theory that writing precedes speaking, a claim refuted by every child and by the thousand spoken languages that have no written languages'.[22] For Wellek, Derrida isn't just obscurantist or mistaken, but stupid. And Wellek's criticism anticipates what would later be said of the notion of Derrida as a 'virus', spreading itself and infecting others:[23] 'If this were an isolated instance of the whim of a learned man, it might be harmless. Unfortunately, it has been widely imitated, with less wit and learning, and has encouraged utter caprice, extreme subjectivity, and hence the destruction of the very concepts of knowledge and truth.'[24] Again, we are given a picture of Derrida as a monstrous *threat*, emerging from the continent to undermine the Anglo-Saxon values of knowledge, truth and rational discourse.

0.1.2 The *New York Review of Books* Affair

Within a year of the 'Cambridge affair', Derrida found himself embroiled in another, this time Stateside. Some background to set the stage is in order (for a full account, see *Points* 422–454). In 1987, Victor Farias published *Heidegger et le nazisme* – a book that received much attention in France as it sought to 'unveil' Heidegger's complicity with National Socialism in the 1930s.[25] Farias's account, which appeared 'new' to those not engaged with Heidegger scholarship, seemed to underwrite a dismissal of the Heideggerian corpus *tout court*, suggesting that the taint of Heidegger's Nazism excused us from the burden of grappling with his thought. Derrida could not accept such a facile conclusion, and stated as much both in *Of Spirit* (appearing just a few days after Farias's book appeared in France), and then in an interview with Didier Eribon, published in *Le Nouvel Observateur* (now republished in *Points* 181–190). When in New York some time later, Derrida found an English translation of this interview included in a volume edited by Richard Wolin.[26] Derrida's text – which was subjected to vigorous critique by the volume's editor – was included in the book, and translated, without the editor soliciting or securing Derrida's permission.[27] Derrida protested, through a lawyer, but without taking legal action; as a result, Columbia University Press withdrew the book and it was published in a second edition, without Derrida's text, by MIT. When Thomas Sheehan reviewed the book for the *New York Review of Books*, a third of his review was devoted to this 'Derrida affair', and for the next several months the Letters column of *NYRB* was the site of an animated, at times nasty, exchange.

Even scholars without any interest or time for deconstruction couldn't help hearing rumblings about the supposed 'death of the author' linked to Jacques Derrida (and Barthes and Foucault). As we've already seen, the term had become synonymous with supposed claims that interpretation was without criteria, that authorial intent played no role in the understanding of texts, and that authors exerted no control over their texts. So when Jacques Derrida, in a very public forum like the *NYRB*, asserted his *rights* as an author, critics who had bought this myth were quick to seize upon the oh-so-poetic irony: 'Here is Jacques Derrida', they seemed to say, 'the hermeneutic monster who has rent asunder any relationship between texts and authors, all of a sudden asserting his rights *as an author!*' Indeed, in one of his letters, Wolin doesn't miss a chance to turn the deconstructive tables and suggest a certain performative contradiction between Derrida's philosophical claims and his authorial practice: Derrida, Wolin noted, 'seemed so preoccupied with the *legal* aspects of the situation (*faire valoir mes droits* seemed to be his favorite refrain) and with the prerogatives of "authorship" (in a rather *anti-deconstructionist spirit*, I must add; for how can he consider himself the sole author of and possessor of rights to *an interview*, which is, after all, a joint venture?)'.[28] The effect of such a move was a *domestication* of the Derrida-monster, albeit a domestication that relied upon precisely what it sought to tame.

Both of these 'affairs' offer two manifestations of the 'Derrida' myth and give us a sense of how the academy has responded to the threat of the Derrida-monster, even if the monster is of their own creation.

0.2 Demythologizing 'Deconstruction'

When faced with such aggressive and vitriolic responses to his work – even academic pogroms of a sort – Derrida formulates the matter in terms that invoke the monstrous, the *threat* of the monster. 'What can these people have felt threatened by to lose their self-control in this way' (*Points*, 403)? Those external scholars who intervened in the Cambridge proceedings did so 'on the pretext of saving or immunizing Cambridge against evil, contagion, decadence' (*Points*, 403) – trying to prevent by any means the spread of the Derrida virus. In response to such protective measures, Derrida does not seek to undercut the monstrosity of deconstruction. His response is not quite, 'I'm not a monster', but rather, 'I'm not the monster you think I am; I'm not *that* kind of monster'. And in fact, he might continue, 'in creating your Derrida-monster and spinning the "Derrida" myth, you've actually been at work *domesticating* deconstruction by reducing it to something silly, absurd, or foolish. By attributing the most ridiculous claims to "deconstruction", you've sought to tame the *real* threat that deconstruction poses.' Thus Derrida does not deny that deconstruction has a certain monstrosity about it:

> it's often the active involvement of students and younger teachers which makes certain of our colleagues nervous to the point that they lose their sense of moderation and of the academic rules they invoke when they attack me and my work. If this work seems so threatening to them, this is because it isn't simply eccentric or strange, incomprehensible or exotic (which would allow them to dispose of it easily), but as I myself hope, and as they believe

more than they admit, competent, rigorously argued, and carrying conviction in its re-examination of the fundamental norms and premises of a number of dominant discourses, the principles underlying many of their evaluations, the structures of academic institutions, and the research that goes on within them (*Points*, 409).

What, then, *is* 'deconstruction?' Who is Jacques Derrida? What is he about? If the 'Derrida' myth gives the lie, what are we to make of Derrida? If the Derrida-monster is not the monster we thought it was, what is the nature of its monstrosity? What *does* deconstruction threaten? What kind of monster is Derrida? One of our goals here is to dispel the 'Derrida' myth by better understanding the nature of deconstruction's monstrosity. And what we will find is not exactly a 'friendly' monster, but perhaps something quite akin to Frankenstein's monster: a creature with deeply affirmative, positive desires.

Derrida, however, often seeks to dispel the myths around deconstruction by a kind of *via negativa*, enunciating what deconstruction is not.[29] And the catalogue is often quite lengthy, as a number of things have been attributed to deconstruction. Derrida commonly emphasizes the following *nots*:

- *Deconstruction is not a 'method'*. By this, Derrida means to indicate that deconstruction is not a 'technique' that could be reduced to a formula or set of rules, then 'applied' to any text or context in a programmatic way. Indeed, such a notion – fostered, no doubt, by undergraduate introductions to literary theory – is one of the primary ways that the 'Derrida' myth has been spread.[30] First, and most basically, Derrida underscores that 'deconstruction could not be reduced to some methodological instrumentality or to a set of rules and transposable procedures'; this is because there is a sense in which 'each deconstructive "event" remains singular'.[31] But secondly, and most provocatively, Derrida stresses that 'deconstruction is not even an *act* or an *operation*';[32] that is, deconstruction is not even something that we *do*. Rather, deconstruction happens *in the middle voice*, as it were: *Ça se déconstruit*. It deconstructs itself. Deconstruction is not the effect of a master interpreter who comes and does something *to* a text, nor the result of bringing external tools or appliances to work 'on' a text. Rather, deconstruction happens *within* texts, from inside, out of their own resources. There is a sense, then, in which we the interpreters are only witnesses (or perhaps, to invoke the Socratic metaphor, 'midwives') to a text's deconstruction of itself.[33]

- *Deconstruction is not a merely negative 'destruction'.* This is perhaps how the term has been most commonly misappropriated, as a mere synonym for destruction, or meaning simply 'to take apart'. This is to miss the movement of the *con* in the word: deconstruction is a double-movement of dismantling with a view to rebuilding. Thus, Derrida emphasizes that behind his adoption of the term 'deconstruction' we should hear the echoes of Heidegger's notions of *Destruktion* or *Abbau*, which are not simply negative, but also reconstructive (so the *Destruktion* of Western metaphysics is not simply the rejection or annihilation of metaphysics, but a critical reconstituting). Thus, recalling that 'deconstruction' was a term adopted in the context of 'structuralism' as the dominant discourse in the human sciences, Derrida emphasizes that 'the undoing, decomposing, and desedimenting of structures, in a certain sense more historical than the structuralist movement it called into question, was not a negative operation. Rather than destroying, it was also necessary to understand how an "ensemble" was constituted and to reconstruct it to this end.'[34] Despite reports to the contrary, deconstruction is fundamentally interested in institutions – in breaking open institutional frameworks, not in the name of anarchy, but with a view to more just institutions. 'Deconstruction concerns, first of all, systems. This does not mean that it brings down the system, but that it opens onto possibilities of arrangement or assembling, of being together if you like, that are not necessarily systematic' (*Points*, 212).

- *Deconstruction is not a 'master' name.* Derrida was always surprised at how this one term – 'deconstruction' – got taken up so quickly and so widely. 'When I chose this word, or when it imposed itself upon me . . . I little thought that it would be credited with such a central role in the discourse that interested me at the time.'[35] In fact, 'this word, at least on its own, has never appeared satisfactory to me (but what word is), and must always be girded by an entire discourse'.[36] Thus, one has to understand the term within its context, since 'the word "deconstruction", like all other words, acquires its value only from its inscription in a chain of possible substitutions, in what is too blithely called a "context" '. The context of the term is a string of other terms which are quasi-substitutes (though none have been taken up like 'deconstruction'); these would include '*écriture*', 'trace', 'différance', 'supplement', 'hymen', '*pharmakon*', 'margin', etc.[37]

- *Deconstruction is not a nihilism.* Many have taken Derrida to be advocating a kind of apolitical aestheticism 'beyond good and evil' and have thus levelled the charge of nihilism against deconstruction. Taking deconstruction to be opposed to any sense of meaning or truth, they see in Derrida a celebration of a play of forces without end – presenting deconstruction 'as a sort of gratuitous chess game with a combination of signs, closed up in language as in a cave'.[38] But Derrida patently refuses the label. 'Deconstruction is not an enclosure in nothingness, but an openness towards the other.'[39] This openness towards the other, we will see below, names the ethico-political heart of deconstruction.[40] Thus, far from being a new nihilism, Derrida emphasizes that deconstruction is not even a relativism: 'I take into account differences', he contends, 'but I am no relativist.' Relativism is a 'doctrine', a 'way of referring to the absolute and denying it; it states that there are only cultures and that there is no pure science or truth. I never said such a thing. Neither have I ever used the word relativism.'[41]

- *Deconstruction is not anti-philosophical.* While deconstruction questions philosophy, and calls into question both the practices and institutions of philosophy as it has been handed down in the West, it is not opposed to philosophy *as such*, nor is it opposed to the university *as such*. Indeed, it seems clear that critics who have levelled such charges have remained ignorant of Derrida's long-standing investment in the institutions of philosophy and his advocacy for the discipline (in his involvement with GREPH, the *Groupe de recherche sur l'enseignement de la philosophie*) and the Collège International de Philosophie. Much of Derrida's professional life has been devoted to the culture and practices of educational institutions – and the place of philosophy within them – from grade school to postgraduate levels. He has been intimately involved with programmes to expand philosophy's presence in the grade school curriculum (in his work with GREPH) and was one of the key figures involved in the launch of the Collège International de Philosophie, a unique institution of inter-disciplinary research.[42] This does not mean, of course, that deconstruction is friendly to current or given configurations of academic institutions or contemporary philosophical practice. As Derrida remarks, 'deconstruction can also serve to question the presumption of certain university and cultural institutions to act as the sole or privileged guardians and transmitters of meaning. . . . There is in deconstruction something which challenges every teaching institution. It is not a question of calling for the destruction of such institutions, but rather of making us aware of what we are in fact doing when we subscribe to this or that institutional way of reading literature [for instance].'[43] Derrida undertakes such questioning, not *against* philosophy, but in the name of philosophy and of a university 'to come' – 'indissociable from the great question of *democracy to come*' (*Points*, 338).

In this brief sketch of what deconstruction is *not*, we have already begun – in good apophatic fashion – to get a sense of what deconstruction *is*. Deconstruction is a deeply affirmative mode of critique attentive to the way in which texts, structures and institutions marginalize and exclude 'the other', with a view to reconstructing and reconstituting institutions and practices to be more just (i.e., to respond to the call of the other). So while it is a mode of radical critique, it is also moved by affirmation: 'I cannot conceive of a radical critique', Derrida confesses, 'which would not be ultimately motivated by some sort of affirmation, acknowledged or not.'[44] The critique is affirmative in the sense that it is responding to something other: the critique is undertaken with a view to something to which we are *responsible* and also with a view to a certain *future*, a vision of what is 'to come'.[45] 'I mean,' Derrida continues, 'that deconstruction is, in itself, a positive response to an alterity which necessarily calls, summons or motivates it. Deconstruction is therefore vocation – a response to a call.'[46] Here Derrida indicates (already in 1981) that deconstruction is fundamentally a *political* project: a way of engaging texts, institutions and practices that is primarily motivated by alterity – the 'call of the other', as he puts it. But far from being a 'method', let alone a set of 'doctrines', there is an admittedly *formal* character to deconstruction which then inhabits different events in different ways. We would do better to think of deconstruction as a *stance* or *sensibility*, which has a great range of possible sites. As such, deconstruction – like any other powerful critical stance – has a certain *transferability* or portability. 'I think there are some general rules, some procedures that can be transposed by analogy . . . but these rules are taken up in a text which is each time a unique element and which does not let itself be turned totally into a method' (*Points*, 200). For instance, the formal nature of deconstruction explains why it has been a powerful influence on more specific, concrete critical theory, such as post-colonial theory, feminist theory or critical race theory. It also explains why a certain deconstructive sensibility could be taken up by a distinctly Christian cultural theory (e.g., in the work of Graham Ward).

It is important for us to appreciate the *originally* political character of deconstruction. Some have suggested a kind of turn or *Kehre* in Derrida's thought (invoking a Heideggerian analogy), from an early, apolitical, *ir*responsible aestheticism to, in his later work (roughly 1990 onward), a more political, ethical concern. But this is a false distinction insofar as Derrida's concern with the 'other' has motivated his work since the earliest texts on Husserl and phenomenology. Already in 1975 Derrida asserted that it 'has been clear from the beginning' that 'this political deconstruction' is about 'the deconstruction of political structures' (*Points*, 28). It was not a matter of deconstruction *becoming* political; it has always been such. Derrida didn't 'get politics' like one is said, in the American south, to 'get religion' (which Derrida also 'got'); on the contrary, Derrida emphasizes that 'philosophical activity does not *require* a political practice; it is, in any case, a political practice' (*Points*, 70). So when a questioner suggests that with respect to the 'political field', Derrida has 'never taken up noisy positions there', Derrida's response is a direct undoing of the Derrida 'myth': 'Ah, the "political field"! But I could reply that I think of nothing else, however things might appear' (*Points*, 86). We will see below that even the earliest work on phenomenology and literature is deeply concerned with doing justice to alterity, and thus a certain politics.

0.3 The Lens of Alterity: Deconstruction and the Other

We have already seen that deconstruction is an affirmative response to the call of the other, and thus is an inherently ethical and political *vocation* in response to the other. And I have suggested that one of the tasks of this book – with a view to 'introducing' Derrida – is to demythologize the received picture of Derrida – a 'Derrida' taken up by both critics and devotees. In order to do so, we need to stage a critical engagement with Derrida's corpus, extending from his earliest work in phenomenology and philosophy of language in the 1960s to his most recent work in ethics, politics and religion. Given Derrida's own account of deconstruction, in the organization of the book and subsequent expositions I will employ the notion of the 'other' or the concept of 'alterity' as an interpretative lens that will help open up the various themes and fields of Derrida's work as well as lay out a fundamental continuity from Derrida's earliest to later work.[47] Deconstruction, from the beginning, has been a response to the other. For instance, even when Derrida speaks about 'reference' with respect to language, he articulates it in terms of alterity. 'It is totally false', Derrida emphasizes, 'to suggest that deconstruction is a suspension of reference. Deconstruction is always deeply concerned with the "other" of language.'[48] To mistakenly assume, as many have, that deconstruction denies reference beyond language would fail to see, above all, that such a supposed linguistic idealism would be a realm of sameness, whereas it is clear, even to Derrida's critics, that deconstruction is concerned above all with difference – that is, *the other*. So if deconstruction offers something like a 'philosophy of language', it is precisely its concern with alterity that generates an account of what is usually called 'reference' – language's relation to the 'other' of language.

To say that deconstruction is a response to alterity could be another way of saying that deconstruction, from the beginning, has been a 'Jewish science'.[49] From the beginning, we might say, Derrida has been a Levinasian – indebted to the work of Jewish philosopher Emmanuel Levinas whose meditations on 'the Other' focus on Hebrew exemplars of destitution: 'the widow, the orphan, and the stranger' (Exod. 22.21–22). 'The Levinas who most interested me at the outset', Derrida would later note, 'was the philosopher working in phenomenology and posing the question of the "other" to phenomenology.'[50] But Derrida's 'Jewish' concern with otherness also grows out of a certain experience of *being* other – of being a stranger and thus being subject to exclusion.[51] As an Algerian Jew, Derrida experienced the pain of expulsion from French schools and the deprivation of French citizenship – the stigma of being a domestic foreigner, being an outcast while yet encircled.[52] Or as he puts it elsewhere in 'Circumfession', 'I always got the feeling of being an excluded favorite' (*Circ*, 279). This sense of Derrida's own otherness is conveyed in an episode recounted by Ivan Kalmar. Comparing Derrida's 'Circumfession' to Heinrich Heine's *Confessions* (a late disclosure of the importance of 'Jewishness' in Heine's life), Kalmar considers the early Derrida's lack of disclosure about his own Jewishness:

> Derrida may have had good reason not to speak too loudly of his Jewishness, as I once had an opportunity to see for myself. I was in Paris, having dinner in a Latin Quarter restaurant with a well-respected French professor of American literature. The conversation veered to connections between French and American specialists, and I commented on the fact that Derrida was much more popular in North America than in France. 'Of course,' replied the man, 'Derrida isn't French.' 'What is he, then?' I asked,

completely puzzled. The professor refused to elaborate. At the time I did not know that Derrida was Jewish.[53]

Indeed, Derrida suggests a fundamental link between Judaism and alterity in his thought. 'I often feel', he commented in 1981, 'that the questions I attempt to formulate on the outskirts of the Greek philo- sophical tradition have as their "other" the model of the Jew, that is, *the Jew-as-other*.'[54] This *being other* gives birth to a philosophical project: deconstruction as vigilance *for* the other.[55] Derrida's project – from the earliest work on Husserl and phenomenology to the most recent reflec- tions on hospitality and religion – is fundamentally an account of *alterity* undertaken in response to the obligation to the other. The lens of 'the other', then, also helps us to discern how and why deconstruction is a fundamentally *affirmative* strategy. So far from being merely a critical 'method', let alone a purely negative mode of destruction, deconstruc- tion is a *calling*, a vocation, which undertakes an intense investigation of texts, structures and institutions in order to enable them to respond to the call of the other. Deconstruction is a way of making room for the other, and so fundamentally a kind of hospitality and welcome.

The hermeneutical lens of alterity and 'the other' is bi-focal, illumin- ating Derrida on two different levels. On the one hand, we will consider 'the other' as that which animates the calling of deconstruction and orients Derrida's critical theory across a range of themes, texts and figures; on the other hand, the lens of alterity will also open up another Derrida – an *other* 'demythologized' Derrida, what we might consider 'a' Derrida 'after theory'.[56]

This lens of the 'other' thus organizes the following chapters, pro- ceeding from Derrida's earliest work on phenomenology and language[57] (Chapter 1), his interest in literature and its relation to philosophy (Chapter 2), and his most recent work explicitly engaging ethics, politics and religion (Chapter 3). We could also suggest that Chapters 1–3 roughly correspond to a kind of classical philosophical 'trivium': meta- physics, epistemology, ethics. Chapter 4 then provides a brief survey of Derrida's relation to others in the philosophical tradition and con- temporary theory. This chapter might be understood as a kind of expanded, annotated bibliography that provides the reader with a map to direct further engagement. Finally, in Chapter 5 we return to expand on themes explored in the book in an 'interview' that interrogates the very genre of the interview, as a kind of 'case study' of deconstruction.

Chapter 1

Words and Things: Phenomenology's Other

*First of all what is it 'to write?' How is it that the fact of
writing can disturb the very question 'what is?'*
—'The Time of a Thesis: Punctuations', p. 37

1.1 In the Beginning was the Word

When confronted by the 'event' designated now by '9/11', Derrida's
immediate response was to address the question of *language*: 'I believe
always in the necessity of being attentive *first of all* to this phenomenon
of language, naming, and dating . . . Not in order to isolate ourselves in
language [contra the 'Derrida' myth], as people in too much of a rush
would like us to believe, but on the contrary, in order to try to understand what is going on precisely *beyond* language.'[58] Thus Derrida, 40
years into his career, continues to return to what originally animated his
work: questions about *language* undertaken with a view to what is *other*
than language, what is *beyond* language.

'In the beginning was the word', would be a fitting epigraph to what
might some day be Jacques Derrida's *Oeuvres complètes*. But why this
primary focus on language? And more particularly, why the fixation on
writing? While Derrida's work cannot be reduced to its context or
sources, the broader context of this interest is what has been commonly
called the linguistic turn in twentieth-century philosophy, a turn made
decisively by Ludwig Wittgenstein and Martin Heidegger. Heidegger
famously re-inscribed Aristotle's claim that 'man' is a rational animal
(*zoon logon ekhon*) by retrieving a sense of *logos* more intimately tied to
language: humans – these beings who 'have *logos*' – are those beings 'who
have the ability to *speak*'.[59] But we must appreciate the way in which this
linguistic turn runs counter to a long tradition in Western thought
that has tended either to forget or to denigrate language: *forgetting* that

philosophy only 'happens' in the medium of a discourse (recall, as an exemplar, the Socratic dialogues) and, whenever it does turn to the question of language, regularly *denigrates* its 'secondariness' (*OG* 14) as a fall from pure access to Truth. This forgetting and denigration of language maps onto a general philosophical attitude toward embodiment and the alterity of being-in-relation to others. The connection is a natural one: the world of signs – whether graphemes or phonemes – is a world of sensuous phenomena that activate and depend upon the body. There would be no language without air and ears, without marks and tablets. Thus, language is inextricably linked to matter and materiality, to bodies which have ears to hear and eyes to read. Moreover, language as a 'public' phenomenon – shared with others in a community – is an essentially *relational* phenomenon and thus necessarily involves *others*. Insofar as the philosophical tradition has devalued language it has also devalued the 'media' of language – bodies and matter. Or, conversely, insofar as a long-standing rationalism (and dualism) in the Western philosophical tradition has denigrated bodies and materiality, the negative accounts of language are a symptom of deeper metaphysical commitments.

For Derrida, the place of language in the philosophical systems of the West (from Plato to Hegel) functions as a micro-cosmic crystallization of larger metaphysical assumptions. Language, then, is a way into larger questions of metaphysics, ontology, and what we might loosely call 'philosophical anthropology'[60] or 'philosophy of mind'.[61] And insofar as philosophers from Plato onward have reserved their most hostile evaluations for *writing*, Derrida is especially concerned with theoretical accounts of writing – or the place of writing in theoretical frameworks – as a site to 'detect' deeper philosophical assumptions. The 'case' of writing, then, is a kind of portal into philosophical and theoretical systems. Reflecting on his early work, Derrida notes that his analyses detect not only across the history of philosophy but also across the 'human sciences' (linguistics, anthropology, psychoanalysis) 'an evaluation of writing, or, to tell the truth, a devaluation of writing whose insistent, repetitive, even obscurely compulsive, character was the sign of a whole set of long-standing constraints'.[62] But keeping in mind our account of how deconstruction works (from the inside, in the middle voice), Derrida is interested in finding those disruptive sites within the philosophical tradition which challenge its own claims *from the inside* – those places where the 'other of language' (the alterity of bodies and others, and the bodies of others) interrupts the assumed ontology in a dominant Western tradition from Plato through to Hegel. But again, as we've emphasized above, this is an ultimately affirmative and productive project: looking for these disruptions in order to open up philosophy to an*other* way of thinking, a revaluing of language and writing which will be a micro-cosmic inbreaking of another way of thinking about embodiment, community, and our responsibility to the Other.

In this chapter we will trace, roughly chronologically, Derrida's early analyses of writing and language. We will first take up the argument of Derrida's first work, the 'Introduction' to his 1962 translation of Husserl's *Origin of Geometry*: a work that spawned Derrida's initial interests in elaborating a 'theory of literature' as the outworking of 'the un-thought out axiomatics of Husserlian phenomenology'.[63] This deconstruction of Husserl – reading Husserl against Husserl – is next undertaken on a different 'site' in Derrida's *Speech and Phenomena*, which focuses on Husserl's own account of language. We will then trace the central lines of one of the 1967 works, *Of Grammatology*. Here we see Derrida taking up these themes in the history of philosophy, but also expanding the view to include other human sciences, particularly the anthropology of Levi-Strauss. Across these sites, we will keep an eye on the Other and the way in which Derrida's early phenomenology and 'theory of literature' are at the same time an ethics and politics.

1.2 Writing: The Very Idea

1.2.1 'Away with the Body': Why Socrates Didn't Write[64]

As we have already noted, in the history of Western philosophy, language (and especially writing) has been associated with the mundane, material, and downright deceptive sphere of empirical, embodied experience. The vocal noises uttered by the tongue, or the scribbles and marks etched by the hand, are inextricably linked to bodies, which are themselves inextricably linked to the world of matter which is primarily a world of *change*. Governed by temporality, the material world of bodies (and thus ears and hands, shouts and scrolls) is given to the vagaries of generation and decay, coming-to-be and passing-away. How could such shifting sands ever be a foundation for *knowledge*, for what I know today would not be true tomorrow, or what is known in one generation could have passed away in the next?[65] So one of the primary moves of philosophy since its inception has been to shift the object of philosophical knowledge out of the mundane, muddy, corruptible world of bodies to the eternal, unchanging world of 'ideas', or what Plato sometimes calls the 'Forms'. Since ideas are immaterial, they are not governed by temporality and therefore not subject to generation and decay; that is, they are not created or invented. Thus, once I know the *idea* of something, I've secured a mode of knowledge that is not given to change. While I might 'know' that this tree in the garden is green, in fact that claim does not count as knowledge *proper* (or 'intelligible' knowledge) because the assertion could tomorrow be false: the autumnal processes of change could set upon the organism overnight, and I will awake to find the tree a shade of yellow. In contrast, once I know an *idea* – the 'essence' of something, what makes it to be what it is – that will not be given to change. If today I know what justice is, when I awake tomorrow the idea of justice remains the same. If when I was a youth I grasped the idea of the Pythagorean theorem, that remains knowledge for me today. The fundamental move of philosophy, then, is to guard knowledge from the vicissitudes of embodiment by locating its site, as it were, in the eternal realm of immaterial *ideas*. Philosophy thus conceived is always already 'idealist'.

1.2.2 Husserl's Archaeology of Geometry

Enter Husserl, two millennia after Plato: while not a 'Platonist' *simpliciter*, Husserl shares with this long philosophical tradition a fundamental interest in *ideas*, or what he will call 'idealities'. But Husserl offers us a Platonism with a twist.[66] In a later text on *The Origin of Geometry*, he undertakes what appears to be a paradoxical inquiry into the *history* of idealities, following the lead of Galileo. So here we hit upon a remarkable notion: that something 'ideal' and 'universal' (and considered to always be the 'same') would have a 'history'. What could that mean? We need to first appreciate that 'geometry' here includes 'all disciplines that deal with shapes existing mathematically in pure time space' (*IHOG*, 158) or what Husserl will also call 'idealities'.[67] The question of its origin is not a question of who the first geometers were, or when the first proofs were formulated, but rather concerns 'that sense in which it appeared in history for the first time – in which it had to appear' (*IHOG*, 158). This ultimately becomes a question of *tradition*, where geometry is but one example of what is handed-down. Geometry, then, is a kind of case study for other idealities (among which Husserl includes 'the constructions of fine literature' [*IHOG*, 160]).

So there is a tradition of geometry. Geometry undergoes the same progress and growth as other sciences: knowledge 'grows into' a projected horizon. The growth of this science is one of projection and realization. But this is where unique questions arise. 'This process of projecting and successfully realizing occurs, after all, purely within the *subject* of the inventor, and thus the meaning, as present *originaliter* with its whole content, lies exclusively, so to speak, within his mental space' (*IHOG*, 160). So Euclidean geometry begins within the subjectivity of Euclid, for example. But, Husserl cautions, we ought not to confuse 'geometrical existence' with mere 'psychic existence', as though geometry were 'subjective'.[68] Rather, geometric existence is quintessentially 'objective': the truths of geometry are 'there for "everyone" ' (*IHOG*, 160): 'Indeed, it has, from its primal establishment, an existence which is peculiarly *supertemporal* and which – of this we are certain – is accessible to all men [*sic*]' (*IHOG*, 160, emphasis added). And so we have what appears to be a paradoxical situation: geometry both has a history and is supertemporal.

Idealities, such as geometric truths, exist independent of individual constitution. They are 'phenomena' whose fulfilment is adequate to intention; in other words, they are entirely given to us without remainder. (This is in contrast to physical objects, for instance, which are only given to us in 'adumbrations': I can only see one side of the cup at a time. But the truth of the Pythagorean theorem, as a 'phenomenon', is fully given to me when I understand it. It has no 'sides'. There is no absence or lack of givenness.) This 'objectivity' – as a mode of being – 'is proper to a whole class of spiritual products of the cultural world, to which not only all scientific constructions and the sciences themselves belong but also, for example, the constructions of fine literature' (*IHOG*, 160). From this Husserl concludes that phenomena of this type cannot be 'repeated' in many exemplars. For instance, 'the Pythagorean theorem, [indeed] all of geometry, exists only once, no matter how often *or even in what language* it may be expressed. It is identically the same in the "original language" of Euclid and in all "translations" ' (*IHOG*, 160). So such phenomena are unaffected by translation because their 'being' is supratemporal and thus unaffected by their temporal manifestations. Indeed (looking ahead to *Speech and Phenomena*), we might say that what is at stake here is a relationship between soul and body (and a very Platonic relation at that). 'The sensible utterances have spatiotemporal individuation in the world like all corporeal occurrences, like everything embodied in bodies as such; but this is not true of the spiritual form itself, which is called an "ideal object" ' (*IHOG*, 160–1).

Here Husserl makes an interesting observation: 'In a certain way ideal objects do exist objectively in the world, but it is only *in virtue of* these two-leveled repetitions and ultimately *in virtue of* sensibly embodying repetitions' – i.e., language (*IHOG*, 161, emphasis added). So on the one hand he seems to say that such objectivities are unaffected by linguistic embodiment, but on the other hand he seems to point to linguistic embodiment as their condition of possibility, that 'in virtue of' which they 'exist'. Here, Husserl hits upon the problem he wants to pursue: 'how does geometrical ideality (just like that of all sciences) proceed from its primary intrapersonal origin, where it is a structure within the conscious space of the first inventor's soul, to its ideal objectivity' (*IHOG*, 161)? In other words, how does a geometrical truth achieve objectivity ('there for everyone'), beginning from its psychic existence within the subjectivity of its 'inventor'? This occurs, Husserl suggests, '*by means of language*, through which it receives, so to speak, its linguistic living body [*Sprachleib*]' (*IHOG*, 161). Language, then, is a kind of *incarnation*.

But this raises a second question: How does language do this? How does embodiment in language make the geometrical truth 'objective'? While this ultimately raises questions about the origin of language itself, Husserl first deals with the question of the 'relation between language, as a function of man within human civilization, and the world as the horizon of human existence' (*IHOG*, 161).[69] Language creates community, which provides the conditions for sharing the geometrical insight (*IHOG*, 162). So the geometer who hits upon the Pythagorean theorem can express it to others, and insofar as it can be communicated intersubjectively via language, it is in a sense 'objective': that which is 'internal' can be 'expressed' externally.[70] But this brings Husserl back to the second question above: 'how does the intrapsychically constituted structure arrive at an intersubjective being of its own?' (*IHOG*, 163). How does it achieve objectivity?

What is originally and vividly 'self-evident' for that first geometer, can be *reactivated* later. In other words, Euclid's scribbles on a napkin, or even a string on his finger, can later be an occasion to remind him of his original insight. However, this still does not take us to others. That occurs by means of *language*: once we recall the 'function of empathy and fellow mankind as a community of empathy and language' then we will see that 'the contact of reciprocal linguistic understanding, the original production and the product of one subject can be *actively* understood by others' (*IHOG*, 163). So that which begins in the mind of the first geometer becomes objective by means of language, by communication. 'In the unity of the community of communication among several persons the repeatedly produced structure becomes an object of consciousness, not as a likeness, but as the one structure common to all' (*IHOG*, 163–4).

However, while this is the first movement towards objectivity – from one person to the community – a second movement is required, since even that first community of geometers will pass away. 'What is lacking is the *persisting existence* of the "ideal objects" even during periods in which the inventor and his fellows are no longer wakefully so related or even are no longer alive' (*IHOG*, 164). What then? How will the Pythagorean theorem, which has attained objectivity by means of a linguistic community, survive the death of these interlocutors? By means of *writing*. 'The important function of *written*, documenting linguistic expression is that it makes communications possible without immediate or mediate personal address; it is, so to speak, *communication become virtual*' (*IHOG*, 164, emphases added). Here we have a first suggested link between writing and 'the death of the author'. The ideality or ideal object thus becomes 'sedimented' in writing: 'the writing-down effects a transformation of the original mode of being of the meaning-structure, [e.g.,] within the geometrical sphere of self-evidence, of the geometrical structure which is put into words' (*IHOG*, 164). This sedimentation, however, can be reactivated or de-sedimented by the reader. So while this geometrical truth – an ideal object – can become sedimented in written language, it can be reactivated in its original self-evidence. But note that this reactivation is effected *by the reader*. So we need to distinguish between merely '*passively*' understanding the expression and [*actively*] making it self-evident by reactivating its meaning' (*IHOG*, 165, emphasis added). He later compares this to, on the one hand, superficially reading the newspaper and 'taking in' the news, and on the other hand being 'moved' by such, reactivating the experience itself (*IHOG*, 167). The 'seduction of language' tends to create a community of readers who are only passive and do not reactivate meaning – who do not, in Husserl's terms, return to 'the things themselves'. Echoing Heidegger's critique of *Gerede* or 'idle talk',[71] Husserl notes that '[g]reater and greater segments of life lapse into a kind of talking and reading that is dominated purely by association' (*IHOG*, 165). So writing is both necessary and seductive.

The positive role of writing is seen in the progress of geometry. If the science had to reinvent itself, in its entirety, at each stage, it would never grow or progress (*IHOG*, 166–7). But because of 'the peculiar "logical" activity' tied to language and writing, by means of 'explication' the reader can reactivate an original 'self-evidence': 'What was a passive meaning-pattern has now become one constructed through active production' (*IHOG*, 167). This makes possible a kind of 'infinitization' of the individual, allowing him to transgress his 'obvious finitude' by a mechanism of self-evidence which defies time (*IHOG*, 168).

We have thus witnessed an interesting twist on the perennial philosophical desire for the eternal idea: in Husserl's archaeology of geometry – as a case study of idealities in general – he ends up recognizing that the materiality of *writing* is the condition for the eternal verities of geometry (*IHOG*, 169). From the view of a long Platonic tradition this must sound like heresy, for it suggests (to invoke an analogy with Platonic warrant) that the body is the condition for the soul.

1.2.3 Deconstructing Euclid

If deconstruction is always attentive to the ways in which philosophy's 'others' come along to interrupt its best laid plans, we can see how this little fragment of Husserl's caught the eye of a young Jacques Derrida. Here is a project with a long philosophical pedigree – the grasping of eternal, unchanging *ideas* – admitting to a dirty little secret in the family tree: that the corruptible material of writing is its mother. Bastard children produced by the copulation of eternal and temporal, body and soul, idealities – and so the philosophical project itself – have a tainted legacy.

1.2.3.1 Language, Incarnation and Objectivity

Derrida unveils a certain lingering 'Platonism' in Husserl's philosophy of language insofar as Husserl wanted to maintain 'a certain nondependence' between the 'word' and its 'material incarnations' (*IHOG*, 66–9). Though Husserl points to the dependence of idealities upon language, these 'ideal formations are rooted only in language in general, not in the factuality of languages and their particular linguistic incarnations' (*IHOG*, 66).[72] It is almost as if Husserl shrank back from the radicality of his thesis; Derrida, on the other hand, wants to pursue this to its more radical conclusions. For instance, Husserl wants to maintain a distinction between what he calls 'free idealities' and 'bound idealities': *free* idealities (such as 'logicomathematical systems and pure essential structures') are 'bound to no territory, or rather, they have their territory in the totality of the universe and in every possible universe'.[73] Free idealities, then, are the *purest* idealities, purified of any taint of material connection: these are the closest ancestors to Plato's Forms. *Bound* idealities, on the other hand, 'carry reality with them and hence belong to the real world'; they are 'bound to Earth, to Mars, to particular territories, etc.'.[74] Tainted by such a connection to territory and materiality, bound idealities (such as cultural phenomena, including 'literary objects') lack the purity of, say, geometric ideal objects. But Derrida's reading of the *Origin of Geometry* will destabilize just this distinction: on the basis of Husserl's own assertions, Derrida will point out the way in which *all* idealities are *bound* idealities. The contamination, as it were, of territory and bodies, goes all the way down.[75]

What intrigues Derrida is the way in which Husserl, on the way to attaining Objectivity by asserting both this distinction and this relation of non-dependence between idealities and language, finally achieves Objectivity precisely by recourse to language! 'Husserl then seems to *redescend* toward language as the indispensible medium and condition of possibility for absolute ideal Objectivity. . . . Thus, does Husserl not *come back* to language, culture, history, all of which he reduced [bracketed] in order to have the pure possibility of truth emerge? Is he not "bound" again to lead into history that whose absolute "freedom" he just described' (*IHOG*, 76)? Isn't this a little like leading the Israelites *back* to Egypt? Yes, Husserl might think, but this is also the final step to pure Objectivity. Without its 'going out' in language (which here must seem like a 'going back'), the ideal object remains enslaved, trapped in the psychological life of the 'first geometer'. In fact, this discloses a 'juridical and transcendental *de*pendence' (*IHOG*, 76): even if it is the case that 'geometrical truth is beyond every particular and factual linguistic hold as such' (and Derrida does not seek to deny this), in order for this truth or ideality to achieve the 'omnitemporality' that Husserl asserts – in order, in other words, for this truth to not remain trapped within 'the psychological life of a factual individual' – it is necessary, *for the sake of Objectivity*, for the geometrical truth to be embodied in language (*IHOG*, 77).

> Whether geometry can be spoken about is not, then, the extrinsic and accidental possibility of a fall into the body of speech or of a slip into a historical movement. . . . The paradox is that, without the apparent fall back into language and thereby into history, a fall which would alienate the ideal purity of sense, sense would remain an empirical formation imprisoned as fact in a psychological sub-jectivity – *in the inventor's head*. Historical incarnation sets free the transcendental, instead of binding it (*IHOG*, 77).

So here we see an instance where what philosophy wants to exclude –

language and its hook to body, territory, materiality – nevertheless reasserts itself *within the philosophical system* as the very condition of possibility for what philosophy wants.

1.2.3.2 And the Word was made Flesh: Writing and Incarnation

As we saw in Husserl's *Origin*, for geometry to achieve Objectivity, it is not enough for the first geometer to *speak*; in order for geometrical truths to achieve enduring objectivity ('persisting, factual existence'), they must undergo documentation in *writing*. As Husserl noted, this documentation of geometry in writing is 'communication become *virtual*' (*IHOG*, 164, emphasis added). Derrida focuses on this virtuality, noting that this '*virtuality*, moreover, is an ambiguous value: it simultaneously makes passivity, forgetfulness, and all the phenomena of *crisis* possible' (*IHOG*, 87). In other words, writing is both a blessing and a curse – or, to adopt a concept from elsewhere in his early writings, writing is *pharmacological*, both poison and cure (see 4.1.1).

The 'virtualizing' of communication in writing occurs by creating the possibility for communication where the speaker is absent (i.e., not *present*): 'By absolutely virtualizing dialogue, writing creates a kind of autonomous transcendental field from which every present subject can be absent' (*IHOG*, 88). In other words, writing crystallizes the necessity of language functioning as a *public* property, which cannot be reduced to a 'private language' (as Wittgenstein demonstrated), but neither can it be reduced even to a 'code' shared by two people. With respect to language, the 'third' is always present: writing must have a kind of universal legibility that transcends a merely dual relation. In other words, writing[76] must *in principle* be able to operate in the absence of both the first geometer and his first interlocutor. It is this absence of the present subject which hails the achievement of Objectivity, but it also signals the death of the author. It creates, in fact, the possibility of a 'subjectless transcendental field' (*IHOG*, 88).

But the result is once again the inevitable logic of incarnation (and hence incarnation of logic) as the condition of possibility for Objectivity/Truth. 'The possibility or necessity of being incarnated in a graphic sign is no longer simply extrinsic and factual in comparison with ideal Objectivity: it is the *sine qua non* condition of Objectivity's internal completion.' (*IHOG*, 89) If Objectivity 'is not in a position to be party to an incarnation . . . then Objectivity is not fully constituted' (*IHOG*, 89). Here, Derrida makes an important note about the nature of this *incarnation*: it is 'more than a system of signals [*signalisation*] or an outer garment' (*IHOG*, 89). In highlighting this, Derrida effects a deconstruction of the philosophical desire for pure, disembodied objectivity by noting the way in which philosophy's desire requires (and cannot escape) the link to incarnation and embodiment. But this does not spell the end of philosophy; rather, it opens up the possibility for reconfiguring philosophical desire in productive ways.

Derrida explores this productive, deconstructive tension when he raises what we might call the question of 'preincarnate' Objectivity. 'Does not this formulation give the impression that ideal objectivity is fully constituted as such *before* and *independently of* its embodiment, or rather, before and independently of its *ability to be embodied*' (*IHOG*, 90)? Calling into question Husserl's suggestions that this is a relation of non-dependence, Derrida here wants to contest Husserl with Husserl – the Husserl who asserts a relation of non-dependence with the Husserl who asserts the mutual dependence between Objectivity and language, specifically writing. For instance, 'Husserl insists that truth is not fully objective, i.e., ideal, intelligible for everyone and indefinitely perdurable, as long as it cannot be said *and* written' (*IHOG*, 90). The 'freedom' of truth from any particular linguistic incarnation is made possible precisely by its achieving objectivity *in language*. Again (cf. *IHOG*, 77), this is a matter of paradox. 'Paradoxically, the possibility of being written permits the ultimate freeing of ideality' (*IHOG*, 90). By becoming embodied, sense becomes nonspatiotemporal. This indicates writing's pharmacological nature for Husserl: 'writing defines and completes the ambiguity of all language' (*IHOG*, 92). This again raises the question of truth's *relation* to writing as both dependent and independent. 'Truth *depends* on the pure possibility of speaking and writing, but is *independent* of what is spoken or written, insofar as they are in the world. If, therefore, truth suffers in and through its language from a certain changeableness, its downfall will be less a fall toward language than a degradation within language' (*IHOG*, 92). Thus Derrida's reading of Husserl is a 'case' of deconstruction at work: closely considering the philosophical desire that animates Husserl's project (and it is a desire with a long pedigree in Western philosophy) – specifically the desire to cancel embodiment and materiality in order to achieve truth and objectivity – Derrida's reading of the *Origin of Geometry* does not 'do' anything *to* the text, but rather is a witness to what is already at work within the text, *viz.*, a paradoxical tension that requires as a condition of possibility precisely what it wants to escape. Derrida attests to the way in which philosophy's *other* (embodiment, materiality, language) always already inserts itself into philosophy. So even Derrida's very technical, almost tedious, analysis of the fine points of Husserl's phenomenology can be seen as a concern with alterity, with philosophy's other.

1.3 Talking to Oneself: The Critique of Husserl

We see this alterity announce and impose itself in a different way in Derrida's *Speech and Phenomena*, a detailed critique of Husserl's theory of signs in the *Logical Investigations* (1900/1901). If the other was linked to embodiment and language in the 'Introduction' to the *Origin of Geometry*, in *Speech and Phenomena* the other will reveal itself in terms of *absence*. But I will argue that the hermeneutical key in this context is to understand *absence* as a synonym for *transcendence*. So what might appear, on a first reading, to be an almost nihilist absorption with absence will turn out to be an ethical concern for the relation to the Other and the place of community in the constitution of the subject.

1.3.1 Husserl's Theory of Signs

The longest and richest tradition of philosophical reflection on language is what we would now loosely describe as 'semiotics' – an account of language in terms of *signs* (*semeia*). While the notion of semiotics is most often linked to twentieth-century figures such as Ferdinand de Saussure or C. S. Peirce,[77] this tradition of reflection has a long pedigree reaching back through Augustine to the Stoics.[78] One of the most powerful and influential restatements of such an analysis of language was offered by Husserl, most especially in his earlier work, the *Logical Investigations*.[79] In order to set the stage for Derrida's critique in *Speech and Phenomena*, we will once again undertake an opening exposition of Husserl.

In the first of the *Logical Investigations* ('Expression and Meaning'), Husserl seeks to map the different modes of expression and speech by asserting a number of distinctions. For Husserl, the overarching category is that of *signs*, so what we get in the first investigations is not really his account of language, but more specifically (yet more broadly) his theory of signs – of which language is a subset. Within the broad category of 'signs' (*Zeigen*), Husserl asserts a first, fundamental distinction between those signs which *express* something – an 'expression' (*Ausdruck*) – and those signs which do not express or 'mean' something – what he calls 'indications' (*Anzeigen*). Expressions are 'significant' insofar as they 'signify' or 'mean' (*Bedeuten*) something, whereas indications are only 'indicative' and serve merely as pointers (*LI*, 269). However, one should not over-state or misunderstand this distinction between 'expression' and 'indication'. For instance, the two are not mutually exclusive: it is possible, Husserl notes, for a sign to be indicative but also 'happen to fulfill a significant' (i.e., expressive) function as well. Moreover, it is not the case that expression is really a particular kind of indication.[80] Indeed, Husserl's most surprising (and most contested) claim is that there can be modes of expression which do not involve any aspect of indication; in other words, there is a sphere – what Husserl calls 'isolated mental life' – in which there is meaning without indication.

Indications are pointers that 'stand for' something else; in this sense, Husserl notes, 'a brand is the sign of a slave, a flag the sign of a nation' (*LI*, 270) – the indications aid us in recognizing something to which the sign is attached. In some cases this attachment is contingent, even arbitrary (as in the case of a flag or brand); but other attachments of signs to their referents are more 'natural'; it is in this sense that we can say 'Martian canals are signs of the existence of intelligent beings on Mars', or 'that fossil vertebrae are signs of the existence of prediluvian animals' (*LI*, 270). In short, smoke is a sign of fire in the sense of being an *indication* (*Anzeige*). The relation between the indicative sign and its referent is *motivational*: what is *given* (the indicative sign) motivates me to consider what is not given, but only indicated in its absence: the referent. On the podium in Greece, the flag of the United States motivates the consideration of a nation-state on the other side of the globe, etc. Essential to the nature of indication, then, is an *absence* of the referent; indication operates on the basis of a certain lack.

Indicative signs are to be distinguished from *expressions* which are '*meaningful* signs' (*LI*, 275). Thus, Husserl wants to reserve the term 'expression' for a specific instance of signification, drastically narrowing what we might describe, in ordinary language, as an indication. For instance, we often speak of 'facial expressions', but on Husserl's register these are not properly *Ausdrucken* ('expressions') because, according to him, such bodily signs 'involuntarily accompany speech without communicative intent' (*LI*, 275).[81] 'In such manifestations', he continues, 'one man communicates nothing to another: their utterance involves no intent to put certain "thoughts" on record expressively, whether for the man himself [i.e., the one making the bodily gesture], in his solitary state, or for others. Such "expressions", in short, have properly speaking, *no meaning.*' (*LI*, 275, emphasis original). In other words, they are not properly 'expressions' at all because they are not communicative. The question is, are these bodily gestures still a mode of *language*? Could there be an instance of non-communicative, non-expressive *language*? What would that be? We will return to this below.

When Husserl considers expression, his focus is on *speech* because it is in speech that we find *intention*: a speaker, by means of a sign, means to communicate something to a listener. The connection between sign and referent with respect to expression is, we might say, 'tighter' than it is with indication; as Husserl puts it, in speech the signs given (the 'expressions') are 'phenomenally one with the experiences made manifest in them in the consciousness of the man who manifests them' (*LI*, 275). There is almost a sense in which the referent inheres in the expressive sign in a way it does not in the indicative sign. Indeed, he goes on to describe an expression as 'a verbal sound *infused* with sense' or meaning (*LI*, 281, emphasis added). Thus, Husserl privileges speech as the site of expression.

However, here we find an interesting twist (which is also the fulcrum of Derrida's critique). Speech is the best exemplar of expression for Husserl, but not all speech is communicative for him. In fact, insofar as speech is *communicative* (that is, insofar as it involves the intersubjective exchange of expressions), it is necessarily implicated with *indication*. 'All expressions in *communicative* speech function as indications' (*LI*, 277). This is because there is a kind of essential *absence* in the intersubjective relation between speaker and listener. Expressions in speech 'serve the hearer as signs of the "thoughts" of the speaker . . . as well as of the other inner experiences which are part of his communicative intention' (*LI*, 277). The word-signs that I utter are given to the hearer and thus are *present* to the hearer, but they serve to *indicate* what can never be present to that other person, *viz.*, my inner thoughts and consciousness. Nevertheless, insofar as these utterances are intentionally given by me in order to communicate or express meaning, they count as expressions. Communicative speech involves the interweaving of both expression and indication.

But what other kind of speech could there be? If intersubjective communication always involves indication, could there be a kind of expression which isn't always already 'bound up' with indication? Could there be a kind of 'pure expression'? For Husserl, yes, and we find this in 'solitary mental life', in the inner soliloquy of consciousness (*LI*, 278–9). Properly speaking, for Husserl (who again, we must recall, does not admit any unconscious), we do not 'talk to ourselves' in our interior mental life;[82] we do not need to employ signs (as indications) of our own inner experiences. This is because he sees interior mental life characterized by a kind of immediate self-presence which does not admit any absence or lack. There are no secret parts of consciousness for Husserl; I am master of my thoughts and intentions. So insofar as indication is a kind of sign *given* to point to what is *absent*, such signs would be superfluous for interior consciousness. The main point is that Husserl sees this interior soliloquy of consciousness as the site of 'pure' expression (*LI*, 279–80).

1.3.2 The Sounds of Absence: Speech and Transcendence

If deconstruction is a response to the call of the other, where do we hear alterity calling in Husserl's semiotics? First, once again, we see a central distinction made by Husserl (between 'expression' and 'indication') that is destabilized by some of his own conclusions. Indeed, the core thesis of *Speech and Phenomena* is that there is an essential 'entanglement' (*Verflechtung*) between expression and indication.[83] But more importantly, what will be at stake here is the question of how we think about the nature of human intersubjectivity. The problem with Husserl's account of signs is not merely an internal theoretical instability; rather, it issues in a picture of selfhood and identity which retreats into the most classical notions of isolation and privacy. In other words, Derrida's critique of Husserl's semiotics is at root *ethical*. By opening it to critique, he means above all to open it up to the *essential relationality* of being-human, getting us to 'recognize an irreducible nonpresence as having a constituting value' (*SP*, 6). The insularity of a self-present ego is disturbed 'at the origin' – what Derrida will describe, paradoxically, as an original supplement. In this case, the phenomenological ego is haunted by a nonpresence, an absence, perhaps even a *transcendence* – another, an Other. Further, and more radically, the phenomenological ego is in fact *constituted* by such nonpresence. In particular, Derrida signals the question of the appresentation of the other ego as a key moment of this interruption (*SP*, 7). It is within this horizon of the question that he will turn to an analysis of the 'sign' (*SP*, 6–7).

We will best read *Speech and Phenomena* if we read it as a kind of Levinasian meditation on the originary relation to the Other which constitutes the subject as subject. If Derrida points out what we might call the 'semiotic conditioning of consciousness' – which we'll unpack below (I.3.2.2) – that is simply a way of pointing out the way in which we are always already constituted by others and thus responsible *to* others.

1.3.2.1 'Phonocentrism' and 'The Metaphysics of Presence'

Husserl's theory of signs is symptomatic of what Derrida has famously called 'the metaphysics of presence' (*OG*, 49; *SP*, 26). But what does that mean? Let's consider an analogy and then a case study. First, we can find an analogy in Emmanuel Levinas's critique of 'ontology' in the Western tradition. For Levinas, philosophy – in both its ontology and epistemology – has privileged 'the Same', the sphere of the knowing subject which assimilates all that is other. For instance, in order for something (or someone) to be known, the phenomenon must submit itself and conform to the conditions of the knowing subject. As a result, what is known – the 'other' – must lose its alterity and divest itself of otherness in order to 'appear' within the sphere of the Same. In other words, the philosophical tradition has tended to privilege that which can be made present within the sphere of the Same, commensurate with the categories of philosophical theory. What is not commensurate with these categories, what fails or refuses to *appear*, is precisely that which is *absent* – that which cannot or will not be made *present*. But then what is *absent* is that which is *other* – otherwise than the categories of rational knowing, phenomenological appearance, etc.[84] By privileging presence, and that which can be made present, the ontological tradition has also privileged the Same, and thereby marginalized that which is other, absent, and cannot 'appear'. The 'metaphysics of presence', then, is a kind of shorthand for naming the ontological xenophobia that has characterized Western philosophy, and which has undergirded the social and political xenophobias of the West.

Now, following Derrida, let's consider Husserl's theory of signs as a 'case' of this metaphysics of presence. In his account, Husserl links 'indications' to *absence*: indications are the kinds of pointers we have when the 'thing' (referent) is missing or absent. But precisely because of this inextricable link between indication and absence, Husserl asserts that indicative signs don't *mean* anything: they lack *meaning*. Meaning, then, can only be linked to *presence*, and that's what we get in 'expressions'. While Husserl concedes that sometimes (often?) expressions are 'interwoven' [*Verflechtung*] with indication, he does not think that such an interweaving is essential. Rather, as we saw above, he believes that we can carve out a region of expression which is purified of the taint of indication; in other words, in the soliloquy of 'interior mental life' Husserl locates a realm of *pure* self-presence, uncorrupted by the absence of indication. But notice, then, how we have come to a place described by Levinas as the sphere of 'the Same': in order to secure presence and remain undisturbed by absence, Husserl retreats to a deeply private interiority, shut off from absence precisely by shutting out others. (We will return to this final point in 1.3.2.2 below.)

In *Speech and Phenomena*, Derrida will challenge the metaphysics of presence by calling into question Husserl's distinction between indication and expression – or more specifically, questioning Husserl's contention that the two can be un-woven, un-*Verflechtung*. 'Husserl's whole enterprise', Derrida contends, 'would be threatened if the *Verflechtung* which couples the indicative sign to expression were absolutely irreducible, if it were in principle inextricable and if indication were essentially internal to the movement of expression' (*SP*, 27). Derrida's project is to demonstrate the irreducibility of this interweaving.

I would suggest a couple of 'layers' to Derrida's critique in *Speech and Phenomena*. The first layer of Derrida's exposition and critique focuses on Husserl's claims regarding an essential link between expression and *speech*, and more specifically, speech as the privileged site of 'meaning' (recalling that meaning is always linked to expression for Husserl). As Derrida observes, for Husserl expression is always inhabited and animated by a meaning because it never takes place outside oral discourse (*Rede*) (*SP*, 34). 'What "means", i.e., *that which* the meaning means to say – the meaning, *Bedeutung* – is left up to whoever is speaking, insofar as he says what he *wants* to say, what he *means* to say' (*SP*, 34). Thus Husserl concludes that all speech counts as expression – and this is the case whether or not such speech is actually uttered (*LI*, 275). So all the aspects of the 'physical incarnation of the meaning' ('the body of speech') are 'if not outside discourse, at least foreign to the nature of expression as such, foreign to that pure intention without which there could be no speech' (*SP*, 34). In short, the physical aspect of language is relegated to indication and 'retains in itself something of the nature of an *involuntary* association' (*SP*, 36) – akin to Husserl's account of bodily gestures which don't 'mean' anything. That is, the bodily manifestation of intentionality in the flesh of words also exceeds the 'control' of the speaker; once I have spoken, my words take on a life of their own and I can no longer control their meaning.

What Husserl excludes, then, is 'the whole of the body and the mundane register, in a word, the whole of the visible and spatial as such' (*SP*, 35), such as facial expressions and gestures. Recalling our discussion of *Origin of Geometry* above, we can hear echoes of a certain Platonism at work here. Indeed, Derrida suggests that what is at stake is an *opposition* between body and soul. 'The opposition between body and soul is not only at the center of this doctrine of signification, it is confirmed by it;

and, as has always been at bottom the case in philosophy, it depends upon an interpretation of language' (*SP*, 35). Visibility and spatiality represent the death of self-presence. Bodily indications such as gestures and facial expressions lack meaning: 'Nonexpressive signs mean (*bedeuten*) only in the degree to which they can be made to say what was murmuring in them, in a stammering attempt' (*SP*, 36); indication lacks intention, or what Derrida calls *vouloir-dire*, 'wanting to say'. (But as we'll see below, it is not only these marginal signs like gestures which are thus excluded: *speech itself* must also befall the same fate since it too remains an essentially embodied, material *medium*.)

Thus, in his quest for pure meaning, Husserl retreats within the inner sanctum of 'solitary mental life'. To reach 'pure expression', Husserl must bracket all that is other (*Fremde*) – in a move analogous to the later reduction to the 'sphere of ownness' in his *Cartesian Meditations* – and reach 'solitary mental life' (*SP*, 41). But this raises the question: if expression only takes place in 'solitary mental life', does this mean that when I 'speak' to myself I communicate something? Husserl answers in the negative (*LI*, 279); in other words, I do not employ *signs* in solitary mental life. As such, 'in the end the need for indications simply means the need for signs' (*SP*, 42); to bracket indication, then, is to bracket signs. 'For it is more and more clear that, despite the initial distinction between an indicative sign and an expressive sign, only an indication is truly a sign for Husserl' (*SP*, 42). So 'expression', in a sense, does not employ signs. And yet, expression remains linked to the *voice* and speech. The result is what Derrida calls 'phonocentrism': the determination of being as presence or ideality and the valorization of *speech* as the site of presence (in contrast to writing) and therefore immediacy (*SP*, 74–5). *Voice* is taken to be the 'medium' which does not mediate, the medium which 'does not impair the presence and self-presence of the acts that aim at it' (*SP*, 75–6).[85] Here we see Husserl's Platonism again – the body being only an apparition: in voice we see expression 'transforming the worldly opacity of its body into pure diaphaneity' (*SP*, 77). Derrida's project is 'to question the phenomenological value of the voice, its transcendent dignity with regard to every other signifying substance. We think, and will try to show, that this transcendence is only apparent' (*SP*, 77). Derrida wants to question the privileging of voice as a site of immediacy, demonstrating that the 'apparent transcendence' of the voice is just that: only an appearance (*SP*, 77).

How does voice achieve this privileged status? How is speech accorded the status of 'immediate presence', whereas writing is consigned to 'secondarity' and mediation? Derrida suggests two links. First, it seems to result from 'the fact that the phenomenological "body" of the signifier seems to fade away at the very moment it is produced; it seems already to belong to the element of ideality' (*SP*, 77). In other words, sound seems more ethereal, and thus closer to the philosophical dream of the Forms and 'pure' knowledge. Because the materiality of sound is not as solid as that of, say, writing, it lends itself to the illusion of being ethereal and immaterial, suggesting its own 'effacement of the sensible body' such that the audible word is no longer considered sensible (i.e., affecting the senses). But this ignores the fundamental sensibility of sound and voice, tongues and ears. Second, sound is connected with ideality because of the (mistakenly) perceived *presence* that characterizes oral discourse. The speaking subject is thought to be *present* to me in a way that an author is not. While I can read Derrida's book a world away, it would be better to hear him 'live'. Thus, speech seems to rely upon an order of *proximity* which guarantees presence (*SP*, 77). But Derrida questions such a naïve notion, and does so *on Husserlian grounds*, for it is Husserl more than anyone who emphasized the way in which the other (the alter ego) remains essentially absent from my consciousness and thus can never be present but only 'appresented'.[86] The underpinnings of phonocentrism, then, are in fact illusions regarding the immateriality of sound and the supposed immediacy of oral discourse. In *Of Grammatology*, to which we'll turn in 1.4 below, Derrida launches a more sustained critique of phonocentrism, but elements of the critique are broached in *Speech and Phenomena*.

1.3.2.2 Speech, Thought, and Community: The Semiotic Conditioning of Consciousness

A second layer of Derrida's critique brings us back to the more ethical, Levinasian aspect of his project. If he first criticizes Husserl's 'phonocentrism', his second critical thrust focuses on the implications of this for thinking about intersubjectivity, community and ethics – though it must be conceded that these themes are addressed obliquely in the early work. In particular, Derrida will suggest that Husserl inscribes a kind of ethical solipsism into the heart of phenomenology, (unsuccessfully) retreating from a relation to the (absent, transcendent) Other.

Recall Husserl's move in the *Logical Investigations*: conceding that all speech linked to communication remains tainted by indication, and hence absence, Husserl brackets (i.e., puts out of play) all that is linked to communication, and hence all that is linked to community – to intersubjective relationships. Without the distinction between indication and expression, and the separability of the two, '[e]very expression would thus be caught up, despite itself, in an indicative process' (*SP*, 21). As such, the expressive sign would be a species of the genus 'indication'; and then 'we would have to say in the end that the spoken word, whatever dignity or originality we still accorded to it, is but a form of gesture. In its essential core, then, . . . it would belong to the general system of signification and would not surpass it. The general system of signification would then be coextensive with the system of indication' (*SP*, 21). But *this is just what Husserl contests*. Note, then, that it is Husserl that wants to maintain the 'purity' and privilege of spoken language, reserving a privileged presence in speech. And it is here that Derrida wants to point out the contamination and infection of absence. In order to retain this privileging of expression and speech, Husserl must demonstrate that 'expression is not a species of indication' (*SP*, 21). In order to make this case, Husserl would have to find a case in which expression is disentangled from indication, 'a phenomenological situation in which expression is no longer caught up in this entanglement, no longer intertwined with the indication' (*SP*, 22). Insofar as all communicative expression ('colloquy') would always already be infected by 'indication' (for reasons noted above), Husserl must locate a 'pure' expression in *soliloquy*, a 'language without communication, in speech as monologue' as found in 'solitary mental life' (*SP*, 22). 'By a strange paradox, meaning would isolate the concentrated purity of its *ex-pressiveness* just at that moment when the relation to a certain *outside* is suspended' (*SP*, 22). Thus it is demonstrated by a kind of reduction to interiority which brackets all exteriority, and hence all communication/colloquy.

But can this be sustained? Will not the privacy of this 'sphere of ownness' be interrupted by another, an Other? Husserl in a sense grasps just this threat: this is why, in his search for a region of 'pure meaning' (and hence pure self-presence), he is obliged to put out of play ('bracket') any aspects of expression which are intertwined with the absence of indication. But what does this entail? It requires bracketing everything and anything that belongs to *communication* because as soon as speech is communicative, it involves another – and insofar as it involves another, it is confronted by an essential *absence* (*SP*, 37). Here we can finally trace the Levinasian line we suggested above: if there is an allergy to absence in Husserl's phenomenology, it comes down to an allergy to alterity; and we see this powerfully illustrated in Husserl's exclusion of any communicative (and hence intersubjective) expression in order to secure a pure and undisturbed self-presence. In other words, 'decontamination' is needed to achieve purity. In order to do so, Husserl will bracket from 'expression' 'everything that belongs to the *communication* or *manifestation* of mental experiences [to another]' (*SP*, 37). This will require a reduction to privacy and the exclusion of all intersubjectivity; that is, the elimination of all 'nonpresence' – which here represents all otherness, all alterity (*SP*, 37). Recalling that 'the difference between indication and expression was functional or intentional, and not substantial' (*SP*, 37; cf. 20), Husserl can now exclude as indications elements of substantial speech; in particular: '*All speech inasmuch as it is engaged in communication and manifests lived experience operates as indication*' (*SP*, 37–8). Excluded, then, are all forms of discourse which are intersubjective; even though Husserl concedes that expression is originally intended to serve the function of communication, it is not *pure* in functioning this way: 'only when communication is suspended can pure expression appear' (*SP*, 38). Thus, all the 'goings-forth (*sorties*) effectively exile this life of self-presence in indications', indicating, in fact, 'the process of death at work in signs' (*SP*, 40). 'As soon as the other appears, indicative language – another name for the relation with death – can no longer be effaced' (*SP*, 40).

Why is communication 'bracketed' in the attempt to distil 'pure' expression? What is it about communication which 'contaminates' expression? What happens in communication? For Husserl, communication represents a *loss* of pure presence. 'Sensible phenomena (audible or visible, etc.) are animated through the sense-giving acts of a subject, whose intention is to be simultaneously understood by another subject. But the "animation" cannot be pure and complete, for it must traverse, and to some degree lose itself in, the opaqueness of a body' (*SP*, 38; *LI*, 277). The intersubjectivity of communication demands a mediation which constitutes a loss of full-presence. Thus, Husserl's phonocentrism and privileging of pure self-presence ends up seeing the other (absence, alterity) as a *threat*, an occasion for loss. In the end, we're not far from Sartre: contamination, it seems, is other people.

But Derrida pushes this critique one step further: it is not just that pure self-presence is a retreat from intersubjectivity (and hence, Levinas would add, a retreat from responsibility); more radically, the very notion of pure self-presence cannot be maintained.[87] And in making this point, we again see the middle-voice nature of deconstruction, for Derrida will challenge Husserl with Husserl, reading his philosophical project against some of his own claims. While Husserl retreats to the solitude of soliloquy in an interior mental life, he admits into this region two factors that undermine its isolation: speech and time. First, Husserl grants a central role to a kind of speech in the identity of the ego. Though he says, 'properly speaking', one does not 'talk to oneself', he nevertheless concedes that 'one of course speaks, in a certain sense, even in soliloquy' (*LI*, 279). He accounts for this by making a distinction between 'effective speech' (of the communicative sort) and 'imagined speech' (that of soliloquy). But the distinction does not hold, Derrida concludes, because 'as soon as we admit that speech belongs essentially to the order of representation, the difference between "effective" speech and the representation of speech becomes suspect, whether the speech is purely "expressive" or engaged in "communication" '(*SP*, 50–1). In other words, insofar as Husserl admits speech into solitary mental life, he necessarily opens the door to the other, for speech as a mode of language is a cultural, 'public', phenomenon. If the ego's own solitary consciousness operates on the basis of a kind of speech, then that means that language is a condition of consciousness. So, contrary to Husserl's notion of a pre-linguistic, 'pure' consciousness, Derrida points to what we might call the *semiotic conditioning of consciousness*: thought does not proceed without language (broadly understood), and insofar as language is a communal product, the ego depends upon others for thinking. As he puts it elsewhere, '[t]he other is in me before me: the ego . . . implies alterity as its own condition. There is no "I" that ethically makes room for the other, but rather an "I" that is structured by the alterity within it, an "I" that is itself in a state of self-deconstruction, of dislocation' (*Taste*, 84). Thus, even the retreat to solitary mental life cannot shut the door to others.[88]

This disturbance of self-presence by the other also has a temporal moment: what Derrida analyses under the rubric of the *Augenblick* (the 'instant', invoking a Kierkegaardian echo). In Chapter 5 of *Speech and Phenomena*, Derrida demonstrates – on Husserlian grounds – the way in which perception depends upon that which is *not* present, temporally speaking, *viz.*, the past and the future. Thus again, the self is constituted by a difference, an absence, an alterity. In fact, memory and expectation (retention and protention) are the conditions of possibility for perception in the present (*SP*, 64). 'As soon as we admit this continuity of the now and the not-now, perception and non-perception, in the zone of primordiality common to primordial impression and primordial retention, we admit the other into the self-identity of the *Augenblick*. . . . This alterity is in fact the *condition for* presence, presentation, and thus for *Vorstellung* [representation] in general' (*SP*, 65, emphasis added). This then 'strikes at the very root of the argument for the uselessness of signs in the self-relation' (*SP*, 66). The result of this deconstructive reading is the production of an alternative account. The goal of the deconstruction of Husserl is to make room for the Other: alterity as the condition for self-consciousness; transcendence as the condition for immanence; the sphere of the Same constituted by the original in-breaking of the Other.

1.4 Writing Speech: On Language, Violence and the Other as Other

I have tried to show the way in which Derrida's earliest work on key, technical aspects of phenomenology are motivated by the central calling of deconstruction – making room for the other. Derrida is an advocate for alterity, attentive to the ways in which philosophical systems like phenomenology marginalize that which is other, and more importantly, the way in which this translates into social and political practices. If the focus has been on issues of language, and writing in particular, this is because Derrida discerned the remarkable way in which the evaluation of writing could be a window into the soul of a philosophical system from Plato to Husserl.

In *Of Grammatology*, another of the 1967 works, Derrida demonstrates how similar mechanics of exclusion are at work in discourses far removed from the arcane world of the Husserl archives. In particular, Derrida takes on two paragons – the paradigmatic French Enlightenment figure, Jean-Jacques Rousseau and the contemporary (at the time) leading voice of structuralism, Claude Lévi-Strauss – in order to show how a similar 'metaphysics of presence' infects both of their 'systems'. And once again, it is the question of writing that will function as a micro-cosmic portal into much broader themes and categories. As with Husserl, the evaluation of writing in Rousseau and Lévi-Strauss will be a symptom of much deeper metaphysical (and ethical) commitments. *Of Grammatology* opens by naming this complex of metaphysical commitments 'logocentrism' and immediately links it to a social programme of 'ethnocentrism': 'not only from Plato to Hegel', but even 'from the pre-Socratics to Heidegger', the 'history of truth' has always been linked to 'the debasement of writing, and its repression outside "full" speech' (*OG*, 3). This *logo*centrism, which privileges the voice (*phone*) as a medium of presence (and thus privileges phonetic writing) gives birth to an *ethno*-centrism which links the power of speech and phonetic writing to certain (Western) cultures. Thus, logocentrism, Derrida asserts, is 'nothing but the most original and powerful ethnocentrism' (*OG*, 3). So to deconstruct the metaphysics of presence that undergirds logocentrism is to really target the violence and colonialisms of *ethno*centrism. If Derrida works through the discourses of linguistics and philosophy, his ultimate target is ethical – a whole range of social and political practices.

The core theme of logocentrism, which we've seen at work in Husserl, and will see at work in Rousseau and Lévi-Strauss, is a privileging of the *voice* (*phone*) as a site of pure presence and a kind of non-medium that effects the transmission of thought *without mediation*, and hence untainted by the contingencies of culture. 'Full speech' or 'originary speech' is 'shielded from interpretation' (*OG*, 8) because 'the essence of the *phone* would be immediately proximate to that which within "thought" as logos relates to "meaning" ' (*OG*, 11). This complicity of voice with presence and immediacy has a long pedigree, finding articulation in Plato's *Phaedrus* (see 4. 1.1) and Aristotle's *De Interpretatione*. For Aristotle, Derrida comments, if spoken words are taken to be the 'symbols of mental experience', it is because 'the voice, producer of *the first symbols*, has a relationship of essential and immediate proximity with the mind' (*OG*, 11). Speech is a kind of mirror of reality which reflects it without any reflection or inflection, im-mediately, by a mode of 'transparence' (*OG*, 11). And this paradigm is taken up, with little challenge, by the structural linguistics of Ferdinand de Saussure (*OG*, 29–30).

Writing, in contrast, is taken to be an interruption and violence that befalls this pristine purity of speech. The logocentric tradition 'debases writing . . . as mediation of mediation and as a fall into the exteriority of meaning' (*OG*, 13). Writing, even if it is deemed 'necessary', is nevertheless seen as a corruption – a 'dangerous supplement' – that inserts the word into the dangerous labyrinth of signs and signification. In short, with writing comes the advent of mediation (interpretation, the play of meaning, and the conflict of interpretations) which comes as a threat to the unity of self-presence and speech. Thus, the 'dangers' of writing are denounced as an evil, a contamination and corruption, from Plato to Saussure. 'Already in the *Phaedrus*, Plato says that the evil of writing comes from without (275a). The contamination by writing, the fact or the threat of it, are denounced in the accents of the moralist or preacher by the linguist from Geneva. The tone counts' (*OG*, 34). Writing is seen as nothing less than a 'sin', the inversion of the 'natural' relationship between soul (speech) and body (writing). To return to the opening interest in *ethno*centrism – the social and political effects of logocentrism – we must appreciate that this devaluing and denigration of writing both assumes and produces apolitical stance. Saussure, for instance, 'is faithful to the tradition that has always associated writing with the fatal violence of the political institution' (*OG*, 36). Indeed, we will see momentarily that this view of writing as violence and contamination harbours a notion of intersubjectivity which sees the other always as a violation of the self's privacy and enclosure. In short, it produces a deeply anti-communal account of intersubjectivity which sees *any* relation to the other as always already violent. Moreover, the ethnocentrism of such distinctions rears its head in the evaluation of cultures through this grid. We see this allergy to alterity unpacked in Derrida's critical expositions of Rousseau and Lévi-Strauss. Derrida engages them retrogressively, being led back to Rousseau *through* structuralism.

1.4.1 Lévi-Strauss: Structuralism as Ethnocentrism

Derrida sees logocentrism at work in one of the most influential structuralist theorists at the time, Claude Lévi-Strauss, and shows the complicity of structuralism with a set of very old metaphysical assumptions by considering Lévi-Strauss's account of the 'proper name' in his study, 'The Writing Lesson'. There, Lévi-Strauss recounts a situation he witnessed during his time with the Nambikwara tribe. His work there was complicated by 'certain problems of language. They are not allowed, for instance, to use proper names.' When he was once playing with a group of children, one little girl was struck by another. The victim came to the anthropologist and began to whisper a 'great secret' in his ear, but Lévi-Strauss could not make out what she was saying. Eventually, the perpetrator discerned what was happening and, in response, tried to tell him another secret. 'After a little while', he recounts, 'I was able to get to the bottom of the incident. The first little girl was trying to tell me her enemy's name, and when the enemy found out what was going on she decided to tell me the other girl's name, by way of reprisal' (cited at *OG*, 110–11).

The 'lesson' that Lévi-Strauss draws from this (by analogy) is the corruption of nature by the introduction of writing. The introduction of the proper name into the public domain of language violates and corrupts the purity of an absolute (but also primitive) idiom, just as the 'introduction' of writing corrupts the purity of speech. As Lévi-Strauss interprets the scene, the violence of naming is occasioned by a foreigner, someone from the 'outside', an exteriority. The purity of the tribe is contaminated by the presence of an outsider. 'This incapacity [for writing]', Derrida notes, 'will be presently thought, within the ethico-political order, as an innocence and a non-violence interrupted by the forced entry of the West' (*OG*, 110).[89] This violence of naming, occasioned by the foreigner, is akin to the violence of *writing*, itself foreign to language, exterior to the purity of speech. But precisely by ascribing this violation to an exteriority, Lévi-Strauss sees it as *accidental*; so also, the violence of writing – with its 'public' system of marks and interpolation of mediation – is thought to be accidental and contingent.

If writing is linked to mediation and the necessity of interpretation, and this is considered a violence, then Derrida's claim is that this violence is *original*. 'The death of absolutely proper naming, recognizing in a language the other as pure other, . . . is the death of the pure idiom reserved for the unique. Anterior to the possibility of violence in the current and derivative sense, the sense used in "A Writing Lesson", there is, as the space of its possibility, the violence of the arche-writing, the violence of difference, of classification, and of the system of appellations' (*OG*, 110). Given that even speech invokes 'a system of linguistico-social differences' (*OG*, 111), to be in community with others is to already be implicated in structures of violence. This violence of naming, then, is not an accidental feature of writing as an exteriority that befalls language; rather, it is inscribed into the very nature of language (and insofar as consciousness itself is 'semiotically conditioned' it is inscribed into the very core of consciousness):

> To name, to give names that it will on occasion be forbidden to pronounce, such is the originary violence of language which consists in inscribing within a difference, in classifying, in suspending the vocative absolute. To think the unique *within* the system, to inscribe it there, such is the gesture of arche-writing: arche-violence, loss of the proper, of absolute proximity, of self-presence, in truth the loss of what has never taken place, of a self-presence which has never been given but only dreamed of and always already split, repeated, incapable of appearing to itself except in its own disappearance (*OG*, 112).

Thus, while Derrida seeks to call into question the politics of ethnocentrism that undergirds (and is undergirded by) logocentrism, and though he seeks to call into question classically liberal notions of the autonomous individual who only 'later' is inserted into intersubjective relationships which will always be a threat, the picture of intersubjectivity that Derrida paints here is one of an *essential* and original inter-relationality, but one that understand these relations as always already violent – thus perhaps retaining some vestiges of the liberal notion of autonomy.[90]

1.4.2 Rousseau: The Other as Necessary Supplement

Derrida goes on to show how deeply ingrained logocentrism is in the Western tradition by unveiling its operations in one of the saints of French liberalism: Jean-Jacques Rousseau. We have already seen the way in which Lévi-Strauss replays Rousseau's classical distinction between a pure, innocent 'nature' and the interruption of a violent 'culture' – linking writing to the later imposition of culture onto the purity of a natural speech. 'Thus we are led back to Rousseau', Derrida notes. 'The ideal profoundly underlying this philosophy of writing is therefore the image of a community immediately present to itself, without difference, a community of speech where all the members are within earshot' (*OG*, 136). But another side of Rousseau intensifies the problem by also emphasizing that such an interruption and violation is nevertheless *necessary*: paradoxically, writing will be seen as both necessary and a supplement (*OG*, 144). But while Rousseau intends to think of the supplement as an *addition*, his texts cannot avoid the sense in which the supplement is a *replacement*. The supplement comes as a 'necessary evil' to supply what is lacking in nature (*OG*, 146–7). But as a result, we must conclude that the supplement is *original*: 'there is *lack* in Nature and . . . *because of that very fact* something *is added* to it'. Thus, 'the supplement comes *naturally* to put itself in Nature's place' (*OG*, 149). What does this mean for the case of writing? That the supposed supplementarity of writing – introducing mediation, absence, and the play of signifiers – is original, inscribed into the origin of language *as such*. This is why 'Rousseau considers writing as a dangerous means, a menacing aid, the critical response to a situation of distress. When Nature, as self-proximity, comes to be forbidden or interrupted, when speech fails to protect presence, writing becomes necessary' (*OG*, 144). A kind of writing (what Derrida will call 'arche-writing') is inscribed at the origin, which is another way of saying that mediation goes all the way down. But it is important to recall the correlations we've established above between absence and alterity, between the mediation of a network of signifiers and the intersubjective communities of which they are a part. So to emphasize that mediation goes all the way down is another way of saying that the self is always already communal, situated in relationships to others to whom we are called to be responsible.

1.4.3 *Arche*-writing and *Differance*: Why 'There is Nothing Outside of the Text'

The phonocentrism of the Western philosophical tradition – 'from the *Phaedrus* to the *Course in General Linguistics*' (*OG*, 103) – privileges voice as the site of immediacy and pure self-presence, and thus denigrates writing as a violation of this presence, introducing mediation and the play of signifiers. But Derrida's analyses of Plato, Husserl, Rousseau, and Lévi-Strauss have demonstrated the way in which this mediation and play affects not only writing, but *language in general*; he has thus sought to turn phonocentrism/logocentrism back upon itself. 'The secondarity that it seemed possible to ascribe to writing alone affects all signifieds in general, affects them always already, the moment they *enter the game*. There is not a single signified that escapes, even if recaptured, the play of signifying references that constitute language' (*OG*, 7). So what the logocentric/phonocentric tradition took to be a contamination introduced by the mediation of writing is, instead, an *original condition*: all language is characterized by the mediation and interpretive play of signifiers that was thought to be confined to writing. In order to indicate the originality of this condition of mediation, Derrida introduces the notion of an *arche-writing* as the condition of possibility for language as such, including speech (*OG*, 56). This is not, as the 'Derrida' myth has it, the silly notion that before there was speech there was writing, or that a literate culture preceded oral culture. 'Writing', in the term *arche*-writing, refers to this condition of mediation, which is now seen to be original to language *as such*.[91] So, in the terms that Rousseau ascribes to writing, one would have to say that all of language is a kind of 'writing'. 'Language is not merely a sort of writing', Derrida comments, 'but a species *of* writing' (*OG*, 52). *Arche-writing* is a synonym for what Derrida elsewhere calls *différance* (see *SP*, 129–160). As the condition of possibility for language (and thus writing 'in the vulgar sense'), arche-writing 'cannot, as the condition of all linguistic systems, form a part of the linguistic system itself and be situated as an object in its field' (*OG*, 60). So, too, with *différance*: it is 'neither a word nor a concept', Derrida stipulates; rather, it is the (quasi)condition of possibility for words and concepts (*SP*, 130). The French *différer* carries with it the dual sense of (1) *differing*: distinguishing, marking a distinction or inequality; and (2) *deferring*: 'the interposition of a delay', a temporal 'spacing' which 'puts off until "later" what is presently denied, the possible that is presently impossible' (*SP*, 129). So on the one hand *différer* indicates *nonidentity*, on the other hand, 'the order of the *same*'; yet, they share a common root. This common root, 'this *sameness* which is not *identical*', is 'called'[92] *différance*. This neologism (inserting the 'a') is meant to refer to this dual movement of temporal and 'spatial' spacing. Difference 'points out the irreducibility of temporalizing' (*SP*, 130). And this spacing – the difference in time and the differences that mark the space between signs – is that which makes signification possible.

> Difference is what makes the movement of signification possible only if each element that is said to be 'present', appearing on the stage of presence, is related to something other than itself but retains the mark of a post element and already lets itself be hollowed out by the mark of its relation to a future element (*SP*, 142).

So once again, Derrida explains spacing or difference in terms of alterity, and the account of writing parallels the account of the 'other' in the critique of Husserl. While the logocentric tradition asserted the 'absolute exteriority of writing' as 'outside' speech – indeed, as the 'sickness of the outside' (*OG*, 313) – Derrida's account in *Of Grammatology* calls into question this distinction between interiority and exteriority. But even more radically, he seeks to show the way in which this exteriority is the condition of possibility for exteriority: 'it does not suffice to show, it is in fact not a question of showing, the interiority of what Rousseau would have believed exterior; rather to speculate upon the power of exteriority *as constitutive of* interiority' (*OG*, 313, emphasis added). Thus one could suggest that 'the absolute *alterity* of writing might nevertheless affect living speech, from the outside, within its inside' (*OG*, 314), just as we saw the alterity of the other (in space and time[93]) *constituting* the conscious ego.

This assertion regarding the primordiality of mediation, spacing, differance is the horizon for Derrida's oft-misunderstood claim that 'there is nothing outside of the text' [*il n'y a pas de hors-texte*], which is better translated, 'there is no outside-text'. The *hors-texte* is the buffer of blank pages at the beginning and the end of a book, the sheets that are without text. Derrida's assertion that there is no outside-text means that there is no aspect of our 'experience' – that interpretive way in which we navigate our being-in-the-world – that escapes the play[94] of signifiers or the conditioning of *différance*. To say that there is nothing outside the text is to say that there is nothing outside of textuality – there is no engagement with or inhabitance of the world which doesn't live off the mediation of signs. Thus, elsewhere he reformulates the claim as 'there is nothing outside of context' (*Linc*, 136), or 'there is nothing but context' (*Taste*, 19). There is no 'access' to either the world *or ourselves* which is not subject to the differings and deferrings of difference; as such, the world and even consciousness are never simply or fully 'present'. That is not to say, of course, that they are simply *absent* or lost either (as some mistakenly conclude). Derrida is not out to deny the reality of a world outside of texts, nor is he out to demolish the self or self-consciousness – only to point out its conditions and limits. *Arche-writing* or *différance* names one of the primordial conditions, and 'this implies that the subject (self-identical or even conscious of self-identity, self-conscious) is inscribed in the language, that he is a "function" of the language. He becomes a *speaking* subject only by conforming his speech . . . to the system of linguistic prescriptions taken as the system of differences, or at least to the general law of differance' (*SP*, 145–6). The subject's self-consciousness is constituted by a relation to an outside, to a community of others which grants language. The subject is constituted by the Other.[95]

Recalling the orienting motivation regarding *ethno*centrism, Derrida argues that what's really at stake here is *ethics*, or better, the conditions of ethics – the nature of intersubjective relations. 'There is no ethics', Derrida asserts, 'without the presence *of the other* but also, and consequently, without absence, dissimulation, detour, difference, writing. Arche-writing is the origin of morality as of immorality. The nonethical opening of ethics. A violent opening' (*OG*, 140). How so? Because arche-writing is another way of naming the fundamental and primordial *relationality*, even *communality* which constitutes being human – being in relation to others and obligated to others.

We have begun to see the shape of what we might call Derrida's 'ontology' – or what he might prefer that we call 'a general grammatology' (*OG*, 43). In the place of a metaphysics of presence is a quasi-ontology of the trace (or presence-in-absence), and instead of an isolated, self-conscious subject fully present to itself in the interiority of a pure consciousness, Derrida sketches a subject who is constituted by a relation to an exteriority – the alterity of the Other in the communal networks of signification. In this chapter we have also tried to sketch the crucial phenomenological beginnings of Derrida's work as the horizon for deconstruction, with a particular interest in the early analyses of language, speech, writing, and textuality. Throughout, we've had our eye on the other, seeing the way in which phenomenology's others (the other person, but also writing) interrupts the discourse of philosophy. Derrida, we might say, is a chronicler of and witness to these interruptions of alterity. In the next chapter we will consider some of the implications of this for what might be described as Derrida's 'epistemology' – his account of literature and interpretation.

Chapter 2

The Other (as) Literature: Critical Literary Theory

> *For I have to remind you, somewhat bluntly and simply,*
> *that my most constant interest, coming even before my*
> *philosophical interest I should say, if this is possible, has been*
> *directed towards literature, towards that writing which is*
> *called literary.*
> —'Time of a Thesis: Punctuations', p. 37

When Derrida registered his first thesis topic (under Jean Hyppolite), the title was 'The ideality of the literary object'.[96] Working 'in a context that was more marked by the thought of Husserl than is the case today', Derrida's project was interested in 'bending, more or less violently, the techniques of transcendental phenomenology to the needs of elaborating a new theory of literature'.[97] Thus, our analyses of Derrida's 'phenomenological beginnings' in Chapter 1 both anticipate and set the stage for a consideration of literature, as he himself recounts. The early work on Husserl – even questions about science and geometry (*Taste*, 44) – opened a way into questions about the literary object as a 'bound ideality'; and thus the question of writing opens onto the question of literature: 'What is literature? And first of all what is it "to write"? How is it that the fact of writing can disturb the very question "what is"? and even "what does it mean"? To say this in other words – and here is the *saying otherwise* that was of importance to me – when and how does an inscription become literature and what takes place when it does?'[98] The question of literature builds on the question of writing and anticipates questions about the event. But the question of literature, or the provocation of literature, is also another instance of alterity that has occupied deconstruction: literature as philosophy's other.

2.1 Philosophy's Others: Literature, for example

2.1.1 Making Room: Literature and the Future of Philosophy

Deconstruction, as Derrida puts it, seeks to make room for the other – to insert itself in the chinks and cracks of institutional armour in order to open up spaces for that (and those) which have been excluded. Deconstruction thus implies a deconstruction *of* philosophy, which is not simply a *de*struction (it doesn't trumpet the 'end' of philosophy) nor simply *anti*-philosophical. Rather, deconstruction is interested in opening philosophy up to its future by opening it up to its other – to the non-philosophical, or better, that which is *otherwise-than*-philosophical. This exposure to an exteriority or alterity is crucial to the (non)method of deconstruction. 'I have attempted more and more systematically to find a non-site, or a non-philosophical site, from which to question philosophy. . . . My central question is: from what site or non-site (*non-lieu*) can philosophy as such appear to itself as other than itself, so that it can interrogate and reflect upon itself in an original manner?'[99] One can see this strategy across Derrida's corpus:

- In his essay 'The Ends of Man' – which is something of a report on French philosophy given in the shadow of the Paris student riots of May 1968 – Derrida considers not only the past and present of French philosophy, but also its future. Seeing opportunities for new trajectories – signified by a certain 'trembling' – Derrida asserts that 'a radical trembling can only come from the *outside*. . . . This trembling is played out in the violent relationship of the whole of the West to its other, whether a "linguistic" relationship, or ethnological, economic, political, military, relationships, etc.' (*MP*, 134–5). One of the ways to effect this radical trembling from outside, he concludes, is 'to change terrain' – to look at old ground from the vantage point of a new site (*MP*, 135).
- The productive possibilities of the non-philosophical other are central to what is perhaps Derrida's finest piece of work: 'Violence and Metaphysics', his first extensive engagement with the work of Levinas. In the opening section of the essay, which functions as a methodological prolegomena, Derrida considers 'nonphilosophy' to be both philosophy's 'death and wellspring' – that which it has sought to exorcise, but at the same time that which launches and nourishes it (*WD*, 79). And since philosophy in the West bears the marks of its

Greek origin, since philosophy is 'primarily Greek', 'it would not be possible to philosophize, or to speak philosophically, outside this medium' (*WD*, 81). But could one conceive philosophy *otherwise*? This, Derrida will show, is precisely what Levinas suggests – and he outlines the possibility of another philosophy by exposing philosophy to its Other: the Hebrew. The Hebraic thought of the prophetic 'summons us to a dislocation of the Greek logos' (*WD*, 82). Thus, Derrida reads *Totality and Infinity* as an exercise in exposing philosophy to its other, exposing the Greek to the Jew. But again, this is a constructive project: it is not about abandoning the Greek. 'Nothing can so profoundly *solicit* the Greek logos – philosophy – than this irruption of the totally-other; and nothing can to such an extent reawaken the logos to its origin as to its mortality, its other' (*WD*, 152).

The non-philosophical other, then, is a catalyst for philosophy to reconsider itself, or a mirror that enables philosophy to engage in self-examination. The goal of such a project is not to shut down philosophy, but rather to open it up to new practices – to invent a new future for philosophy.[100] In 'Tympan', Derrida explicitly considers literature as a privileged other of philosophy. While philosophy from its inception has insisted upon 'thinking its other', it is just this kind of *thinking* that appropriates the other and nullifies its alterity: '*To insist* upon thinking *its other*: . . . In thinking it *as such*, in recognizing it, one misses it. One reappropriates it for oneself, one disposes of it' (*MP*, xi). Thus, philosophy has sought to maintain its relationship to the non-philosophical by construing it as the *anti*-philosophical and setting the rules of engagement in terms of 'knowledge' (*MP*, xii). In other words, the deck is stacked in such a way that philosophy always wins and the rational trumps what it construes as irrational. The question for Derrida is 'can one, strictly speaking, determine a nonphilosophical place, a place of exteriority or alterity from which one might still treat *of philosophy*' (*MP*, xii)? Or will it not be the case that philosophy has so constituted the field that it can always already absorb any exteriority *on its own terms*? In order to 'critique' philosophy, then, one must be more cunning, and more oblique.[101] A frontal assault is too easily absorbed by the system. Instead, Derrida suggests a kind of indirect discourse (*pace* Kierkegaard): '[B]y relating [philosophy] to something to which it has no relation, is one not immediately permitting oneself to be encoded by philosophical logos, to stand under its banner? Certainly, *except* by writing this relationship following the mode of a nonrelationship about which it would be demonstrated simultaneously or *obliquely* . . . that no philosopheme will ever have been prepared to conform to it or translate it' (*MP*, xiv). It will be a matter of exposing philosophy to its other *in a way that* 'overflows' philosophy's categories of absorption (*MP*, xiv, xxiii): 'to avoid frontal and symmetrical protest, opposition in all the forms of *anti-*, or in any case to inscribe *antism* and overturning . . . in an entirely different form of ambush, of *lokhos*, of textual maneuvers' (*MP*, xv). It is in this sense that Derrida is interested in the 'margins' of philosophy: neither simply inside or outside, the relation of the margin to the text of philosophy is oblique and complicated. Thus, the studies gathered together in *Margins of Philosophy* 'ask the question of the margin. Gnawing away at the border . . . they are to blur the line which separates a text from its controlled margin' (*MP*, xxiii). They interrogate philosophy by recalling that 'beyond the philosophical text there is not a blank, virgin, empty margin, but another text, a weave of differences of forces without any present center of reference' (*MP*, xxiii). It must be remembered, however, that by opening up the text(s) of philosophy to their margins, the point is a productive one: to open up a new future for philosophy, for 'the margin is no longer a secondary virginity but an inexhaustible reserve' (*MP*, xxiii). It will be an oblique exposure to philosophy's other – to its 'outside', its margin – that will signal an *other* philosophy, the possibility of 'doing' philosophy *otherwise*.

Why literature, then? If philosophy is opened up to a new future – opened to being constituted otherwise – by an exposure to its non-philosophical other, why is literature privileged in Derrida's project? To answer these questions, we need to first understand why philosophy has traditionally been so interested in exiling literature outside the walls of the rational city. Why has philosophy been so allergic to literature and poetry? Why does it pose such a threat? And why is it seen as such a dreaded contamination? This brings us back to logocentrism and philosophy's desire for immediacy (and univocity). Literature might be seen as the first paradigmatic field of alterity for Derrida (a later exemplar would be religion) precisely because it is that which philosophy has been most interested in exorcising. Literature is philosophy's other according to philosophy's own account. Thus, Derrida recalls a classical antagonism in the history of philosophy, *viz.*, the confrontation between philosophy and poetry, logic and rhetoric. The first thing we should do in founding the good *polis*, Plato suggested, was exile the poets[102] (*Republic*, Books VI and VII). The temptations and dissimulations of rhetoric are to be countered by the good sense of logic (*Phaedrus*). This devaluation of rhetoric and poetry, Derrida would argue, is yet another outworking

of the logocentrism that undergirds the metaphysical tradition. Literature – which we could take as a shorthand for rhetoric and poetry – is
one of those modes of language which 'overflows' the philosophical
ideal of univocity – the ideal of stable, unitary meanings and one-to-one
correspondences between words and things. But literature lives off analogy and equivocity, the play of meaning embedded in language, the
almost   infinite   possibilities   of   de-contextualization   and   recontextualization. If the philosophers – guardians of univocity – were
charged with policing the use of language, that would spell the end of
poetry and literature. But precisely because of this, staging a confrontation between literature and philosophy can open up the possibility of
philosophy engaging in self-criticism, interrogating this longstanding
ideal of univocity. As we will see below, one of the effects of exposing
philosophy to literature is that, when philosophy looks into the mirror of
literature, it will see something of itself. 'Without mixing them up',
Derrida cautions, 'and without reducing the one to the other, perhaps it
may be said that *there is always*, in what we call "philosophical", an
adherence to natural language, a profound indissociability of certain
philosophemes from the Greek, the German, the Latin, which is not the
literary part of philosophy, but is instead something that philosophy
shares with literature' (*Taste*, 11). In the same way, there is something
that is 'translatable' in literature – something that at least bears an
affinity with the univocal – and thus participates in something common
to philosophy. Thus, we should not be surprised that 'if we look more
closely, we shall find a Platonic literature that is not the literature of
Hegel, and a Shakespearean philosophy that is not the philosophy of
Dante' (*Taste*, 12).

Though part of the 'enormous research programme' that is deconstruction will call into question the tidy categories of academic scholarship (*Taste*, 12), it must be noted that Derrida does *not* simply advocate an
inversion of the relation between rhetoric and logic. If he is interested in
exposing philosophy *to* literature, even exposing the literary moment *of*
philosophy, this is not at all meant to *reduce* philosophy *to* literature – as
Rorty mistakenly has suggested.[103] 'I have never tried to confuse literature and philosophy', Derrida reiterates, 'or to reduce philosophy to
literature.'[104] More importantly, Derrida has never advocated – like
Rorty – a move to literature as a retreat to privacy or as an exercise in
private irony. 'Someone like Rorty', Derrida comments, 'is perfectly
happy that we should give ourselves over to literature – on the understanding that it is a private matter, a private language, and that taking
shelter in a private language is just fine. I have tried to emphasize that

deconstruction has nothing whatsoever to do with privatizing philosophy, letting it take shelter in literature' (*Taste*, 10). Deconstruction's
interest in literature is not a way of letting philosophers play in the
corner while the important matters of business take place in the public
sphere (conducted in a univocal language). Rather:

> the texts that are *apparently* more literary [as suggested by Rorty],
> and more tied to the phenomena of natural language, like *Glas* or
> *La carte postale*, are not evidence of a retreat towards the private, they
> are performative problematizations of the public/private distinc-
> tion. . . . *La carte postale*, the very structure of the text, is one where
> the distinction between the public and the private is rightly unde-
> cidable. And this undecidability poses philosophical problems to
> philosophy, and political problems, such as what is meant by the
> political itself.[105]

As we have seen, one of the primary vocations of deconstruction is the
disestablishment of this myth of immediacy – the demythologization of
an account of pure presence, precisely because of the *politics* of such an
ontology and epistemology. With that in view, literature is an exemplary
other which destabilizes the myths of idealist philosophy and functions as
a site for glimpsing another political order, the democracy to come.

2.1.2 The Secret Politics of Literature

It is Derrida's claims regarding the political nature of literature which
are perhaps most intriguing. But we have already seen why this might be
the case: as Derrida tried to show in his readings of Husserl, Rousseau,
and Lévi-Strauss, the philosophical penchant for immediacy and purity
produced (and was produced by) a political interest in keeping the space
of the social homogenous – a 'sphere of the Same'. As such, the community is walled off by rigid boundaries of exclusion and marginalization. This is well illustrated in Derrida's reading of the Tower of Babel
narrative (Gen. 11), where he suggests that the Semites' desire to impose
one language is an imperial agenda that Yahweh comes to interrupt, in
the name of pluralism.

> In seeking to 'make a name for themselves', to found at the same
> time a universal tongue and a unique genealogy, the Semites want
> to bring the world to reason, and this reason can signify simul-
> taneously a colonial violence (since they would thus universalize

their idiom) and a peaceful transparency of the human community. Inversely, when God imposes and opposes his name, he ruptures the rational transparency but interrupts also the colonial violence or linguistic imperialism.[106]

By calling into question the linguistic ideal of immediacy and one (univocal) language – which is, in a way, at root a desire to be *without* language – deconstruction has sided with Yahweh at Babel. If Derrida has seemed to introduce 'confusion' into philosophy, it has been this kind of prophetic confusion which is really an affirmation of plurality and difference, opening up the space for others within the community to *speak otherwise*, to speak 'in other tongues'.[107] Literature, we might suggest, is a kind of glossolalia that destabilizes hegemonic communities by rupturing the univocal ideal of language.

Literature, then, is a site of alterity and otherness – but precisely because it is the embodiment of *singularity*. If the 'ethics of deconstruction' is an ethics of obligation to the Other, this is because the Other is not merely an 'individual' (one of many), but a *singularity*, utterly unique. This is the theme that Derrida has most deeply absorbed from Kierkegaard. Already in 'Violence and Metaphysics', Derrida appealed to Kierkegaard (*contra* Levinas) as something of a witness to 'subjective existence': 'It is as subjective existence', Derrida responds to Levinas, 'that the other does not accept the system. . . . The philosopher Kierkegaard does not *only* plead for Sören Kierkegaard, . . ., but for subjective existence in general' (*WD*, 110). It is precisely this 'subjective existence' of the Other – the fact that the Other is an-other Ego – which demands respect. Thus, Derrida returns to Kierkegaard much later, in *Gift of Death*, to articulate the sense that 'every other is wholly other' [tout autre est tout autre] precisely because every other is *singular* and *secret*.[108] But Derrida also links this singularity, and Kierkegaard, to his interest in literature. Speaking of Kierkegaard ('to whom I have been most faithful'), Derrida remarks: 'for me', literature 'represents this singularity of experience and of existence in its link to language. In literature what always interests me is essentially the autobiographical – . . . the autobiographicity that greatly overflows the "genre" of autobiography' (*Taste*, 41). Thus 'memoirs . . . are the general form of everything that interests me' (*Taste*, 41).[109] Literature, Derrida seems to suggest, always has a moment of this autobiographicity that is linked to the secrets of subjectivity. Indeed, 'the autobiographical is the locus of the secret' (*Taste*, 57). And once again, this returns to the political: if 'I have a taste for the secret', Derrida testifies:

it clearly has to do with not-belonging; I have an impulse of fear or terror in the face of a political space, for example, a public space that makes no room for the secret. For me, the demand that everything be paraded in the public square and that there be no internal forum is a glaring sign of the totalitarianization of democracy. I can rephrase this in terms of political ethics: if a right to the secret is not maintained, we are in a totalitarian state (*Taste*, 59).

So the link between singularity and the secret – both of which Derrida relates to literature – has a political edge that cuts two ways: on the one hand, Derrida is interested in opening up socio-political spaces for those secret singularities which have been excluded and marginalized; on the other hand, he is wary of a public space which demands that one give up all secrets to enter, for to do so would be to relinquish one's singularity – which is to give up one's alterity. The 'culture of privacy' retains the homogeneity of the public sphere by requiring the other to keep her secret at home, in private.[110]

But how exactly does the secrecy of singularity relate to *literature*? Derrida draws the link in stages: literature, far from being a private retreat, has since its (recent) invention been an indisputably *public* institution. More specifically, it is an inherently *democratic* institution because 'what defines literature as such' is 'the principled authorization that anything can be said publicly'.[111] Literature releases language from the policies of the reigning regime and the policing of philosophical univocity and thus is a revolutionary stance with respect to both the political and the philosophical: on the one hand, because literature is able to say anything in the public sphere, 'it is inseparable from human rights, from the freedom of expression, etc.'; on the other hand, literature also 'allows one to pose questions that are often repressed in a philosophical context'.[112] If Derrida wants to then speak of the secret in this regard, it is because 'the right to say anything is said in keeping the secret'.[113] Literature is a kind of public clandestine – the right to say anything and thus the right to keep a secret, to *not* say anything. But even what it says testifies to the singularity of secret subjectivities. Literature is language run up against the alterity of the other, which clears a public space for the other to be manifest, but also guards the other's secrets. The secret, here, is 'not the secret of representation that one keeps in one's head and which one chooses not to tell, it is rather a secret coextensive with the experience of singularity'.[114] Literature is a way of (not) telling secrets.

2.2 Post Cards from the Edge: A Metaphor for Metaphoricity

2.2.1 The Irreducibility of Metaphor: or Why Plato Never Gets out of his Truck

Philosophy has long been interested in effacing this alterity and overflow of literature, excising the contamination of rhetoric in order to distil the purity of logical concepts. In particular, philosophy has refused to traffic in *metaphor*, which is fuelled by difference, preferring the vehicles of 'natural language' or 'literal meanings'. But like the desire for a pure self-presence or the immediacy of a pure speech, Derrida is witness to the originary interruption of metaphor in the discourse of philosophy. Drawing out a picture sketched in Anatole France's *The Garden of Epicurus*, Derrida opens his most intense consideration of metaphor by suggesting that one of the first movements of philosophy is one of *forgetting* – an obliteration of its debt to metaphor. The character Polyphilos recounts a reverie about 'the language of metaphysics': Metaphysicians, he suggests, are like:

> knife-grinders, who instead of knives and scissors, should put medals and coins to the grindstone to efface the exergue,[115] the value and the head. When they have worked away till nothing is visible in their crown-pieces, neither King Edward, the Emperor William, nor the Republic, they say: 'These pieces have nothing either English, German or French about them; we have freed them from all limits of time and space' (cited at *MP*, 210).

An original meaning is put to work by philosophy, and thereby 'becomes a metaphor', but then its metaphoricity is almost immediately forgotten. 'The metaphor is no longer noticed, and it is taken for the proper meaning.' A most proper philosophical concept like *ousia* ('being'), for instance, began as a more humble term related to property and wealth; but it has now been the property of philosophy for so long we are apt to forget its material origins. So, in a way, the metaphor of *ousia* is stretched to such an extent that its hook to property is severed and the word is cut loose *as if* it were only a philosophical concept. Indeed, '[p]hilosophy would be this process of metaphorization which gets carried away' (*MP*, 211). Such a notion echoes a famous Nietzschean image, which Derrida eventually cites: 'What then is truth? A mobile army of metaphors, metonymics, anthropomorphisms: in short, a sum of human relations which became poetically and rhetorically intensified, metamorphosed, adorned, and after long usage, seem to a nation fixed, canonic and binding; truths are illusions of which one has forgotten that they *are* illusions; worn out metaphors which have become powerless to affect the senses.'[116]

In order to facilitate such forgetting, and as a result of such a tradition of obliteration – 'in order to reduce the labor of rubbing' – the metaphysicians 'prefer to choose the most worn out words from natural language: "they go out of their way to choose for polishing such words as come to them a bit obliterated already" ' (*MP*, 211). What is it that has been rubbed off? It is precisely the play of multiple meanings, the rich productive density that generates multiple references – the *sensus plenoir*. This stems, once again, from philosophy's desire for the comfort and familiarity of univocity. Indeed, according to philosophy, '[u]nivocity is the essence, or better, the *telos* of language. No philosophy, as such, has ever renounced this Aristotelian ideal. This ideal is philosophy' (*MP*, 247). Metaphor, on the other hand, 'is plural from the outset' (*MP*, 268). In trying to efface metaphor, what philosophy is really interested in is halting dissemination and the proliferation of meaning. This interest produces the 'movement of metaphorization': 'origin and then erasure of the metaphor, transition from the proper sensory meaning to the proper spiritual meaning by means of the detour of figures' (*MP*, 226). But then this movement of metaphorization is 'nothing other than a movement of idealization' (*MP*, 226): a means of dis-incarnating the word, de-contextualizing it with the dream of removing it from context altogether, to the abstract ether of the ideal which secures its *one*, proper meaning.

It is just this philosophical desire and movement that deconstruction contests. Derrida's interest in metaphor is another means of exposing philosophy to its other. So it is not just a matter of metaphor 'playing exclusively the role of a pedagogical ornament' (*MP*, 221). Derrida's project resists just such a reductionism which makes metaphor simply a vehicle for propositions – a mode for 'expressing' ideas – as if the very notion of an *idea* 'did not have an entire history of its own (to which Plato is no stranger), and as if an entire metaphorics, or more generally, an entire tropic system, had not left several marks within this history' (*MP*, 223; cf. *MP*, 254). For such a notion of expression or vehicle assumes the classic philosophical claim that 'the sense aimed at through these figures is an essence rigorously independent of that which *transports* it' (*MP*, 229). Derrida is calling into question this possibility of detaching philosophical 'ideas' from their metaphorical vehicles by pointing out the way in which metaphor is irreducible. To run with the metaphor (!) a bit, we might say that these philosophical ideas are welded to the seats of their vehicles and always already bear the imprint of the vehicle. Even in the rarified air of philosophical conceptuality one does not escape the earthy stuff of metaphor. Metaphor goes all the way down.

For instance, a philosophical discourse *on* metaphor could never get outside metaphor; its categories would already assume metaphor (*MP*, 228–9). When Aristotle offers criteria for evaluating obscurity in discourse, he counsels us to check to see if the person is speaking metaphorically. But the very appeal to criteria of clarity and obscurity confirms the irreducibility of metaphor: 'How could a piece of know-ledge or a language be properly [i.e., in its "proper" sense] clear or obscure? . . . All the concepts which have operated in the definition of metaphor always have an origin and an efficacity that are themselves "metaphorical" ' (*MP*, 252). The philosophical ideals of 'clarity' and 'obscurity' bear a metaphorical origin in experiences of light and dark, seeing and blindness, now translated into philosophical concepts. So, too, the Platonic 'idea' remains marked by the embodied origin of sight, seeing, and the eyes in one's head (*MP*, 254). Even the 'exact' sciences – or what we call the 'hard' sciences, which supposedly avoid the 'fuzzi-ness' of tropes and metaphors – are deeply marked by the play of metaphorical language and give in to the temptation to 'take the meta-phor for the concept' (*MP*, 261). Derrida notes cellular theory as an example: when the nomenclature of the 'cell' was invoked to name this phenomenon, the term brought along with it (and imposed upon it) all kinds of notions of sociality, cooperation and association (*MP*, 261).[117] While the whole philosophical account of metaphor assumes the notion of a sense which is 'proper' or 'literal', it is precisely the 'abyss of metaphor' which philosophy cannot escape.[118] Even its most rigorous criteria and ideals (clarity, the idea, etc.) are 'borrowed dwellings' (*MP*, 253). Thus, what philosophy seeks to repress returns to the heart of philosophy.[119]

Deconstruction, by exposing philosophy to the other of literature, aims to point out what Derrida calls the 'generalization of metaphoric-ity' first suggested by Nietzsche (*MP*, 262). This might be translated as the claim that metaphor goes all the way down: we never get *through* the play and slippage of metaphoricity to arrive at the one, univocal, stable 'literal' sense. Thus, the claim that metaphor goes all the way down is synonymous with the claim that there is nothing outside of the text; generalized metaphoricity is another name for *arche*-writing. We see these two themes come together in the opening pages of *Of*

Grammatology. From Plato's *Phaedrus* through to Rousseau, writing *as metaphor* is opposed to writing in the *'literal' sense*, without recognizing that what is ascribed to the 'good' writing imports a metaphor which draws on the 'literal' writing which it condemns. For example, in the *Phaedrus* Plato opposes the 'writing of truth in the soul' (a 'good' writing) to the bad writing of literal, sensible marks on a page (*Phaedrus*, 278a). Bad writing introduces 'metaphoric mediation' which corrupts the immediacy of the soul's knowledge of itself. But what is happening when this 'truth' of the soul is described *as* a writing? Or when, in the Middle Ages, the fallen, mediated writing of books is contrasted with the 'book of Nature and God's writing', what are we to make of this appeal to an original metaphor of writing? 'Of course', Derrida notes, 'this metaphor remains enigmatic and refers to a "literal" meaning of writing as the first metaphor. This "literal" meaning is yet unthought by the adherents of this discourse' (*OG*, 15). Deconstruction seeks to think this unthought originary role of metaphor as a generalized metaphoricity – a metaphoricity that goes all the way down and thus undoes the classical oppositions between immediate writing in the soul and mediated writing on the page. Even the writing in the soul, we might say, is subject to the play of signifiers and the mediation of textuality. Thus, the generalization of metaphoricity is another way of articulating what we called above the semiotic conditioning of consciousness.

2.2.2 Post Cards: Performing the Metaphor

It has been widely recognized that much of Derrida's work in the 1970s departed from the more staid, traditional philosophical genres of philosophical literature (as we ironically call it). The genre of 'professional' philosophy remained wed to the ideal of univocity, and though Derrida's earliest works 'gnawed at the margins' of this, works such as *Speech and Phenomena* and the *Introduction to Husserl's Origin of Geometry* could still be seen operating inside the strictures of this genre. They contested the ideal of univocity, but strategically, from the inside. The triptych of works in 1972 (*Margins of Philosophy*, *Dissemination*, and *Positions*) challenged the strictures of the genre more directly, with more creative, playful strategies – such as the parallel columns in 'Tympan', or the non-traditional structure of *Dissemination*.[120] From the perspective of the analytic philosophy police, this was the beginning of the end. This trajectory in Derrida's work hit full stride later in the decade with the publication of *Glas* and *The Post Card*. And Derrida's interest in 'autobiographicity' became autobiographical in his 'Circumfessions' – a heretical (even 'sinful'[121]) tribute to Saint Augustine's *Confessions*, written in the mode of confession and seeking to (not) tell some secrets – 'one undecipherable secret per jar'.[122] Each of these works seeks to *perform* Derrida's point about literature and philosophy: to create something of a lab where the theses of 'White Mythology' could be effected. If Derrida 'argued' that metaphoricity goes all the way down – that there is an irreducibly literary moment to philosophy (and vice versa [*Taste*, 11]) – works such as *Glas* and 'Envois' in *The Post Card* seek to inhabit this play, not merely comment on or observe it from the outside.

Take, for example, *Glas* which, at the first encounter, is a bewildering, dizzying work that resists the typical univocal genre of professional philosophy. (Even the very materiality of the oversize book resists being easily placed on the shelf with other philosophy texts.) The 'book' takes the parallel-column scheme of 'Tympan' and multiplies it: on the left is an extensive, albeit non-traditional, exposition of Hegel (including attention to marginal, early texts); on the right is an engagement with the French literary figure Jean Genet; and interrupting the columns are snippets from letters, journals and other 'private' genres. The book resists any simple philosophical translation, let alone a reduction to a collection of theses or propositions. It also lacks the traditional apparatus of footnotes and references that form the standard parameters of philosophical 'literature'.[123] The work is, we might say, an 'event', which requires an exposure across these columns, across these genres and fields. This is not to say, of course, that *Glas* doesn't have a claim to make, that it's merely philosophical frivolity dressed up in literary garb. Such an evaluation remains tied to just the classical opposition that Derrida seeks to challenge. 'The deconstruction of philosophy does not renounce truth', Derrida emphasizes, 'any more, for that matter, than literature does' (*Taste*, 10). There is in *Glas* a 'reading' of Hegel and Genet, and there is a reading of philosophy and literature being performed in the space between these columns. As such, what *Glas* offers is, at least, a tangible picture of the programme sketched in 'Tympan': an exposure of philosophy to literature, to it's other, *for the sake of* philosophy *and* literature. Later commenting on *Glas*, Derrida remarks:

> It is neither philosophy nor poetry. It is in fact a reciprocal contamination of the one by the other, from which neither can emerge intact. This notion of contamination is, however, inadequate, for it is not simply a question of rendering both philosophy and poetry *impure*. One is trying to reach an additional or alternative dimension beyond philosophy and literature. . . . In *Glas*, consequently, I try to

compose a *writing* which would traverse, as rigorously as possible, both the philosophical and literary elements without being definable as either. Hence in *Glas* one finds classical philosophical analysis being juxtaposed with quasi-literary passages, each challenging, perverting and exposing the impurity and contradictions in their neighbor; and at some point the philosophical and literary trajectories cross each other and give rise to something else, some *other* site.[124]

The product of such a contamination and exposure, Derrida concedes, is something of a 'monster' with respect to the staid traditions of philosophical discourse: 'a monstrous mutation without tradition or normative precedent'. *Glas* isn't the sort of book that gets reviewed in *Ratio* or *Philosophy and Phenomenological Research*.

If *Glas* stages a literary performance of deconstruction's quasi-theses regarding philosophy and literature, *The Post Card* provides both a performance and a metaphor for Derrida's claim regarding the irreducibility of metaphor and mediation. 'Envois' is a collection of notes, post cards, or love letters, sent to an anonymous lover; and yet here we have this private correspondence, published, for all to see. As we saw earlier, with this genre Derrida problematizes the public/private distinction – but in doing so, points to something fundamental about language: as soon as there is language, there is publicity, a way in which even intimate expressions put into language are necessarily inserted into a public space, capable of being read by others, for such legibility (or 'iterability') is an essential feature of language. (With Wittgenstein, Derrida rejects the possibility of a 'private language'.) In this sense, every missive is like a post card: lacking the privacy and (en)closure of an envelope, it can be read by just anyone, in very different contexts, and thus could generate an almost endless number of readings and speculations. This universal legibility that characterizes the post card is an integral feature of language itself, and thus language (whether speech, writing, or gesture) is a public space of mediation which always already introduces the play of signifiers and calls for interpretation. Like a metaphor, the post card has a tenuous, almost detached relation to both its sender *and* its intended recipient(s) – it is sent out into the world, through many hands, into new contexts of reception (all along the way), and is thus capable of generating other meanings quite beyond the 'control' of the sender/speaker/author.

Thus the *postal system* is a metaphor for generalized metaphoricity. Language, the stuff of both philosophy and literature, is a medium of spacing, play and interpretation, and like the postal system, it is not infallible:

> If the post (technology, position, 'metaphysics') is announced at the 'first' *envoi*, then there is no longer A metaphysics, etc., . . . nor even AN *envoi*, but *envois* without destination. For to coordinate the different epochs, halts, determinations, in a word the entire history of Being with a destination of Being is perhaps the most outlandish postal lure. There is not even the post or the envoi. . . . In a word, . . . as soon as there is, there is *différance* . . . and there is postal maneuvering, relays, delay, anticipation, destination, telecommunicating, network, the possibility, and therefore the fatal necessity of going astray, etc. (*PC*, 66).[125]

All of our sendings are posted, inserted into the mediation of the postal system, and thus given over (but also therefore entrusted) to this system of relays (and delay), sending (and loss). Because it is inscribed in the public, post-card-like surface of language, it is capable of being read by others – and thus capable of being read differently, in a different context, assuming a different authorial context, missing the allusions or reading a metaphor otherwise. Of course, there remains a desire for a direct connection, without mediation: 'Would like to address myself', the sender confesses, 'in a straight line, directly, without *courrier*, only to you, but I do not arrive, and that is the worst of it. A tragedy, my love, of destination. Everything becomes a post card once more, legible for the other, even if he understands nothing about it' (*PC*, 23). Even if one were to write 'in code', to encrypt the messages for the private opening of another, such a code necessarily requires the iterability of a language, and is thus capable of being broken and deciphered by others (*PC*, 11). Thus, 'within every sign already, every mark or every trait, there is distancing, the post, what there has to be so that it is legible for another, another than you or me, and everything is messed up in advance, cards on the table. The condition for it to arrive is that it ends up and even that it begins by not arriving' (*PC*, 29). The iterability that is an essential feature of language entails a deep metaphoricity that means language always overflows itself. Even philosophical 'concepts' are, at bottom, post cards.

2.3 Reference to the Other: Interpretation, Context and Community

2.3.1 Reference and the Ethics of Interpretation

The essential postal mediation that Derrida points out in *The Post Card* gives rise to quite extravagant suspicions concerning deconstruction and the question of *reference*. If metaphor goes all the way down, then it would seem that there is nothing – no 'literal' or 'proper' sense – to halt the play of signifiers. On this postal account of mediation and iterability, anything (even philosophical concepts) could be read just any way by anybody: what's stopping them? If we can't police interpretation with the stable boundaries and laws of literal meaning or authorial intent, it would seem that what we are left with is linguistic and interpretive anarchy. Thus, deconstruction has been taken to be the rather extreme, yet sophomoric, assertion that 'anything goes'. (And there has been no shortage of 'readings' by assistant professors of English at the Modern Language Association that contribute to this picture.[126])

But it is simply mistaken – yes, a *bad* reading of Derrida – to conclude from the generalization of metaphor that there are no criteria for reading, even reading *well*. So too, one should not conclude from the claim that 'there is nothing outside of the text' that there are no limits that impinge upon the reader as obligations. Indeed, on the very same page that Derrida states *il n'y a pas de hors-texte*, he emphasizes that one must 'respect' the strictures of a classical exposition. 'This moment of doubling commentary should no doubt have its place in a critical reading. To recognize and respect all its classical exigencies is not easy and requires all the instruments of traditional criticism. Without this recognition and this respect, critical production would risk developing *in any direction at all* and authorize itself to *say almost anything*' (*OG*, 158, emphasis added). But Derrida notes this possibility and temptation in order to avoid and resist it. Even if a 'deconstructive' reading seeks a critical, productive reading, this must be one that respects a first 'faithful' reading.

Deconstruction, then, is not license to make a text say just anything at all, and if it is interested in the *play* of signifiers, this does not underwrite silliness or frivolity. Most importantly, it must be noted that the claim that 'there is nothing outside of the text' and the assertion that metaphor goes all the way down does *not* entail a denial of *reference*. Indeed, to deny reference would be to shut down alterity by shutting up language within its own sphere of the same. Derrida is clear and pointed on this matter:

> It is totally false to suggest that deconstruction is a suspension of reference. Deconstruction is always deeply concerned with the 'other' of language. I never cease to be surprised by critics who see my work as a declaration that there is nothing beyond language; it is, in fact, saying the exact opposite. The critique of logocentrism is above all else the search for the 'other' and the 'other of language'.[127]

Granted, deconstruction calls into question simplistic, traditional notions of reference as an easy correspondence of an inside with an outside, or notions of the text's mirroring reality. Reference never gets to a simple, pure 'outside' which is not always already implicated in a network of signifiers, but that does not mean that there is not reference; it is just that such reference is always a bit slippery – mediated and undecidable. And this is true even in literature; though literature is the right to say anything, this right also comes with responsibilities and obligations. If 'referentiality' is an important 'guardrail' on interpretation, it is important to see that referentiality is co-extensive with language *as such*: 'referentiality is not simply part of everyday, serious language; there is also referentiality in fiction, even though it is a *different kind* of referentiality'.[128]

2.3.2 Context and Community as Interpretive Guardrails

If the other of language (reference) imposes a limit upon interpretation, then we can see a second limit (or obligation) on interpretation in the function of *context*. If deconstruction is *not* license to say just anything, and demands respect for the other of language in reference, it also requires respect for context and the communities which constitute the conditions of context. As Derrida reiterated (in response to Searle), the oft-misunderstood phrase 'there is nothing outside the text' means nothing other than 'there is nothing outside of context' (*Linc*, 136). Indeed, from the early essay 'Signature Event Context' we can already see that deconstruction is deeply interested in interrogating the limits and possibilities of context, that 'the problem of context' (*MP*, 310) might be another way to conceive the central vocation of deconstruction.

Now, as with the appeal to reference, there can be no simple, naïve sense of context here. Derrida's point is to emphasize that because of the post-card-like iterability of all utterances or 'speech acts' (whether spoken or written), there is always a necessary possibility of their being *de*-contextualized, and *re*-contextualized (indeed, they can never be *without* context). Moreover, a context can never be fixed or stabilized: contexts overflow our determination of them (both in the sense that the *now* of a context is always changing, and in the sense that as finite beings we cannot 'master' a given context). A context is never 'complete' or 'saturated' – we can never have what Austin calls a 'total context' (*MP*, 322). However, at the same time, Derrida will emphasize that it is the determination of a context which makes communication possible (yes, Derrida thinks communication *is* possible). 'This is inevitable', Derrida remarks; 'one cannot do anything, least of all speak, without determining . . . a context' (*Linc*, 136). Just because contexts are always already *under*-determined does not mean that they are *in*determinate.

So despite emphasizing the impossibility of a total context, Derrida does not decry the determination of context *as such*. In fact, Derrida is not even opposed to 'interpretive police' as such; rather, he patiently describes the way in which the determination of a given community can then determine the context of utterance, thus producing criteria for good and bad interpretations, true and false interpretations (*Linc*, 146). 'Otherwise', he notes, 'one could indeed say just anything at all and I have never accepted saying, or encouraging others to say, just anything at all, nor have I argued for indeterminacy as such' (*Linc*, 144–5). What Derrida is opposed to, then, is not the determination of communities *as such*, but rather to the naïve assumption that no such determination has taken place – that these communities or rules are 'natural' or 'self-evident' (*Linc*, 146). So, for instance, the academic community is defined by a certain *telos*, certain procedures, a certain consensus. 'I believe that no research is possible *in a community* (for example, academic) without the prior search for this minimal consensus' (*Linc*, 146, emphasis added). Therefore, with the determination of the community, we have in place certain rules which are to 'govern' interpretation, and it is these 'rules' which Searle violated (*Linc*, 146).

It is in this context that Derrida speaks in a positive manner regarding a kind of interpretive police. A question put to him by Gerald Graff seems to equate the 'political' with the 'repressive', suggesting that any determination of rules must be inherently repressive and a function of a kind of police-state (*Linc*, 131). Derrida, however, rejects this equation. 'I would hesitate before associating the police, directly and necessarily, as you seem to do . . . with a determinate politics, and in particular, with a repressive politics' (*Linc*, 132). Restrictions and rules as such, enforced by police, are not inherently repressive; as he mundanely notes, '[a] red light is not repressive' (*Linc*, 132; cf. 138, 139). Certainly such restriction is not *neutral* – it is a political gesture (*Linc*, 132, 135–6) – but such non-neutrality should not be confused with repression. Indeed, Derrida explicitly notes that not all determinations of context are repressive. 'I never said that the police as such and a priori, or "the very project of attempting to fix the context of utterances", is "politically" suspect. *There is no society without police*' (*Linc*, 135). So communities 'fix' contexts and contexts determine 'meanings' – in the sense that they can choose to halt the play of recontextualization.

With this account of context in place we can consider the question of authorial intent: what, then, is the link between the determination of meaning by communal contexts and the discernment of authorial intent? Does Derrida's account of iterability preclude authorial intent? Simply, no. Rather, Derrida would emphasize two points. First, the author's intention(s) is one of an array of possible meanings for a given utterance. This follows from iterability and the structural possibility of decontextualization which is a necessary condition of possibility for language. Thus, when the author of the 'Song of Songs' pens the line 'Your hair is like a flock of goats' (6:5), the author's *intended* meaning is one of many possible meanings of this grapheme (and whether the Puritans' interpretation was included in the author's intention would be a matter for discussion). But second, there *can* be a determination of one (or several) meanings *as* the author's intended meaning *within the consensus of a communal determination*. The author's intent is not something that is 'perspicuous' or *Zuhanden*, to be simply read off of the lines of a text. Discerning the author's intentions can only unfold as a *communal* discernment, insofar as the community 'saturates' a context, to use Derrida's term. In other words, the author's intention is not something that exclusively occupies the space of an utterance, or self-evidently inheres in a given text. But it *is* something that can be communicated via a text or utterance and would be discerned from *within* the determination of a particular community. The 'author's intention', then, is not some magical hermeneutic grail which escapes the conditioning of context and textuality; but neither is it sheer myth.

Deconstruction's account of interpretation – including the interpretation of literature – is governed by a deep respect for the other of language which translates into an ethical respect for what we've suggested are 'limits' to interpretation: reference, context and community. This ethical impetus of alterity is explored beyond questions of interpretation in Derrida's more focused consideration of politics, ethics and religion, to which we turn in Chapter 3.

Chapter 3

Welcoming the Other: Ethics, Hospitality, Religion

> *Insofar as it has to do with the ethos, that is, the residence, one's home, the familiar place of dwelling, inasmuch as it is a manner of being there, the manner in which we relate to ourselves and to others, to others as our own or as foreigners,* ethics is hospitality.
> —On Cosmopolitanism and Forgiveness, *pp. 16–17*

For those who had bought into the 'Derrida' myth and vilified (or, in some cases, celebrated) the vices of the Derrida-monster – the nihilistic beast that inspired an apolitical aestheticism in the hearts of professors of English everywhere – Derrida's presence at a 1989 Cardozo Law School conference on 'justice' was at least puzzling, and for some, downright shocking. And when he had the audacity to announce that 'deconstruction is justice' (*FL*, 15), it was hailed as an event that marked a decisive *turn* in Derrida's work. So many (including key interpreters such as Rorty, Critchley and Rapaport) have interpreted this as a 'shift' in Derrida's work, a kind of repentant *Kehre* by which Derrida emerged from absorption in the aestheticism of a private irony to finally deal with 'public' political questions. But as we've already seen in Chapters 1 and 2, deconstruction has been political since its inception. So it isn't the case that Derrida's work *became* political in the 1990s; rather, it would be better to say that the topics of his analysis shifted from the deeper metaphysical assumptions that undergird the political (the dualism that produces structures of exclusion and marginalization; logocentrism *as* ethnocentrism) to those institutions and sites that we more regularly regard as 'political' (matters of law, justice, ethics, religious wars, etc.). Derrida's deconstructive gaze turned from the theoretical frameworks that shape our given institutions to consider (and disturb) the institutions themselves.

Around this same period, we find that religious themes and texts begin to emerge onto the centre stage of Derrida's work. But once again, we shouldn't overinterpret this development; there is no Damascus road experience for Derrida, no garden conversion; Derrida didn't 'get religion' at some kind of philosophical revival. Rather, there is an intimate link between Derrida's work on justice and his interest in religion. The link is the tandem of two of the most important figures that have shaped Derrida's thought: Emmanuel Levinas and Sören Kierkegaard. As he noted in the same 1989 lecture, for Levinas, the relation to the other is a question of justice (*FL*, 22), and Levinas names this relation *religion*. The call that resounds in this relation, what the Other calls us *to*, is hospitality – making room for the Other, receiving the Other as wholly Other. It would then be Kierkegaard that helps Derrida articulate the axiom that *every other is wholly other* (in *Gift of Death*). So the emergence of themes of justice, ethics, religion and hospitality in Derrida's later corpus represents not something new in the heart of deconstruction, but rather an intensification of its original vocation and apostolate as an advocate for alterity. In this chapter we will trace these themes in key works from the last decade or so, beginning with the question of law, moving to a more explicit consideration of the Levinasian moment of Derrida's work, and finally considering the shape of a deconstructive politics in what Derrida calls a 'democracy to come'. This will also give us an opportunity to see deconstruction at work 'on the ground', so to speak, addressing concrete questions of immigration policy, international law and crimes against humanity.

3.1 Deconstruction *as* Justice: A Legal Hauntology

When it comes to matters of law and justice, deconstruction is a gadfly which seeks to do nothing more than remind the powers-that-be of their finitude. Indeed, Derrida remains convinced that we are visited with the most crushing *in*justice precisely when rulers, institutions, and their agents *forget* the finitude of law – forget that our given institutions always already fail to measure up to the call of justice. When the powers-that-be begin enacting policies that traffic under the triumphant banner of 'Operation Infinite Justice', Derrida would like to do nothing more than tap these 'world leaders' on the shoulder and point out the structural impossibilities of such claims, reminding them (and us) of the *limits* of law *in the name of* justice. This reminder – this quasi-prophetic function of simply pointing out the finitude of law – *is* justice: that is why Derrida could proclaim, without prophetic pretension, that 'deconstruction is justice' (*FL*, 15). For to point out the limits of law and given socio-political institutions (the state, international law, the university, etc.) is to have one's eye on something other, that to which they don't quite (ever) measure up. In other words, this painstaking indication of the limits of given institutions lives off what these institutions are *not* (yet), what they fail to be, but to which they are also *called* to be and to which they are responsible. Derrida undertakes the work of deconstruction (of law, for instance) in the name of what is *un*deconstructible (namely, *justice* [*FL*, 14]). Thus, he emphasizes that deconstruction inserts itself into the difference between the two: 'deconstruction takes place in the interval that separates the undeconstructability of justice from the deconstructibility of *droit*' (*FL*, 15). In the language of *Specters of Marx*, we could say that justice *haunts* the law and its institutions, comes back (from its future) to disturb us and keep us awake at night, reminding us that the law has some answering to do *to* justice, that the law answers *to* justice for its *in*justices.

By inhabiting this slippage between law and justice – or more for-mally, between given institutions and institutions 'to come' – Derrida is not interested in simply demeaning the given configurations of our institutions, let alone out to destroy such institutions. Rather, he aims to 'bring them to justice', we might say – which doesn't mean (as in the code of current political parlance) seeking revenge on such institutions or 'hunting them down', but rather calling them to something better, to more just configurations. The ghosts of justice that haunt our current practices and institutions – like the ghosts that haunted Hamlet or Scrooge – come to us with *invitations*: they invite us to see things other-wise, and to then participate in effecting a transformation. Like the 'spectre' of Communism that Marx and Engels claimed was haunting Europe – that is, calling Europe to different configurations, to be an *other* Europe – so deconstruction is a witness to the hauntings of justice (see *The Other Heading*). This is closer to the 'proper' monstrosity of deconstruction – its vocation as a ghoulish threat to those who would identify given configurations of law or given institutions *as just*, as having secured or arrived at justice (as when an American President can calmly appeal to the 'goodness' of America and thus justify the extermination of 'evildoers'). And precisely because the powers-that-be are interested in securing the 'justness' of their policies, any deconstructive threat to such self-confidence is construed as 'relativism' or 'nihilism' (or 'anti-Americanism').

We might say that there is a certain *eschatology* that is central to

Derrida's work, albeit a *quasi*-eschatology.[129] The haunting and destabil-
ization of given laws and institutions is undertaken with a view to a
future 'to come' – characterized, as we'll see, by a certain *messianic* waiting. So while Derrida interrogates 'the idea of an *eschaton* or *telos* in the
absolute formulations of classical philosophy', he emphasizes that this
'does not mean that I dismiss all forms of Messianic or prophetic
eschatology. I think that all genuine questioning is summoned by a certain type of eschatology, though it is impossible to define this eschatology
in philosophical terms.'[130] This eschatology underwrites a prophetic
critique of injustice which, more often than not, is the result of institutions and the powers that govern them *forgetting* the future – forgetting
this eschatological not-yet and identifying given configurations with the
arrival of justice (a kind of realized eschatology). Deconstruction *is* justice because it remembers the future, remembers that justice has not yet
arrived, and reminds us that *we* have not yet 'arrived'; therefore the
institutions and laws we have created fail to measure up, in all kinds of
ways, to the vision of an institutional order 'to come'.

Before exploring this further, it might be helpful to consider a few
concrete examples or 'cases' that will illustrate Derrida's concern and
give a picture of how deconstruction 'operates' on this score.

3.1.1 Opening Borders: Asylum, Immigration and Cities of Refuge

Justice, for Derrida, *is* hospitality: welcoming the other. Thus, he is most
interested in those institutions which are called to be paradigmatic sites
of welcome but which, in their current configurations (undergirded, as
they are, by just the kind of metaphysical assumptions he has called into
question since the 1960s), have become systems of closure, shutting
down hospitality by shutting out the other. Thus he has shown a particular interest in questions of immigration and international law,
heightened no doubt by disturbing tendencies in France (and elsewhere
in Europe, particularly Germany and the Netherlands) which have given
rise to new justifications of xenophobia and shutting down borders in
order to protect against the threat of (especially Muslim) immigrants to
'French identity' (a major theme in Jean-Marie Le Pen's recent cam-
paign). In this context, in 1996, Derrida delivered an important address
to the International Parliament of Writers – an organization that seeks
to be an advocate for writers who are considered dissidents by their
home nations and thus silenced. The Charter of the IPW focuses on
creating a network of 'Cities of Asylum' – drawing on the biblical

notion of 'cities of refuge' (Num. 35.9–32) – where writers could escape oppressive regimes and be welcomed into democratic spaces that would give them voice.

Derrida took this proposal as an occasion for thinking about the very nature and conditions of hospitality as such. Because hospitality *is* ethics for Derrida, what is at stake in considering hospitality *as such* is not just international law or immigration but also the nature of intersubjective relationships. It is in the consideration of hospitality, we might suggest, that we get something like Derrida's philosophical anthropology. By thinking about this in terms of the *city* (the 'city of refuge'), he was taking up an ancient strategy for discussing the nature of the human person: when Plato wanted to discuss the matter of justice, and ultimately the nature of the just person, he first engaged in a thought project: 'first we'll investigate what justice is like in the cities', Socrates asserted. 'Then, we'll also go on to consider it in individuals, considering the likeness of the bigger in the idea of the smaller' (*Republic* 368e–69a). The city, then, was considered as a macro-exemplar of the individual person. In a way, Derrida takes up a similar strategy: 'cosmopolitanism' poses the question of the relation between states and their citizens in a way that will function as a 'large scale' version of the relations between persons on a micro-level. The result is a new 'cosmopolitics' oriented around the core value of *hospitality*.

Derrida suggests that the 'Charter for the Cities of Refuge' is an occasion to re-think the nature of *hospitality* – the 'right to asylum' and the corresponding 'duty to hospitality'. This is occasioned by a particular context: the realities of global violence and persecution, often carried out by and in the name of *the state*, or in a way that the state is powerless to prevent (*OCF*, 5–6). On top of this is the erosion of asylum-granting in Europe and elsewhere. Here, the supposed 'distinction' between economic and political immigration becomes problematic: nation-states will grant *political* asylum 'only to those who cannot expect the slightest economic benefit upon immigration'. But what kind of welcome is that? '[H]ow can a purely political refugee claim to have been truly welcomed into a new settlement without entailing some form of economic gain' (*OCF*, 12)? And if we take the specific case of writers (the focus of the IPW), if a writer is seeking asylum precisely because she or he has been silenced, this silencing is not 'purely' political but obviously also entails an economic impact: the political censorship has also compromised one's profession and livelihood. If the 'Cities of Refuge' will *welcome* writers, this would clearly also entail an economic benefit, since the writers would finally be free to practise their craft.

In light of this context, Derrida (and the IPW) advocate a concrete proposal: *cities* of refuge – a network of cities exercising hospitality that not even a 'government of the world' could realize (*OCF*, 8–9). These cities are to embody what Derrida calls 'an ethic of hospitality' (*OCF*, 16), though it might be said that such a notion is tautologous precisely because *ethics is hospitality* (*OCF*, 17). Hospitality (welcoming the other) is not one kind of ethical thing to do, 'not simply one ethic amongst others'; it is, rather, the condition of possibility for ethics. 'Insofar as it has to do with the *ethos*, that is, the residence, one's home, the familiar place of dwelling, inasmuch as it is a manner of being there, the manner in which we relate to ourselves and to others, to others as our own or as foreigners, *ethics is hospitality*' (*OCF*, 16–17). If ethics is hospitality, and hospitality is welcoming the other, then given what we have demonstrated above (namely, that deconstruction is a way of making room for the other), we could suggest that deconstruction *is* ethics (or, in Derrida's formulation, deconstruction is justice).

However, it is precisely the radicality of the call to hospitality which haunts given structures and institutions of hospitality – haunts our very home, our *ethos*. For Derrida suggests that hospitality is at the core of relationality, and that the categorical imperative of hospitality – what he calls '*the* Great law of hospitality' (*OCF*, 18) – requires *un*conditional welcome and orders 'that the borders be open to each and every one, to every other, to all who might come, without question or without their even having to identify who they are or whence they came' (*OCF*, 18). But insofar as welcoming the other seems to presuppose 'being at home with oneself', which seems to imply a certain sovereignty over the home (*domus*, *dominus*), it would seem that hospitality is doomed to be conditional and limited – and therefore *violent* (*OCF*, 17). Particular acts and institutions of hospitality, undertaken under the necessary conditions of finitude, will be necessarily conditioned and thus fail to measure up to '*the* Great law of Hospitality'. But for Derrida, this (essential) opposition between the unconditional ideal and the conditions of reality, does not issue in either complacency or despair; rather, he finds in this disparity a call and a challenge: to make laws more hospitable. 'It is a question', he concludes, 'of knowing how to transform and improve the law' and how this is possible '*between* the Law of an unconditional hospitality, offered *a priori* to every other, to all newcomers, *whoever they may be*, and *the* conditional laws of a right to hospitality, without which *The* unconditional Law of hospitality would be in danger of dreaming a pious and irresponsible desire' (*OCF*, 22–3). If the conditional laws of hospitality need to be haunted by The Law of Hospitality, it is also true that this

Great Law needs the concreteness of particular laws in order to avoid evaporating into a merely spectral ethereality. (Like Voldemort, Hospitality needs an embodied host, even if the finitude of that host imposes certain limits.)

3.1.2 Opening Ourselves (to Offence): Forgiveness Without Condition

These 'cases' of welcome (immigration, asylum, etc.) give us a more concrete picture of what I have called Derrida's philosophical anthropology – the account of intersubjectivity that both generates and is generated by these instances of relating to others. Clearly, it is not an isolationist picture; rather, it is an account predicated on an original and essential relationality. However, the mode of relationality is decidedly *asymmetrical* and *non-reciprocal*. I find myself originally obligated to an other, an obligation I did not choose. And insofar as the other is absolute, infinite and unconditioned, the mode in which I am to relate to the other is one of absolute, infinite, unconditioned *welcome* – what we might also call, using Derrida's idiom, *pure* welcome. To establish conditions on this welcome would be to reassert a kind of egoism where the sovereign 'I' sets the rules of engagement, where 'I' governs the conditions for relationship. So, on Derrida's account, we cannot properly say, 'you are welcome to come in *if* . . .'

Now, what does this have to do with *forgiveness*? To forgive is, in a sense, to welcome offence – to absorb a violation from another. As a result it is a kind of correlate or analogue of hospitality; and thus 'pure' forgiveness must be as *un*conditioned as absolute welcome. This is why Derrida opposes pure forgiveness to 'language of forgiveness at the service of determined finalities' (*OCF*, 31). Forgiveness in the service of political reconciliation or normalization[131] is always *interested*. If, for instance, the Truth and Reconciliation Commission in South Africa sought to create a space for forgiveness *in order to* achieve reconciliation, then according to Derrida, this would not be authentic or pure forgiveness. If forgiveness is ever *instrumental* to another desired good or end, then it is not 'pure' forgiveness for Derrida. Pure forgiveness is an end in itself (*OCF*, 31–2).[132]

Thus, Derrida announces an *axiom*: 'Forgiveness forgives only the unforgivable' (*OCF*, 32). If we forgive only the forgivable, then that's like Pharisees who love only their friends (Mt. 5). We are called to love our enemies, to forgive the unforgivable. In this context, Derrida criticizes the *economic logic* or logic of *exchange* which is often associated with forgiveness. According to this economic model (an economy of give and take – 'a *conditional* logic'), one gives forgiveness only when the offender *asks* for forgiveness, when the offender *repents* (*OCF*, 34). But such conditional welcome does not properly welcome the other *as* Other; rather, it establishes conditions of welcome that diminish the alterity of the other. The other has to cram itself through hoops of quasi-welcome which strip the other of precisely that alterity which threatens the sovereignty of the welcoming 'I'. As a result, what is welcomed is not alterity, but more of the Same.

But, as with questions of hospitality and immigration, Derrida recognizes a disparity between pure forgiveness and the political possibilities of effecting forgiveness. There is, and will always be, a heterogeneity between forgiveness and politics, because politics is always calculated and interested (*OCF*, 39–40). We cannot confuse 'the order of forgiveness' with 'the order of justice'. Thus, forgiveness has 'nothing to do with . . . the public or political sphere' (*OCF*, 43). However, while these orders remain heterogeneous, they are nevertheless indissociable (*OCF*, 44). Just as The Law of Hospitality needs acts and institutions of (albeit conditioned) hospitality to be effective, so also, in order to be 'effective', the 'purity' of absolute forgiveness must 'engage itself in a series of conditions' (*OCF*, 45). The relation between them, Derrida suggests, is one of *reference*: the concrete practices and 'works' of forgiveness 'refer to' the 'idea' of pure forgiveness (*OCF*, 45).[133] Derrida concedes that this double-bind gives rise to a deep tension, and he 'remains "torn" ' between a hyperbolic vision of 'pure' forgiveness and 'the reality of a society' working at reconciliation (*OCF*, 51). These two poles – ideal and empirical – are 'irreducible to one another' but also 'remain indissociable' (*OCF*, 51). But for Derrida, this disparity is itself a call. 'It alone can inspire here, now, in the urgency, without waiting, response and responsibilities' (*OCF*, 51).

3.1.3 Opening Europe to Its Other

In 1990 – in the wake of the bicentenary of the French revolution, the fall of the Berlin Wall, and discussions concerning the formation of the European Union – Derrida testified to a certain calling or vocation for Europe intimately linked to the other. To respond to the call of the other would be to re-direct Europe, to set its course for an 'other heading' – but one that remained deeply European precisely insofar as Europe, the 'idea' of Europe, *is* responsibility. 'What if Europe were this: the opening onto a history for which the changing of the heading, the relation to the other heading or to the other of the heading, is experienced as always possible? An opening and a non-exclusion for which Europe would in some way be responsible? For which Europe *would be*, in a constitutive way, this very responsibility? As if the very concept of responsibility were responsible, right up to its emancipation, for a European birth certificate?'[134] Given all of the injustice inflicted by 'old' European assertions of a 'New Europe', Derrida suggests that Europe's *identity* is assigned by *alterity*: 'the *heading of the other*, before which we must respond, and which we must *remember*, *of which* we must *remind ourselves*, the heading of the other being perhaps the first condition of an identity or identification that is not an egocentrism destructive of oneself and the other'.[135]

So while there has been a renewed discussion of a distinctly European 'identity', and a particularly French self-congratulation for securing the 'rights of man', Derrida sees in this a distinct challenge, even a double-bind, of constituting an identity (which presumes a unity, one-ness, ipseity) which is in fact constituted *by* alterity, an openness to the other. Europe must respond to an injunction 'to make ourselves guardians of an idea of Europe, of a difference of Europe, *but* of a Europe that consists precisely in not closing itself off in its own identity and in advancing itself in an exemplary way toward what it is not'.[136] If Europe is to be properly Europe, to answer the call to this idea of Europe, it must answer the call of the other by opening itself to the other. Europe's identity entails a *duty*: 'welcoming foreigners in order not only to integrate them but to recognize and accept their alterity'.[137] This 'other Europe', quite simply, is a Europe which exercises hospitality – and which, we should expect, welcomes not only Spain and France, but even Turkey, its 'other'.

3.1.4 Opening the Academy: The University to Come

One of the institutions that has consumed much of Derrida's time and passion is the university and its correlate spaces. But here, too, Derrida discerns a disparity between what the university is called to be and its current configuration, which includes all kinds of mechanisms of exclusion and marginalization. Indeed, despite worldwide acclaim and being welcomed by American universities (with a host of appointments at Yale, UC Irvine, NYU and elsewhere), Derrida's own relation to the university establishment has been somewhat marginal (he was never appointed to a university chair in Paris, but instead spent his time as director of a para-university institution). This has been true since the time of his own education, when he could never quite bring himself to meet the university requirement of a 'thesis' because his own work called into question the university's valorization of the 'thetic', along with its policing of disciplinary boundaries which discouraged transgression. As Derrida later recounted:

> all of this persuaded me that the time was now past, that it was, in truth, no longer possible, even if I wanted to, to make what I was writing conform to the size and form then required for a thesis. The very idea of a thetic presentation, of positional or oppositional logic, the idea of position, of *Setzung* or *Stellung*, that which I called at the beginning the *epoch* of the thesis, was one of the essential parts of the system that was under deconstructive questioning.[138]

Thus, the institutions to which Derrida devoted his life (the Ecole des Hautes Etudes en Sciences Sociales, the Collège International de Philosophie, GREPH, even the 'Humanities' programme at UC Irvine) all undertook quite rigorous interrogations of the staid, stable assumption of the university, the disciplinary nature of scientific research, the constitution of 'subjects' or 'fields', the criteria of 'scholarship', etc.[139] With one deconstructive eye on the current shape of the university, Derrida kept another hopeful eye on an*other* university, a university 'to come' – an alternative configuration of the academy as such.

Thus, Derrida inhabits this space between the past and future, tradition and inauguration. The deconstruction of the university will never be *against* the university as such, nor out to destroy the university. Once again, those who see the Derrida-monster as a threat to the university *as such* are forgetting the future, are working from a realized eschatology which takes the current configuration of the university to be *the* configuration – the divine template dropped from heaven with exemplary instantiations in Berlin, Cambridge and Boston. Derrida's critique of the university, however, is more properly eschatological and remembers the future of the university yet to come. Deconstruction is calling the current configuration of the academy to be open to its future, to welcome a reconfiguration of the university and be hospitable to what is to come.

3.2 Religion *as* Hospitality: Levinas and Kierkegaard as Proto-Deconstructors

If deconstruction is, at root, a kind of theory which testifies to and on behalf of alterity, then – contrary to traditional academic animosity – we ought to expect a certain link between Derrida and religion. Religion – or 'the religious' – has a dual link to alterity: first, like literature, it is another privileged 'other' of philosophy, a non- and other-than-philosophical source of practices, habits and thought that comes as an interruption to the staid rational categories of philosophical discourse (which is why, since Plato, philosophy has seen it as a threat). In this respect, Derrida's engagement with religious texts and phenomena follows the methodological path of two earlier landmarks in phenomenology: the young Heidegger's investigations of the 'facticity' of lived religious experience and Levinas's 'rupturing' of Greek registers of philosophy with the Hebraic cadences of prophecy (*WD*, 79–82).[140] Second, religion (or what we might even call 'religious experience') is fundamentally about the in-breaking of transcendence and alterity, which is at the same time a call to be responsible for the Other: the revelation of the Wholly Other is attended by the command to consider every other wholly other, such that there is a certain slippage between God and neighbour. In his eulogy of Levinas, Derrida alludes to both of these alterior moments of the religious as noted by Levinas: '[I]f we are able to have commerce with this unknowable, it is precisely in fear or in anguish, or in one of those ecstatic moments that you just refused as being non-philosophical; it is there that we have some presentiment of the Other – it seizes us, staggers and ravishes us, carrying us away from ourselves.'[141] Thus, from its inception, deconstruction has evinced a certain collusion with religion – first (not entirely mistakenly) identified as a quasi-negative theology, taking up religious themes and texts throughout the 1970s and 1980s, Derrida's work would later come to be identified with a certain Judaism with a prophetic edge.[142] His extended engagements with Augustine (in 'Circumfession'), Kierkegaard's Abraham (in *Gift of Death*) and questions of religious fundamentalism (in 'Faith and Knowledge') were the logical outworking of trajectories laid down in his earliest work, *viz.*, the concern with alterity we have pursued in the previous chapters.[143] The more extensive presence of religious themes in Derrida's corpus is also a result of the intensification of debts to two key influences on his work: the Christian thinker Sören Kierkegaard and Jewish sage Emmanuel Levinas. Thus, we find the formulation of some key axioms of deconstruction in Derrida's productive commentary on these two philosophers.

3.2.1 'The relation to the other, that is to say, *justice*': Levinas

Levinas's concern for the Other – what Derrida calls his 'ethics of ethics' – has inscribed itself into the heart of deconstruction since its inception. Rather than looking for a 'Levinasian turn' in Derrida's thought, we will find that Derrida has long been oriented by Levinas's distinctly Jewish account of alterity – and not only in texts devoted to Levinas's work (such as the early essay, 'Violence and Metaphysics', which evoked from Levinas the later work, *Otherwise than Being, or Beyond Essence*). In fact, what is most theoretically interesting are the ways that Derrida's most rigorous early works are governed by a certain (albeit submerged) Levinasian agenda.[144] In 'Différance', Derrida noted that 'the thought of differance implies the whole critique of classical ontology undertaken by Levinas'; in particular, it is Levinas's notion of the 'trace' that Derrida picks up to think about 'the enigma of absolute alterity, that is, the Other' (*SP*, 152), for it is the notion of the trace which permits the possibility of thinking beyond the binary opposition of presence and absence. Thus, Levinas also orients the discourse of *Of Grammatology* through this role of the trace in the 'deconstruction of presence' (*OG*, 47, 70). But Levinas is also present in the very *ethical* thrust of Derrida's early work. Thus, at the fulcrum of *Of Grammatology*, Derrida suggests that his investigation is concerned with the very condition of possibility of ethics. 'There is no ethics without the presence *of the other* but also, and consequently, without absence, dissimulation, detour, differance, writing' (*OG*, 139–40).[145]

Because of this fundamentally Levinasian orientation of deconstruction, Derrida's quasi-commentaries or expositions of Levinas are insights into his own project; indeed, it is sometimes difficult to distinguish the voices of Derrida and Levinas in these texts. What we get is the amalgam, Levinas/Derrida, with a productive ambiguity between the two. Thus, Derrida's post-mortem reading of Levinas in 'Word of Welcome' provides a helpful portal into key themes in Derrida's later work. We can understand Derrida's project here by a metaphor: recall the games and decoder sets that used to come in cereal boxes. 'Invisible' ink would be made visible by viewing the page through a translucent screen that highlighted what hadn't been previously seen. So also, Derrida's reading of Levinas's corpus through the lens of *welcome* and *hospitality* serves as a screen which highlights aspects of the corpus – and Levinas's overall project – in ways previously unseen. So we can read *Totality and Infinity* as 'an immense treatise of hospitality', Derrida contends, even if no one has ever noticed this before (*Ad*, 21) – not because we can count the number of times the word is used, but rather by noting the 'links and discursive logic' that orient the account.

This (re)reading of Levinas also opens a fundamental form of questioning that dominates Derrida's later work: how can we move from an 'ethics of ethics' to a concrete politics? How should we understand the relationship between ethics as hospitality and a law or politics of hospitality (*Ad*, 19)? Or more concretely: can the ethics of hospitality described by Levinas found a law or politics within a nation or state (beyond the familial dwelling)? Here we hit upon a central aporia that governs Derrida's account of ethics, justice and law: what he calls the terrible ineluctability of the double-bind introduced by 'the third' (*Ad*, 33). The 'third' is something of a technical term from Levinas: if I am infinitely responsible for the Other, then I can never measure up to the call to do justice to this Other, the face that confronts me. But then to top it off, another Other is always already on the scene – 'the third'. If I am infinitely obligated to the 'first'[146] Other, and could never measure up to that 'initial' call to responsibility, then what am I to do with another Wholly Other on the scene? How could I possibly adjudicate between competing infinite obligations? With this 'introduction' of the third (again, chronological terms are deceiving here) come questions about the distribution of responsibility and the adjudication of competing ethical claims. With the third is the advent of politics, civics, and what Levinas calls 'justice' (which is roughly the equivalent of what Derrida calls 'law'). But Derrida argues that 'a sharp distinction must remain between the ethical subject and the civic one' (*Ad*, 32). This is the distinction between a 'purely ethical responsibility' and something like 'political' responsibility (*Ad*, 32). And it is here that Derrida introduces the concept of violence: in fact, he suggests, the interruption of the third actually saves us from the violence of the ethical relation: the third 'protects' us from 'ethical violence itself' (*Ad*, 33), namely, our being consumed by the obligation to the ('first') other. Thus, Derrida suggests that the ineluctability of the third represents 'an initial perjury' – an originary betrayal as the very condition of justice (which is to say, *law* – the finite order of regulation, adjudication, and distribution). Law [*droit*] is a betrayal of justice [*droiture*] (*Ad*, 33). Justice, in this sense, is lamentable, such that we can hear 'the sigh of the just': 'What have I to do with justice' (*Ad*, 34)? To be just and 'law-abiding' would be to fail to discharge one's infinite obligation to the Other. It would be to already have shirked one's responsibility to the Other for the sake of another Other, 'the third'. But as we will see, for Derrida this aporetic situation of betrayal and originary perjury is 'necessary' (*Ad*, 35).

Metaphysics[147] *is* hospitality: that is Derrida's provocative reading of Levinas (*Ad*, 46). But he later glosses this in a way that is not without problems. Drawing on Levinas's metaphysical account of the 'idea of the infinite',[148] Derrida strings together this implication (admitting that one 'might draw' this 'rather abrupt conclusion'): 'hospitality is infinite or it is not at all' (*Ad*, 48). So from the notion of 'welcoming the idea *of* infinity' (my emphasis) Derrida concludes that this requires an infinite welcome (a different genitive), which he takes to mean an *unconditional* welcome (*Ad*, 48).[149] This immediately engenders a question that echoes our question above: '[H]ow can this infinite and thus unconditional hospitality, this hospitality at the opening of ethics, be regulated in a particular political or juridical practice' (*Ad*, 48)? This is both a question of translation and regulation: how can the infinite demands of unconditional hospitality be translated into policy? And how can particular laws and policies be regulated by this 'Great Law' of hospitality?

To grapple with this question of the relation between universality and particularity, Derrida looks to a question posed in one of Levinas's Talmudic commentaries: is there a recognition of the Torah before Sinai (*Ad*, 65)? Does the 'revelation' of our responsibility to welcome the other (the sum of the 'Torah') depend upon the specificity of a contingent revelation given at a particular place, Sinai? Or could there be a 'recognition of the Torah by the peoples or the nations for whom the name, the place, the event *Sinai* would mean nothing' (*Ad*, 65)? If the ethical relation to the other *is* 'religion',[150] as Levinas contends, is there the possibility of a 'religion without religion', or more specifically, a religion (as hospitality) *before* religion (the revelation that inaugurates Judaism)? In the concrete specificity of his Talmudic commentaries, Levinas comes down on the side of universality: 'a hospitality beyond all revelation' (*Ad*, 66). Indeed, the Torah, on this reading, is a proto-Enlightenment ideal such that:

> Levinas orients his interpretation toward the equivalence of *three concepts – fraternity, humanity, hospitality* – that determine an experience of the Torah and of the messianic times even *before* or outside of the Sinai, and even for the one who makes no claim 'to the title of bearer or messenger of the Torah' (*Ad*, 67).

Thus, Derrida – in a 'hypothesis' that is 'obviously not Levinas's' (*Ad*, 67) – refers to this structure of unconditional hospitality as 'a structural or *a priori* messianicity' that is not dependent upon the contingencies of a particular, historical revelation: it bears no holy ties to either a date or place. Election – the election *to* responsibility, called to welcome every Other – is not restricted to 'some particular people or nation'; rather, election is coextensive with the *human* community (*Ad*, 70, 66, 72).

However, if Derrida has unhooked this 'messianic' structure from the determinate revelations of particular religious traditions, the double-bind remains operative. While the source of our infinite obligation to welcome the other has been universalized, this still leaves us in the situation of being called to an unconditioned and infinite hospitality which seems incommensurate with the finite, conditioned nature of positive law (the kinds of regulation and law we find in immigration policy, and even in that law which is called 'international'). So the question remains live: how can we translate the ethics of absolute, unconditioned hospitality into a politics or law of hospitality for particular states and institutions?

In the last section of *Adieu*, we see that the tension between the two can be formulated in terms of the singularity of the Other and the generality of law (*Ad*, 98, 115–16). Insofar as ethics requires absolute response to the singularity of the Other, but laws can only be formulated for a plurality, there is a sense in which laws are doomed to be essentially unethical and inhospitable (though 'just', since justice always operates on the level of the third, of comparison and adjudication). So there is an essential tension (or 'double-bind') between the two to the extent that law must always represent a kind of failure. This is why Levinas suggests that the State 'deforms the I and the other' (*Ad*, 97). Nevertheless, '*it is necessary* to deduce a politics and a law from ethics' (*Ad* 115, emphasis added). So, despite the impossibility of doing this well, of deducing a politics or law that is good, the relation between the two is necessary: politics must be deduced from – and thus haunted by – ethics as hospitality. In fact, and here Derrida lapses into the most classical (Kantian) language, this points to a formal injunction – to deduce politics from ethics – but the content is 'undetermined' (*Ad*, 115). In other words, there is no neat and tidy 'schema' or formula for this deduction. The best we could manage is a kind of casuistry, ending in a decisive 'leap' in the face of undecidability (*Ad*, 116–17). The best that we can do is to find the 'better' decision, which is really only 'the least bad' (112–13, cf. 114); 'it is not good' (*Ad*, 113). Politics, then, is a necessary evil whose advent is the ineluctable presence of the third. But for Derrida, the recognition of this failure is not reason for despair or for abandoning the project; rather, deconstruction seeks to keep its eye on an unconditional hospitality 'to come' as that which funds a critique of our current laws and institutions. This persistent haunting is what keeps law seeking justice, and it is this ghostly gap between the present and the future that deconstruction inhabits *in the name of* a justice to come. Deconstruction is a kind of minion to the haunting ghost of the 'to come'.

3.2.2 Every Other is Wholly Other: Kierkegaard's Abraham

Derrida's reception of Levinas, and hence his deconstructive affirmation of alterity, has always been filtered through Kierkegaard. Already in 'Violence and Metaphysics', Kierkegaard functioned as something of a corrective to Levinas's hyperbole (*WD*, 110–11). But when Derrida turns to an extended meditation on Kierkegaard in *Gift of Death*, it is to extend the Levinasian account of a fundamental, infinite obligation to the other. What he finds highlighted in Kierkegaard is what Derrida defines as the essential *aporia* of responsibility: the situation without (*a-*) a 'way out' (*poros*), the double-bind where one is faced with a decision but does not *know* what to do. Derrida first unpacked this aporetics of responsibility in 'Force of Law' in terms of three aporias, or three moments of the same aporia:

(1) *The epoche or bracketing of the rule.* Responsibility, in contrast to the Kantian notion of 'giving oneself the law', requires that my decision be made without the comfort of simply applying a precedent or the predetermined guidance of a rule. '[F]or a decision to be just and responsible, it must, in its proper moment if there is one, be both regulated and without regulation: it must conserve the law and also destroy it or suspend it enough to have to reinvent it in each case' (*FL*, 23). The judge who judges what is 'just' is thus caught in a double-bind: if he simply applies a rule, then he is merely a 'calculating machine' and does not warrant praise for being just; on the other hand, we would also withhold the label of 'just' if he made no reference to law at all. 'It follows from this paradox', Derrida concludes, 'that there is never a moment that we can say *in the present* that a decision *is* just' (*FL*, 23).

(2) *The ghost of the undecidable.* A second paradox of responsibility is what Derrida calls 'undecidability': the condition for justice and ethical

responsibility is precisely the dual state of *not knowing* what to do but at the same time being *obliged to decide*. 'The undecidable', he cautions, 'is not merely the oscillation or the tension between two decisions; it is the experience of that which, though hetero-geneous, foreign to the order of the calculable and the rule, is still obliged' (*FL*, 24). So a second condition of responsibility is this incommensurability between knowledge and justice: between the calculable register of rational knowledge and the risky, non-rational order of ethics (a distinction not unknown, for instance, to Aristotle, who suggested that if one is looking for precision, look to maths, not ethics). Because one will always, *structurally* (due to finitude), lack full knowledge or a complete context, it follows that there is 'no moment in which a decision can be called presently and fully just' (*FL*, 24) – American presidential self-confidence notwithstanding. Indeed, at the heart of this deconstructive account of ethical responsibility, Derrida notes, is 'the deconstruction of all presumption of a determinate certitude of a present justice' (*FL*, 25). But this deconstruction itself feeds on and 'operates on the basis of an infinite "idea of justice", infinite because it is irreducible, irreducible because it is owed to the other' (*FL*, 25).

(3) *The urgency that obstructs the horizon of knowledge.* The heterogeneity of knowledge to justice, which gives rise to the structural situation of undecidability, means that there is an urgency to justice that does not await the 'filling in' of horizons. Justice, Derrida argues, doesn't wait: 'a just decision is always required *immediately*, "right away"' (*FL*, 26). Justice doesn't wait around for us to furnish ourselves with the impossible ideal of collecting the infinite information required to reduce the decision to a calculation. Indeed, the very finitude of the moment of decision necessarily precludes the possibility of hav-ing the requisite knowledge to calculate what is ethical. But this situation of urgency and not-knowing is the very condition of responsibility.

For Derrida, this aporetic situation of undecidability, of being *without knowledge*, does not spell the end of ethics, but rather its inauguration; indeed, aporia is the *condition of* responsibility. 'For me, the *aporia* is not simply paralysis, but the *aporia* or the *non-way* is the condition of walking: if there was no *aporia* we wouldn't walk, we wouldn't find our way; path-breaking implies *aporia*. This impossibility to find one's way is the condition of ethics.'[151] Or, as he summarizes elsewhere:

> There is responsibility only because there are these aporetic struc-
> tures in which I have to respond to two injunctions, different and
> incompatible. That's where responsibility starts, when I *don't* know
> what to do. If I know what to do, well, I would apply the rule, and
> teach my students to apply the rule. But would that be ethical? I'm
> not sure. I would consider this unethical. Ethics start when you
> don't know what to do, when there is this gap between knowledge
> and action, and you have to take responsibility for inventing the new
> rule which doesn't exist. . . . An ethics with guarantees is not an
> ethics. . . . Ethics is dangerous.'[152]

Many have misunderstood undecidability to mean a radical status of
indecision, a kind of 'paralysis in the face of the power to decide'.[153] But
this is to misunderstand Derrida's point: undecidability does not stand
in opposition to decision, but rather in opposition to a situation of
complete knowledge. To describe a situation (whether ethical or hermeneutic) as undecidable is to denote it as a state of affairs where the
actors lack a saturated context or complete knowledge. Nevertheless,
they are in a position where they *must* make a decision *despite* lacking full
knowledge of the situation. It is precisely this *lack* of knowledge which
makes the situation ethical and makes the actors responsible. 'If you
don't experience some undecidability', Derrida remarks:

> then the decision would simply be the application of a programme,
> the consequence of a premiss or of a matrix. So a decision has to go
> through some impossibility in order for it to be a decision. If we
> knew what to do, if I knew in terms of knowledge what I have to do
> before the decision, then the decision would not be a decision. It
> would simply be the application of a rule, the consequence of a
> premiss, and there would be no problem, there would be no
> decision. Ethics and politics, therefore, start with undecidability.[154]

To decide in such a situation (a situation of *blindness*[155]) is, from the
perspective of 'knowledge', a kind of *madness*. Thus, Derrida sets up
heterogeneity, not between undecidability and decision, but between a
'responsibility which is heterogeneous to knowledge'[156] – which is, in the
end, a quasi-Kantian opposition between faith and knowledge in the
name of justice.[157] 'And deconstruction is mad about this kind of justice.
Mad about this desire for justice' (*FL*, 25).

It is this responsible madness that Derrida finds in Kierkegaard.
Abraham is the paradigmatic exemplar of this aporetic and undecidable
nature of responsibility, working without a net of ethical norms and

rules. All the previous codes and laws which he might have counted on to guide his decision have been transgressed by a singular command from the Wholly Other, but he can't excuse himself by commissioning a study to 'get all the facts'. Recall the scene of Abraham's predicament: Yahweh has promised him that through his 'seed' all the nations of the earth shall be blessed, and only after many years has Isaac, the fruit of his loins, finally been produced. Now, with the boy a youth, Yahweh comes to Abraham with a paradoxical command: he is to sacrifice his only son, the son of his love (Gen. 22). This is a singular call, given only to Abraham, a revelation known only to him – one he can't even share with his son. But here is the aporia: this is a call to transgress every rule Abraham has ever been taught. To respond to this call would be to violate every principle of 'ethics'. And because this call is singular – without precedent and without rule – Abraham cannot appeal to any rule or law that would 'justify' his actions. Indeed, Abraham's situation is such that the universality of 'ethics' is, in fact, a temptation. If Abraham were to act on the basis of knowledge and according to the order of rules, it would signal his *ir*responsibility (*GD*, 24). According to the register of ethics and reasons, to respond to such a call would be sheer madness – but this madness is reckoned to Abraham as *faith*.[158] It is only this faith (beyond and other-than-knowledge) that enables Abraham to respond to the call of the Wholly Other for a 'justice' that transcends and even transgresses ethics.

Much that goes under the banner of 'ethics' – all the sorts of deontological and utilitarian frameworks transmitted in courses on 'ethics' – represents the height of *ir*responsibility, Derrida would suggest (*GD*, 25–6). Ethical theory is for tragic heroes, not knights of faith. For inasmuch as we try to give ourselves rules (*auto-nomy*) and create formulas of justification and legitimation, we are in fact shirking our responsibility. Such 'ethical' frameworks try to undo the aporia of decision and reduce the situation of decision to one of knowledge. In short, all of our ethical theories are ways of trying to cover up the angst that attends undecidability; they are means of trading madness for rationality. Indeed, 'Kierkegaard sees acting "out of duty", in the universalizable sense of the law, as a dereliction of one's absolute duty' to the Wholly Other (*GD*, 63). Thus, 'the activating of responsibility (decision, act, *praxis*) will always take place before and beyond any theoretical or thematic determination. It will have to decide without it, independently from knowledge' (*GD*, 26).

What Abraham pictures for us is our absolute duty to the singular call of the Wholly Other – beyond 'ethics' and knowledge. This more formal formulation of Abraham's situation of responsibility allows Derrida to effect a certain translation of Kierkegaard in a Levinasian direction: if it is the essence of responsibility to respond to the call of the Wholly Other (in Abraham's case, God), then once we appreciate that *every other is wholly other* [*tout autre est tout autre*] we can see that this Abrahamic situation of an infinite responsibility under the conditions of undecidability is, in fact, the situation of everyone. If every other is wholly other, we are all Abraham (*GD*, 78).[159] Even the most banal situations of choosing our vocation (*GD*, 69) or feeding our cats (*GD*, 71) is a Mount Moriah – 'this land of Moriah that is our habitat every second of every day' (*GD*, 69) – charged with the call of the Other which comes to us under the conditions of undecidability.

3.3. The Politics of Deconstruction: The New International and the Democracy to Come

Derrida's 'generation'[160] (Foucault, Deleuze, Lyotard and others) encompassed an epoch of French philosophy that was deeply marked by political interests – with deep links to Marxism, Leninism, and Maoism, as well as the watershed events of 'May '68'.[161] But because Derrida maintained a certain critical distance from these generational badges of political commitment, those working with a disturbing, 'you're-either-for-us-or-against-us' logic tended to construe deconstruction as, at best, *a*political, and at worst, downright 'conservative'. But because it was just this kind of simplistic, binary logic that Derrida sought to deconstruct, any response to such charges could only be oblique and complex, often not satisfying those who were looking for party banners flown high over one's corpus (what Derrida would later call 'a certain Marxist intimidation'[162]). Thus, Derrida's relationship to the philosophical establishment in France – even to those figures he is most associated with in Anglo-American theory – was always somewhat marginal, underwriting his own interest in the politics of marginality and exclusion. Indeed, given our analyses so far of Derrida's work on phenomenology and literature, we could almost deduce the politics of deconstruction: it would be a politics concerned with doing justice to the other and thus criticizing structures and institutions of exclusion, seeking to open them up to another kind of institution – hospitable institutions that make room for the other. And, in fact, when Derrida began to speak more specifically about political institutions in the early 1990s, this is precisely what he unfolded, under two key names: *Marxism* and *democracy*.

3.3.1 Conjuring the Spirit of Marx

In one of Derrida's earliest interviews, reprinted in *Positions*, the interviewers conjure the spectre of Marxism and push Derrida to state his 'position' with respect to Marxism.[163] Behind this persistent questioning was a highly charged context swirling around the critical journal *Tel Quel*, with which Derrida had been associated. Jean-Pierre Faye, formerly one of the editors of *Tel Quel*, left the journal over ideological differences and founded his own journal *Change*. At the time, *Tel Quel* openly supported the French Communist Party, but in September 1969 Faye criticized those who pledged allegiance to Marxism but smuggled into the Parisian left the 'language' of Germany's 'extreme-right', alluding to the role Heidegger played in the theoretical work of figures such as Derrida. A week later, figures from the *Tel Quel* circle responded to Faye's charges, contending that he confused Heidegger with his Nazi interpreters and charging him with defaming Derrida in particular. However, in June 1971 – the same month as Derrida's interview with Houdebine and Scarpetta – *Tel Quel* broke with the Communist Party (declaring itself Maoist), and eventually broke with Derrida as well. It was in this politically charged context that the interviewers pushed Derrida on the ambiguities of his relationship to Marxism. Derrida's responses were cagey and resisted the hegemonic yes-or-no logic of the questions. Nevertheless, he did assert that 'I am not advocating anything contrary to "Marxism", I am convinced of that.'[164] When pressed about the privileged place given to two of the masters of suspicion (Nietzsche and Freud) but the absence of the third person of the infamous trinity (Marx), Derrida responds with something of a promise: 'do me the credit of believing that the "lacunae" to which you alluded are explicitly calculated to mark the site of a theoretical elaboration which remains, *for me*, at least, *still to come*.'[165]

Derrida would fulfil this promise 20 years later, in another political context that seemed almost ironic: for Derrida took up the theme (and mantle?) of Marxism in the wake of the fall of the Berlin Wall, the demise of Soviet communism, democratic resistance in Tiananmen Square, and in the era that Francis Fukuyama proudly proclaimed that the 'end of history' was being realized in globalized capitalism. But the engagement with Marx was not belated; rather, there is a sense in which the articulation of Derrida's relation to Marxism in the wake of Soviet communism opened a space for this relation to finally be articulated in ways that need not conform to the yes-or-no logic of an earlier era. So here, two decades later, Marx comes back (*revenant*) to haunt Derrida: the ghost of Marx poses to Derrida an invitation and an obligation, like the ghost that confronts Hamlet (*SM*, 3).

Deconstruction is not *simply* Marxist, Derrida contends; however, neither is it opposed to Marxism.[166] Rather, deconstruction responds to a certain 'spirit' of Marxism, as 'a radicalization, which is to say also *in the tradition* of a certain Marxism' (*SM*, 92):

> Now, if there is a spirit of Marxism which I will never be ready to renounce, it is not only the critical idea or the questioning stance (a consistent deconstruction must insist on them even as it also learns that this is not the last or first word[167]). It is even more a certain emancipatory and *messianic* affirmation (*SM*, 89).

So it is in deconstruction's incarnation of this Marxist spirit that we find three key, inter-related themes in Derrida's religio-politics: the deeply democratic desire for liberation and emancipation, the Marxist concern for justice and the messianic expectation of a future 'to come'. So, contrary to the anti-eschatological Marxism of Althusser and others, but also contrary to the doctrinaire and dogmatic Marxisms focused on a defined content or Marxist orthodoxy (*SM*, 89–90), Derrida asserts that the 'spirit of Marxism' entails an essentially 'messianic eschatology', albeit an eschatology which brackets determinate content.[168] Thus, we see the coalescence of Derrida's concern with justice, democracy and religion:

> What remains irreducible to any deconstruction, what remains as undeconstructible as the possibility itself of deconstruction is, perhaps, a certain experience of the emancipatory promise; it is perhaps even the formality of a structural messianism, a messianism without religion, even a messianic without messianism, an idea of justice – which we distinguish from law or right or even human rights – and an idea of democracy – which we distinguish from its current concept and from its determined predicates today (*SM*, 59).

Deconstruction is a kind of formalized Marxism which is forthrightly eschatological and messianic, harnessing a vision of a democracy and 'new international' *to come* as the criteria for undertaking a critique of current institutions and law as well as the outline for constructive projects of institution-building. This is not to say, of course, that there is no overlap of 'content'; indeed, Derrida explicitly points to Marx's account of capital as something to be appropriated, but at the same time transformed. 'Is it not necessary to have the courage and lucidity for a *new* critique of the *new* effects of capital (within unprecedented techno-scientific structures)?'[169] And conversely, the hope for *democracy* is not an extra-Marxist imposition: as even the *Communist Manifesto* made plain, one of the key components for realizing a just, classless order was the institution of democracy. Further, Derrida affirms the post-national vision of Marx's 'New International' as the necessary deconstruction of the sovereignty of the (modern) nation-state (*SM*, 94) – here, reading Marx against his Soviet interpreters. There even remains a hint of the manifesto as a genre in Derrida's appropriation of Marx, particularly when he outlines the ten 'plagues of the "new world order" ' (*SM*, 81–4).

However, there is also a fundamental logic of *dis*sociation at work in Derrida's 'spirit of Marxism' whereby he distances himself from the doctrines and dogmatics of a Marxist ontotheology and 'the Party' (*SM*, 74) in the same way that his affirmation of a 'messianic' structure of justice must be dissociated from the determinate doctrines of the various messian*isms* (whether Jewish, Christian or Islamic).[170] Derrida asserts this purely 'formal' Marxism without Marxism (and messianic with messianism) for two reasons: first, because 'content . . . is always deconstructible' (*SM*, 90). The determination and fixation of particular doctrines, programmes, policies and even manifestos are finite demarcations and, like laws of hospitality, can never measure up to the 'Great Law' of justice. Second, if the space of the political is to remain *really* open to the other – and to the future *to come* (which is not simply programmable or foreseeable) – then our waiting must not be conditioned by any particular, determinate horizon of expectation. If we specified beforehand what we were looking for, we would have already set up blinders to an alterity that would have surprised us. The fixing of doctrines and the determination of horizons of expectation thus necessarily translate into structures of exclusion, even if they are erected in the name of justice or utopia. As Derrida summarizes:

> A deconstructive thinking, one that matters to me here, has always pointed out the irreducibility of affirmation and therefore of the promise, as well as the undeconstructibility of a certain idea of justice (dissociated here from law). Such a thinking cannot operate without justifying the principle of a radical and interminable, infinite (both theoretical and practical, as one used to say) critique. This critique belongs to the movement of an experience open to the absolute future of what is coming, that is to say, a necessarily indeterminate, abstract, desert-like experience that is confided,

exposed, given up to its waiting for the other and for the event (*SM*, 90).

As we suggested earlier, Derrida is haunted by (and seeks to haunt us with) the spectre of finitude which calls for a constant reminder of the failure of our given, conditioned institutions: we will only be able to maintain a radical, messianic critique if our waiting for a justice to come remains unconditioned and open to the alterity of a surprise – even if that also means leaving ourselves open to monsters (cf. *Points*, 386–87).

3.3.2 What Are We Waiting For?: The Enlightenment to Come

To many (especially Habermas), Derrida's affirmation of an 'emancipatory' project was a revelation – the surprising hint of deconstruction as an Enlightenment project. Taken to be a paragon of 'postmodernism', most have understood deconstruction as *anti*-modern and thus opposed to the emancipatory, liberal politics of the Enlightenment – as if deconstruction advocated instead an obfuscation or darkening. But Derrida's discourse on justice and his appropriation of Marx signal otherwise, and in the past decade Derrida has explicitly described deconstruction as a kind of 'new Enlightenment': 'I am resolutely in favor', he proclaims, 'of a new university Enlightenment [*Aufklärung*].'[171] If deconstruction embodies and draws on a certain 'spirit of Marxism' this is because it also radicalizes a certain 'spirit of the Enlightenment' – in particular, the critical link between reason and democracy, as well as a desire for universality that translates into a kind of new 'cosmopolitanism'. Deconstruction has an Enlightenment pedigree, which can be seen particularly in Derrida's assertions regarding reason, democracy and universality. But for Derrida, there is something deeply messianic about the Enlightenment (Voltaire notwithstanding), for the Enlightenment is driven by a kind of eschatological desire – a passion for what is 'to come' (*à venir*). Thus, as we already saw in *Specters of Marx*, Derrida does not distinguish between a messianic desire for a kingdom without sovereignty and the Enlightenment desire for a democracy to come. This is because Derrida's radicalized 'new' Enlightenment is driven by a passionate reason that bears affinity to the madness of (fearful, trembling) Abrahamic faith.[172]

So Derrida – long thought the enemy of reason, Enlightenment, and the university (according to the infamous letter to *The Times*) – is, in fact, interested in 'saving the honor of reason' – albeit a more radical reason, an account of reason more closely linked to desire (and hence the body) than the ethereal, mechanistic abstractions of a long philosophical tradition from Plato to Kant.[173] This would be a reason with both an 'interest' and a calling: a reason with a sense of obligation that begins from the Other. This would be a reason that no longer operates on the basis of 'calculation' (our dominant paradigms of reason *reduce* rationality to calculation[174]), but rather a desire for the *in*calculable that has regularly haunted and interrupted the philosophical tradition, even into the Enlightenment. 'The rationality of the rational has never been limited, as some have tried to make us believe, to calculability, to reason as calculation, as *ratio*, as account, an account to be settled or given. . . . The role that "dignity" (*Würde*), for example, plays in [Kant's] *Groundwork for the Metaphysics of Morals* belongs to the order of the incalculable. In the kingdom of ends, it is opposed to what has a price on the market (*Marktpreis*) and so can give rise to calculable equivalences.'[175] In a world governed by the logic and calculability of global capitalism, where the rational is identified with market values, deconstruction is waiting and hoping for a rationality that is oriented by the *in*calculable, that which cannot be reduced to a commodity or price – a rationality which resists such commodification. Such a radicalized reason is deeply *futural*, even eschatological, as opposed to the confident teleologies of a calculative reason:

> We must ask ourselves whether, in their very historicity (for there is an undeniable thought of history in Kant and in Husserl, and even a place for a certain history of reason), these great transcendental and teleological rationalisms grant a thought of – or expose themselves to – that which *comes*, the *event of what comes and of who comes*, of what arrives or happens *by* reason and *to* reason, according to this *coming*, according to this verbal noun that links such notions as event, advent, future, and mutation to a vocabulary of the *coming*.[176]

This will be a rationality open to a future of new configurations, open to the otherness of the future in the hope of a future where every other is welcome. This will require a dissociation of reason and knowledge from its Baconian (and often Draconian) link to *power*, particularly *power-over* and an entire logistics of *sovereignty*. This clearly has implications for the regnant paradigm of the State, for 'all these great rationalisms are, in every sense of this term, rationalisms of the state, if not state rationalisms'.[177] Derrida's desire for an Enlightenment and democracy to come thus requires a deconstruction of sovereignty and all the conditions of the State-form:

> [f]or deconstruction, if something of the sort exists, would remain above all, in my view, an unconditional rationalism that never renounces – and precisely in the name of the Enlightenment to come, in the space to be opened up of a democracy to come – suspending in an argued, deliberated, rational fashion, all conditions, hypotheses, conventions, and presuppositions, and criticizing unconditionally all conditionalities.[178]

Deconstruction, in other words, is out to make trouble for reason, not in order to be irrational, but to get reason (critique, discourse, argument, etc.) to orient itself not to the calculable order of the market but to the incalculable dignity of the Other.

But in order to wait and hope for such an unconditional future, it is necessary to also divest ourselves of horizons of expectation that would condition what could arrive from this future. What we're waiting for is an *event*, but in order make room for its arrival, we must renounce any attempt to divine its advent. An event 'worthy of its name' must be un-foreseeable (and, Derrida adds, 'it is reason itself that orders us to say this, reason that gives us such a thought of the event, not some obscure irrationalism'[179]): the event must 'announce itself as im-possible; it must thus announce itself without calling in advance, without forewarning [*prévenir*], announcing itself without announcing itself, without any horizon of expectation, without *telos*'.[180] The event that we await is the in-breaking of the other *as other*: 'the hope, beyond all "messianisms", of a universalizable culture of singularities'.[181] Deconstruction is the prophet of a new kingdom of ends, seeking to make straight the way for the other to arrive. And the way to do this is by reconsidering the very nature of reason and rationality, not in order to celebrate the *ir*rational, but to open reason (and the university, and public discourse) to its other. 'It is a matter of thinking reason', Derrida contends, 'of thinking the coming of its future, of its to-come, and of its becoming, as the experience of *what* and *who* comes, of what happens or who arrives – obviously as other, as the exception or absolute singularity of an alterity that is not reappropriable by the ipseity of a sovereign power and a calculable knowledge'.[182] Finally, this 'new' Enlightenment affirmation of reason and democracy also requires an affirmation of universality: 'it will have to require or postulate a universal beyond all relativism, culturalism, ethnocentrism, and especially nationalism'.[183] But this will be a universality that stands opposed to the hegemony of 'globalization' which, in the name of a worldwide economy or 'village', seeks to reduce alterity to the sameness of corporate brands, while at the same time tolerating the grossest differences in the utilization of natural resources and distribution of wealth.[184]

So if the event that we await – the democracy/justice/messiah 'to come' – deserves the name *event*, it must be 'im-possible'. This is not garden-variety impossibility, however: 'this im-possible is not privative. It is not the inaccessible, and it is not what I can indefinitely defer: it announces itself, sweeps down upon me, precedes me, and seizes me *here and now* in a nonvirtualizable way, in actuality and potentiality.'[185] The event that would be the in-breaking of a democracy to come is not chronologically future and deferred; rather, its advent would be *kairological* – an interruption of the present.[186] Thus, the im-possibility of the event is not reason for despair, paralysis or indifference; rather, it is this aporetic im-possibility which inspires and infuses the present. So the event is both apocalyptic and banal: 'every time something happens, even in the most banal, everyday experience, there is *something* of an event and of singular unforeseeability about it: each instant marks an event, everything that is "other" as well'.[187] Insofar as every other is wholly other, every other is the Messiah and every greeting an event of a justice to come.

Chapter 4

Derrida on Others: Others on Derrida

Derrida's corpus is an intricate web of debts, legacies and trajectories: his work, we have seen, engages a dizzying range of philosophers from the canon and its margins. And his influence can be seen in almost every discipline and in a number of contemporary theorists. To attempt a comprehensive account of Derrida's debts and legacies would be doomed to failure. So in this chapter, we will take up a more humble task of considering the role of a few privileged 'others' that have left traces on his work and then consider a few schools of thought that have critically engaged Derrida and deconstruction.[188] This chapter is best read as a selective bibliography which provides clues for further reading.

If Derrida's work is animated by the other, it is also true that his corpus 'lives' on others in a way that is almost parasitic ('there is nothing but parasites', Derrida once remarked [*PC*, 10]). It is impossible to separate the themes of Derrida's work from his expositions of others, since almost every text in his corpus hovers on the margins of commentary and finds a springboard in the texts and productions of others.[189] This is because deconstruction is a deeply *historical* strategy and is, perhaps first of all, a kind of history of philosophy that lives on the philosophical tradition. In fact, his 1953–4 thesis on the theme of 'genesis' (not published until 1990) begins by contesting the distinction between 'speculative' and 'historical' philosophy – and it is precisely the phenomenological notion of *genesis* that calls this distinction into question since it points to the history, even genealogy, of speculative thought.[190] If the ego has a history of embodied experience which shapes consciousness, then even 'speculative' thought has a history of its material production which leaves its mark on even the most idealist of philosophies.[191] Constructive philosophy, then, cannot be separated from the history of philosophy. 'I think that in fact every philosopher is both a historian and a speculative thinker', Derrida remarks. 'In my own case, I'd say that I am incapable of distinguishing in what I do between the taking into account of the history of philosophy and a gesture that is not purely and simply historical' (*Taste*, 65–6). For Derrida, texts that have come down to us through the tradition of Western philosophy – texts both in the centre of the canon and on the margins – are deep wells of life. As he once commented, 'all of the great philosophical texts – of Plato, Parmenides, Hegel or Heidegger, for example – are still *before* us', they have a *future*.[192] These texts have an 'opaque and inexhaustible residue' such that, '[b]efore a Platonic or Heideggerian text . . . I feel I am confronting an abyss, a bottomless pit in which I could lose myself. No matter how rigorous an analysis I bring to bear on such texts, I am always left with the impression that there is something *more* to be thought.'[193] Thus, Derrida is happy to suffer the reproach sometimes levelled at him, that he doesn't 'speak for himelf', but rather lives on the texts of others. 'When I read another, something I do all the time and which I have been reproached for, for not writing anything in my own name but being content with writing on Plato, on Kant, on Mallarmé and others . . . – the feeling of duty which I feel in myself is that I have to be true to the other; that is, to countersign with my own name, but in a way that should be true to the other.'[194] There is a way in which every one of Derrida's texts is a collaborative work, and he is happy to explicitly jettison notions of authorial autonomy by being up front about this almost 'parasitic' strategy (though this charge itself lives off of antiquated notions of authorial autonomy).[195] This is not to say that Derrida's relation to the tradition is one of simple repetition or reproduction. Derrida is not simply a 'follower' of Nietzsche or Heidegger. On the contrary, his model of engagement is one of pious infidelity: 'my relation to the masters that you mentioned – Freud, Heidegger – is a relation of fidelity and betrayal; and I betray them because I want to be true to them'.[196] This is because something like 'authentic' following – being an 'acolyte' – requires a certain degree of rupture – of *ana*coluthon: 'to follow in the most demanding and authentic way', Derrida comments, 'implies the "*ana*col", the "not-following", the break in the following, in the company so to speak. . . . [I]n order to follow in a consistent way, to be true to what you follow, you have to interrupt the following.'[197] Derrida will be faithful to the tradition precisely by breaking with it.

In his engagements with the history of philosophy, Derrida's concern with alterity takes shape in two ways: on the one hand, he is interested in finding those places within the philosophical canon, or within the corpus of a philosopher, where the 'other' – what philosophy excludes or represses – refuses to be excluded or domesticated but rather presses itself through the fissures within a mode of thought, interrupting the self-assurances of a closed system. Derrida suggests that 'one can discern signs of such fissures of "differance" in every great philosopher: the "Good beyond Being" (*epekeina tes ousias*) of Plato's *Republic*, for example, or the confrontation with the "Stranger" in *The Sophist* are already traces of an alterity which refuses to be totally domesticated'.[198] Or, to take another example, Derrida has persistently been interested in the way 'woman' or 'the feminine' has constituted an interruption of philosophical and theoretical discourse.[199] The deconstructionist is a kind of seismographer, trying to sense where the pressure of the other is exerting itself on a text or corpus in order to release it in some way. Second, Derrida's engagement with the history of philosophy is interested in the *other* of the philosophical canon, both in terms of engaging figures and texts on the margins of the tradition, as well as sources that are *otherwise-than-philosophical* altogether – such as the literary provocations of Joyce and Jabès, the images of van Gogh, or the poetry of Celan. In what follows, we will briefly consider some of the most important of these relationships with philosophical predecessors.[200]

4.1 Feeding on Others: Derrida and the History of Philosophy

4.1.1 Plato

Though, according to the 'Derrida' myth, deconstruction is out to do away with metaphysics and tradition, it is interesting to note that Plato has been a constant foil and inspiration for Derrida since his earliest works. Indeed, it is Plato who is the source of one of the more famous terms in the deconstructive lexicon: the *pharmakon*.[201] This arises in Derrida's early engagement with the *Phaedrus*, particularly the final section of the dialogue which takes up the question of rhetoric, speech and writing; as such, 'Plato's Pharmacy' reads as a parallel to the critique of Husserl in *Speech and Phenomena*. Indeed, we might say that Plato is a proto-Husserlian (or Husserl is a Platonist): both operate with a metaphysics of presence and devalue writing on this basis. So, like Husserl, Derrida sees in Plato a privileging of *voice* (speech) over *writing*. In particular, he sees Socrates values speech because of its 'immediacy', its presence to itself – or perhaps what we could call its closeness to the Idea, whereas writing is always secondary, further removed from the

Idea itself and thus characterized by absence, lack, nothingness. But as with Husserl, Derrida then challenges Socrates' account, pointing out the way in which speech itself is characterized by all the same problems as writing: it is exterior, sensible, removed from the Idea itself, etc. And if that is the case, then Socrates ought to devalue voice/speech just as he does writing. Behind all of this is a privileging of the interior over the exterior, the intelligible over the sensible, the eternal over the temporal – all of which devalues 'finitude'. Writing (or perhaps better, arche-writing) is thus a kind of *pharmakon*, either poison or cure (Dis, 70).

While Plato plays an important role in the early Derrida's critique of a metaphysics of presence, he continues to have a privileged place in Derrida's later work. If Derrida's early work was interested in exploring what was on the margins of philosophy, we might say that his later work is interested in what lies at the limits of phenomenality – those phenomena which don't quite measure up to the criteria for 'appearance' on phenomenology's terms – things like spectres and ghosts (in *Specters of Marx*), or that which is 'seen' in the blindness of faith, through tears (in *Memoirs of the Blind*). Derrida wants to explore the conditions of phenomenality by exploring its limits and liminal cases, and it is under such a heading that we might consider his later engagement with Plato, specifically the notion of the *khôra* explored by Plato in the *Timaeus*.[202] This is yet another liminal case in the history of metaphysics. Recall the general lines of Plato's ontology, neatly summarized in the 'divided line' discourse, or the allegory of the cave, both in the *Republic* (Books VI and VII): the changing, temporal world that we experience with the senses is given to change and is thus shifty and deceptive; it's not really *real*. Rather, things in this sensible world are copies or imitations of stable, eternal, unchanging Forms in an intelligible world – the world of *being* proper. While I can see and sit upon this couch, the *real* couch is the Form of the couch which is grasped not with the eyes, but the intellect. However, things are not quite as simple as we might think, as Plato introduces further layers to this picture. Notably – and this is a central inheritance of Plato in Levinas – in Book VII of the Republic Plato suggests that even the intelligible world owes its being to something (though 'thing' isn't quite right) *beyond Being*, namely, 'the Good beyond being'. So if metaphysics traffics in the world of the Forms and is equipped with the tools of concepts that are fitted to these entities, philosophy meets its match when it runs up against that which is *beyond* Being: for how could we speak of that which transcends the order of being? If our conceptual arsenal is crafted for the stable world of being, and all of our categories are intended to be employed for things (Forms) that are, how could we even speak of this 'Good beyond being'? Thus, at the heart of philosophy we find a certain infinity, a kind of negativity which exceeds conceptual grasp and thus engenders a negative theology at philosophy's birth.[203]

But Derrida is interested in yet another layer of liminality, a quasi-some(thing) that eludes western ontology; once again, this limit case is found already in Plato's corpus under the name of *khôra* – the 'receptacle' or matrix in which sensible things are inscribed or formed. If the 'Good beyond being' exceeds the ontological table at the top end, *khôra* eludes it at the bottom, without simply falling off into *non*-being. Like the Good, *khôra* is one of philosophy's others that disrupts philosophical categories. And in fact, because both evade the fixity of philosophical concepts and definitions, there is a certain slippage between the two: when we run into that which is *other than* being, and thus resists the ontological categories of philosophy, we cannot easily fix the distinction between the Good and the *khôra*. The inability to name *khôra* raises questions about the very possibility of naming – something close to Derrida's heart.[204] So Plato turns out to be an important ally in the work of deconstruction.

4.1.2 Nietzsche

A persistent trait of the Derrida-monster conjured up by people like Alan Bloom is a deep complicity between Derrida and the monstrous Nietzsche. This usually stems from a fundamental misconstrual of Nietzsche (though the last thing we would want to do is domesticate Nietzsche's monstrosity). What, then, are we to make of Derrida's relation to (and perhaps debts to) Nietzsche?

If deconstruction is construed as a fundamentally Nietzschean project in Anglo-American theory, I think this stems from Gayatri Chakravorty Spivak's influential 'Translator's Preface' to her English translation of *Of Grammatology* – a key document in Derrida's reception in the English-speaking academy.[205] In this introduction to Derrida, Spivak particularly – and justly – emphasizes his debts to Hegel, Freud, Heidegger and Nietzsche, but with a particular emphasis on Nietzsche (*OG*, xxi–xxxviii). As we already saw in 2.2 (above), Derrida enlists Nietzsche's 'mobile army of metaphors' to critique philosophical pretensions to literality and purity. This trenchant critique of regnant paradigms of 'truth' (not truth *as such*, we must note) is further expanded in Derrida's most extensive reading of Nietzsche in *Spurs*. Deconstruction's most Nietzschean debts can be found in its critique of metaphysics (*MP*, 362–3), in its radical perspectivalism – the claim that interpretation goes all the way down (*OG*, 19), and in its genealogical reading of the history of philosophy.

But, these acknowledged debts to Nietzsche notwithstanding, an acquaintance with Derrida's corpus as it now stands (as opposed to that surveyed by Spivak in 1976) would make it difficult to see Nietzsche as a 'central' figure in Derrida's work. We never find Derrida, for instance, employing the 'will to power' as an overarching critical category.[206] While Nietzsche continues to inform Derrida's project (providing, for instance, the tools for a critique of Christian 'sacrifice' in *Gift of Death* and an account of friendship in *Politics of Friendship*), the Nietzschean voice in Derrida seems, not silenced, but at least quieted by the voice of Levinas: the *Übermensch*, we might suggest, succumbs to the Other.

4.1.3 Heidegger

If some have overestimated the role of Nietzsche for Derrida, it would be hard to do the same with respect to Heidegger. But again, the debt is not simple: Derrida concedes that he is 'simultaneously very far from and very near to Heidegger' (*PC*, 66). In *Post Card* Derrida also admits to being haunted by Heidegger's ghost, recounting a (prank) phone call, on 22 August 1979, asking whether Derrida would 'accept' a collect call from Martin. That, of course, is just the question: what will Derrida do with Heidegger's ghost? Does he accept this debt/call? Though he does not accept the call, he cautions: 'All this must not lead you to believe that no telephonic communications links me to Heidegger's ghost, as to more than one other. Quite the contrary, the network of my hookups . . . is on the burdensome side, and more than one switchboard is necessary in order to digest the overload' (*PC*, 21). It has always been Heidegger who opened up the space for deconstruction, even the deconstruction of Heidegger. 'What I have attempted to do would not have been possible without the opening of Heidegger's questions'; but precisely because of 'this debt to Heidegger's thought' Derrida locates *in* Heidegger 'the signs of belonging to metaphysics, or to what he calls ontotheology'.[207] His relation to Heidegger is the epitome of the filial infidelity noted above. Thus, from his earliest work on *Being and Time* (in *WD*), through to *Of Grammatology* and his quasi-apologetic yet deeply critical reading of Heidegger in *Of Spirit*, up to his engagements with the later Heidegger on 'justice' and the 'gift' (in *Specters of Marx* and *Given Time*), Heidegger's work – both early and late – functions as a condition of possibility for deconstruction. The tensions of deconstruction can be seen in the privileged 'others' of Levinas and Heidegger.

4.1.4 Freud

We might say that, if Freud didn't exist, Derrida's critique of Husserl would have to invent him. Derrida's account of consciousness as constituted by an absence and an alterity that exceeds the control of the subject and can never be fully present is a phenomenological reinscription of the unconscious. Thus, we should not be surprised to find Freud a persistent source (and foil) from Derrida's earliest work. However, the relation is always one of critical reception, or unfaithful following. While Freud provided a precursor to the account of arche-writing, Derrida criticizes him for failing to see the radicality of this (in 'Freud and the Scene of Writing' in *WD*); similarly, though psychoanalysis offers an account of consciousness that calls into question classical notions of authorial mastery and intention, and attendant models of interpretation, Freud retains a classical model of hermeneutics which claims that the analyst, as the master hermeneut, can unlock any secrets through a kind of interpretive X-ray vision that escapes mediation (see 'Le facteur de vérité' in *The Post Card*). This give-and-take in Derrida's relation to Freud continues into later work, including other texts in *Post Card*, *Archive Fever*, and most recently, 'Psychoanalysis Searches the States of Its Soul', in *Without Alibi*.

4.1.5 Other Others

We've still only scratched the surface of Derrida's historical sorties with the philosophical canon. We've not discussed important treatments of Aristotle (in *Margins of Philosophy* and *Politics of Friendship*), Augustine (in 'Circumfession' and *Memoirs of the Blind*), Kant (in 'Of an Apocalyptic Tone', *Truth in Painting*, and *Voyous*), or Hegel (in *Margins*, *Writing and Difference*, and especially *Glas*), just to name a few. And there remain the singular influences of literary figures such as Joyce, Mallarmé, Genet, Blanchot and Baudelaire, as well as Jewish thinkers such as Rosenzweig, Cohen, and Scholem. The bibliographies will point to primary and secondary sources that consider these figures.

But given the extensive range of his engagement with the historical canon, certain lacunas in this also become interesting. For instance, in Derrida's corpus we find no extensive engagement with Descartes or Pascal, patron saints of French philosophy. Nor do we find a rigorous confrontation with Sartre. And the 'avoidance' of Wittgenstein is, at least, curious.[208] These are engagements to come.

4.2 Others on Derrida: Responses to Deconstruction

Derrida has had no shortage of either critics or admirers. Most of the critics, however, are responding less to Derrida and more to what we called the 'Derrida' myth or the threat of the Derrida-monster. Insofar as I hope we've shown both of these to be unfounded, we need not spend time cataloguing the multitudes of misperceptions of Derrida – though in different disciplines there still need to be those who will undertake the challenge of correcting these misperceptions. In addition, we need not summarize the wealth of appropriations by Derrida (some of which *also* foster the 'Derrida' myth and feed the Derrida-monster). Instead, here I want to very briefly note four key 'schools' of engagement with Derrida that involve both appropriation and critique.

4.2.1 American Reception: The Yale School

Derrida was introduced to Anglo-American 'theory' through what came to be known as the 'Yale School' – a consortium of literary theorists at Yale that included Paul de Man, Geoffrey Hartmann, J. Hillis Miller and Harold Bloom.[209] Derrida's reception via Yale was not without problems; in particular, it meant that Derrida's own work and project was often simply reduced to whatever de Man was doing. In other words, de Man and the Yale theorists often functioned as a *substitute* for Derrida, especially for those not willing to labour in difficult texts (or in French). Furthermore, this general reception of Derrida through the gates of literary theory tended to be blind to the deep philosophical, and especially phenomenological, milieu of Derrida's work. Thus, we saw a generation of readers of Derrida without training in Husserl and Heidegger (and largely depending, for instance, on Spivak's distillation of these themes). I would contend that much of the misappropriation of Derrida stems from this very a-contextual reading that he received at the hands of assistant professors of English in the 1970s and 80s.

4.2.2 German Reception: Habermas and Gadamer

While Derrida was widely received into Anglo-American thought through the Yale school of literary theory, there was a different reception in philosophy that took up Derrida as an extension of Heideggerian hermeneutics: Gadamer representing a more conservative extension of

Heidegger, and Derrida representing the 'left wing' of this heritage. However, Derrida resisted such interpretations of deconstruction as a kind of hermeneutics, no matter how radical. This was symptomatic of a general dissonance between Derrida and German philosophy, particularly as embodied in Gadamer's hermeneutics and the Frankfurt school of critical theory associated with Jürgen Habermas. The development of Derrida's relationship to both of these 'schools' is intriguing.

Consider first his relationship to Gadamer. In an infamous (non)encounter in 1981, Derrida seemed most interested in distancing himself from Gadamer and the project of philosophical hermeneutics. Whereas Gadamer suggested that interpretation must begin from a fundamental *trust* (not suspicion) and aim for understanding (not dissemination), Derrida – in one of his most Nietzschean moments – suggested that *rupture* was more fundamental than connection: 'one needs to ask', he said, 'whether the precondition for *Verstehen* [understanding], far from being the continuity of *rapport* (as it was described [by Gadamer] yesterday evening), is not rather the interruption of *rapport*, a certain *rapport* of interruption, the suspending of all mediation'.[210] This clearly put Derrida in the camp of those advocating a fundamental hermeneutics of suspicion, and Gadamer found it difficult to even respond.[211] Later, Derrida would admit being puzzled by his own response on this occasion, suggesting it was the product of a certain 'ageless melancholy' and something that he regretted, in a way.[212]

But the trajectory of Derrida's work over the next decade and a half would bring him closer to Gadamer than this abrasive response would suggest. In his work on Heidegger, *Of Spirit*, Derrida explicitly rejected a notion that suspicion comes 'first' or is fundamental; rather, before questioning is a promise: 'the promise which, opening every speaking, makes possible the very question and therefore precedes it without belonging to it: the dissymmetry of an affirmation, of a yes before all opposition of yes and no. . . . Language always, before any question, and in the very question, comes down to the promise.'[213] Thus, before any hermeneutics of suspicion (which is, at heart, a hermeneutics of radical questioning), one must place one's trust in the promises of language.

> Language is already there, in advance at the moment at which any question can arise about it. In this it exceeds the question. This advance is, before any contract, a sort of promise of originary allegiance to which we must have in some sense already acquiesced, already said yes, given a pledge, whatever may be the negativity or problematicity of the discourse which may follow.[214]

This pledge, he goes on to say, is a 'commitment' to what is given in the promise itself. Questioning – the heart and sole of suspicion – does not have the last word, precisely because it does not have the first word, because it is itself grounded in trusting a promise.[215] This pledge happens 'before' the question, even before language, in time immemorial: 'before the word, there is this sometimes wordless word which we name the "yes". A sort of pre-originary pledge which precedes any other engagement in language or action.'[216] By calling into question the priority of suspicion, Derrida articulated a position remarkably similar to that of Gadamer.

The same ambiguity, and perhaps rapprochement, can be found in Derrida's relation to Habermas and the Frankfurt school of critical theory. Initially, the reception of deconstruction in Frankfurt was chilly. According to Habermas's evaluation in *The Philosophical Discourse of Modernity*, postmodernists like Derrida, Foucault and Lyotard, were engaged in a 'total critique' of modernity which, he concludes, must mean that they are opposed to the Enlightenment. But if they are opposed to the Enlightenment, he further concludes, then they must also be opposed to the political ideals of the Enlightenment. Since the Enlightenment is all about liberation from authoritarian structures – in short, *revolution* – then postmodernists must be opposed to revolution and hence 'for' the status quo and the reinstatement of some kind of authoritarian political structure. It is based on this reasoning that Habermas will in fact describe Foucault and Derrida as 'conservatives' or 'neoconservatives'.[217] Conversely, Derrida worried about a creeping homogeneity at work in Habermas's call for 'transparency' and 'the univocity of democratic discussion' (*OH*, 55).

The problem, of course, is with Habermas's starting point: as Derrida will take pains to point out, he does not reject the Enlightenment project *en toto*, but only elements of its rationalism. As we have already seen (3.3.2), Derrida affirms and even radicalizes the Enlightenment. So there is a sense in which deconstruction is attempting to complete, or at least carry on the Enlightenment project of liberation from oppression and hence remains revolutionary, not conservative. With this relation to the Enlightenment clarified, space was opened for a more fruitful dialogue between Frankfurt and Paris. This included the important influence of Walter Benjamin on Derrida's later work (especially in 'Force of Law'), Derrida's expression of affinity with the Frankfurt school in his address upon receiving the Adorno prize[218] (published as *Fichus*), and culminated with a collaborative effort between Derrida and Habermas that produced the 'February 15th' document, 'Europe: Plea for a Common Foreign Policy' in 2003.[219] Like the later Foucault, who expressed a deep affinity with critical theory, Derrida's later work suggests a deep alliance between Paris and Frankfurt.

4.2.3 Anglo-American Responses: Analytic Philosophy

While Derrida has generally been the subject of derision in the circles of Anglo-American or analytic philosophy,[220] there are several noted exceptions, and what appears to be an increasing interest. Perhaps the first engagement to be noted should be Newton Garver's lucid Preface to the 1973 English translation of *Speech and Phenomena*. Clearly meant to offer an apologetic, Garver seeks to situate Derrida in relation to a tradition with an unspotted analytic pedigree: the work of Ludwig Wittgenstein and the analysis of language in his wake (in *SP*, ix–xxix).

The most notable expositor of Derrida with at least analytic 'credentials' would be Richard Rorty. First sketching overlap between Donald Davidson and Derrida's account of language, and respecting Derrida as a reader of Heidegger, Rorty 'translated' a certain Derrida into idioms that were at least intelligible to the lexicon of Anglo-American philosophy. The problem was that the 'Derrida' that survived this translation turned out to be a 'private ironist', whom Rorty praised for retreating from silliness such as the mind/body problem and instead became absorbed with Joyce. Granted, Rorty didn't think this had much public or political cachet, but it was great for weekends at the cottage. The rest of the week it was only Deweyan pragmatism that could get any real (political) work done.[221] As we already saw in 2.1.2, Derrida explicitly rejects this reading, thus confirming that Rorty probably did as much as the Yale School to contribute to the formation of the 'Derrida' myth.

Following in Rorty's wake, but also departing from his model, more recently we have seen some sustained analysis of deconstruction from fairly mainstream analytic philosophers. Samuel Wheeler even has the audacity to describe deconstruction *as* analytic philosophy. The work of Rudolph Gasché prepared the way for this; and in a way, Christopher Norris's persistent notation of links between Derrida and the tradition of Kantian critique feeds into this picture of Derrida as a 'real' or 'serious' philosopher.[222] The collection of studies gathered by Simon Glenndinning is an encouraging sign of a new generation of analytic philosophers who are interested in taking Derrida seriously.[223] In response, Derrida has expressed a certain 'guilt' for not taking analytic philosophy more seriously, and is happy to describe himself as an analytic philosopher. In response to Moore, Derrida remarks, 'when you were defining conceptual philosophy, or analytic philosophy as conceptual philosophy, I thought: well, that's what I am doing, that's exactly what I am trying to do. So: I am an analytic philosopher.'[224] This opens a way of reading Derrida that is only in its infancy, but repays more labour.

4.2.4 After 'Postmodernism': Eagleton, Žižek, Badiou

Finally, we might note a growing movement within theory or 'cultural studies' which has begun to articulate a fairly trenchant critique of Derrida under the guise of a rejection of 'postmodernism'. Seeing deconstruction as part of a broader celebration of particularity, Žižek and Badiou have criticized this kind of theory for rejecting the universality that is required to fund a proper *critique*. Badiou suggests that three, quite different strains of contemporary philosophy – which he names hermeneutic, analytic, and postmodern – all 'hold that we are at the end of metaphysics' and accord a central place to the question of language.[225] But he also contends that these two 'axioms' compromise the very possibility of philosophy as such; in fact, such celebration of plurality and difference plays right into the hands of the market. 'If the category of truth is ignored, if we never confront anything but the polyvalence of meaning, then philosophy will never assume the challenges that is put out to it by a world subordinated to the merchandising of money and information.'[226] Philosophies of difference end up accommodating themselves to the fetishization of a market-driven world. For Badiou, the only way to resist this is to rehabilitate a robust metaphysics.[227] Žižek echoes this concern, suggesting that deconstruction actually opens the space for totalitarianism, rather than offering a counter valence to such violence. Like Badiou, and with Badiou, Žižek asserts the necessity of universal, even extra-linguistic, criteria which he believes Derrida's radical semiotics will not allow.[228] And Terry Eagleton tends to include deconstruction as a form of what he calls 'culturalism' or fetishization of difference which, in its theoretical framework, celebrates the kind of cultural agonism that gives birth to late modern violence, all the while talking about an 'ethics' that is bizarrely Kantian and 'bathed in an aura or religiosity – in a rhetoric of religion which has nonetheless emptied religious language of very much determinate meaning'.[229] This abstraction plays right into the hands of capitalism, which, 'for all its crass materialism, is secretly allergic to matter'.[230] Thus, Eagleton also invokes the reaffirmation of a theory that asserts universality, albeit a 'materialist idea of universality'.[231] In light of this, we might read Derrida's most recent interventions on the 'universality' of the event (in *Voyous*, for instance) as oblique responses to this line of critique.

Chapter 5

Authorship, Sovereignty and the Axiomatics of the Interview: Derrida 'Live'

If deconstruction is opposed to anything, it would be the very idea of 'live theory'. One of the central theses of Derrida's work is the instability of meaning, or perhaps the way in which the meaning of a text or pronouncement exceeds the control of the author or speaker. As such, Derrida would resist the very founding impetus that might engender a series devoted to 'live theory': that perhaps if we could get the author 'live' – if we could land an interview – the author would clear up all of the ambiguities in his very difficult texts. Such a penchant, participating in a certain cult of the interview, exhibits a desire to get *through* texts to the immediacy of the author, to leap over the nagging mediation of books and reading in order to learn what the author 'meant' *first hand*. In its worst form, the ritual of the interview is fundamentally about making things easy and devolves to the level of the soundbite, participating in the fetishization of an author's every word, and thus eager to get him to say something 'new'. This fetishization is at work in interviews that are conducted according to the rule of extracting precious little gems from the philosopher, usually with the question, 'could you talk a little bit about X?' Derrida responds almost angrily when the director of the film, *Derrida*, simply asks him, 'could you talk about love?' 'At least ask me a question', he retorts.

So it is fitting that Derrida was not able (or willing?) to sit for an interview for this volume. That lack tells us more about Derrida's 'theory'[232] than any discussion might have. The absence of a 'new' interview, then, is an opportunity to creatively deconstruct the axiomatics and ritual of the interview. And insofar as this gets at central questions about the nature of authorship, sovereignty, subjectivity, texts and reading, this becomes a performative way into deconstruction 'as such' (if we can say such a thing). So what follows is an interview with Jacques Derrida that never happened, and yet one in which he speaks in the first-person. Drawing on a vast corpus of interviews and other texts, this interview is a new configuration, an invention of sorts, which extends the conversation begun in the previous chapters. Such an exercise risks what deconstruction perhaps fears most: the simple appropriation of the other, making him play a role he has not chosen (Levinas), making him say what I want him to say. We risk this violence in the name of the other, in the name of Jacques Derrida, who always took such risks in reading others with a view to doing justice to the other.

Interview

Perhaps no philosopher has been more interrogated than you – by the press, by academics, even by filmmakers. And yet it seems to me that your work – let's call it 'deconstruction' – calls into question the very axiomatics that motivate most 'interviews'. The press – and young academics – seem eager to 'get an interview' in order to solve the riddle of a text, to bypass the difficulty of reading, to get to an author's 'intentions'.[233]

Interviews motivated by such an axiom – and I agree, it is most – would constitute a kind of violation, a forced entry. It is a mode of 'exposure' that one is pressed into. An interview is an agreement to 'expose oneself to the risks of this tape-recorded surprise' (*Points*, 10). So there is a certain violence to the interview, though not qualitatively different from the violence and risk of exposure that constitutes writing and speech, or arche-writing more generally. We could perhaps say that (too many) interviews are conducted on the basis of this axiomatics of forced exposure – aiming to get inside an author, to break open the secret, and return home with the prize. ('Did you get that?', the journalist will ask the cameraman.)

And you are right: this axiomatics of the interview presupposes a model of subjectivity that 'deconstruction' – if we can use a shorthand – has called into question 'since the beginning' (*Points*, 28), if we can sound so epic. So when a literary magazine interviews me to 'get the latest' on my work, or invites me to a retrospective consideration of one of my publications, they assume that I am somehow master of such works. But all of this – the whole process of production – 'depends on more or less conscious, more or less imaginary calculations, on daily mini-X-rays, on a whole chemistry of information largely under the sway of unconscious drives, as well as affects and phantasms that were already in place before any calculation. In any case, my representation cannot possibly master them; it sheds no more light on them than a flashlight in a prehistoric cave' (*Points*, 12).

So if I reject this axiomatics of the interview, it is because of what I tried to patiently demonstrate in my earliest work on Husserl: that the author (or speaker) is not the master of her or his intentions. The axiomatics of the interview assumes the most classical, most Husserlian notion of authorial self-presence. Deconstruction got its start calling into question just such construals of the authorial subject. It would be giving up the game to play along with it now, for the sake of the press.

Do you think interviews are illegitimate? That would make this a bit of a charade, wouldn't it? Or even worse, the kind of 'performative contradiction' you are so often charged with.

We should be careful not to generalize, not to speak of 'interviews' as a monolithic genre. What I am opposing is a certain axiomatics of the interview, as you called it, that operates with a classical notion of authorship – of the author as master of his texts, which in turn assumes a metaphysics of presence. It assumes that I am master of meaning, lord of language. But I have always insisted that there are important ways in which, as a speaker or author, I am subject *to* (*SP*, 145–6) and governed *by* language (*OG*, 158). In fact, it is precisely this point which underwrites the legitimacy – and necessity – of deconstructive reading. There are always elements of the language and hence text which the author does not command. Inserting a reading into that space between the *vouloir-dire* of the author and that which s/he does not command is when reading becomes *productive*. The author is 'inscribed in a determined textual system' (*OG*, 160) – which is not to say, as so many have wrongly thought, that we are 'slaves' to language; but it does mean that we are 'governed' by a system that exceeds our mastery.

I say this not only as an *a priori* thesis, but as a confession growing out of my own experience as an author and my own relationship to 'my' texts. When we sit down here, and you begin to ask me what I was up to in a text from 1962 or 1967, there are important ways in which I am simply a reader of my texts as you are. And as I tried to suggest in *Of Grammatology*, every 'reading' must 'always aim at a certain relationship, unperceived by the writer, between what he commands and what he does not command of the patterns of the language that he uses' (*OG*, 158). That is true of Husserl and Rousseau, and it is true of Jacques Derrida.

But outside of such an axiomatics of the interview we can find other kinds of interviews, other reasons for conducting interviews which are productive and which I would affirm, even celebrate.

I can understand, then, why you would be uncomfortable with the notion of capturing Derrida 'live'. And yet you continue to grant interviews. (It's interesting, isn't it, that we use the language of giving in this context: one [the interviewee] gives an interview, grants access in some way.) Do you have strategies for resisting this axiomatics of the interview? Is that why you seem to play with your interviewers? Subvert them? Avoid them?

I'm not sure what you mean by 'avoidance' or 'subversion'? Do you think I do you an injustice?

No, no; in fact, I wonder if the subversion of the interrogator might just be justice. If, as you've said, deconstruction is justice, I wonder if the pragmatics and genre of 'the interview' might not be a place where, above all, you've put deconstruction to work. Let's consider just one example, one of your first interviews, in 1975, for Diagraphe.[234] *To call these 'interviews' seems to strain the notion, doesn't it?*

What are you suggesting?

That in giving this 'interview' you were subverting the very possibility of an interrogation. Take just two examples: first, the text really seems to be a monologue. Your questioner seems little more than a foil, and the questions are almost irrelevant to your responses.

I don't think it's fair to say my answers are irrelevant. If I am not immediately forthcoming; if I undertake a certain detour or circuitous route to the question, that is perhaps a performative point. It signals to the interviewer and listeners (or readers) a basic tenet of deconstruction, that 'I cannot, for reasons of principle, have answered your questions. Because of the impossible or inaccessible idiom (what the other has access to that remains hidden from me is still not purely idiomatic), but also because of the difficulty there is in speaking about texts that were *done* in view of such a difficulty' (*Points*, 22).

But secondly, if someone were to step back and consider the scene in which such an interview would be given, it is almost laughable. I mean, did you expect us to believe that you rattled off these massive etymologies from the Littré *(*Points*, 7, 24–5) from memory, in a casual conversation? In what kind of dialogue would this happen?*

Or consider the most intriguing mode of subversion here, which also plays on a theme that has long concerned you: the relation and slippage between speech and writing. In both of these interviews, we find the constant interruption of brackets, brackets within brackets, even brackets within brackets within brackets. How exactly does one speak a bracket? To the tertiary level?[235]

So my only question is: was Diagraphe in on the joke?

Of course, we could engage in a long conversation about jokes, but let's postpone that for now. We could perhaps rather say that there is a 'play' in this mode of engagement. Serious play. You must appreciate that the interrogation of the interview is a situation of *aporia* – of a double-bind not unlike the situation of ethical responsibility. As soon as we inaugurate the ritual of the interview, we activate an entire constellation of duties and debts. 'Here and now an "interview" is taking place, what is called an "interview", and it implies all kinds of codes, demands, contracts, investments and surplus values. What is expected from an interview? Who requests interviews from whom' (*Points*, 9–10)? Just what is being asked – being asked *of* me? And so we engage in this 'theatre' of the literary interview: 'is there anyone who does not expect me to defend, justify, consolidate things that I have done these last years and about which you have asked me certain questions, having yourselves an interest (a legitimate one, you think, and so do I, which is why we are doing this together) in our gaining some ground when the whole thing is over' (*Points*, 10)? So the interview is in some sense a site of interrogation *by* the other, and as such, the interviewee is a kind of Abraham, responsible but also unable to respond in a way that does justice to the situation.

I don't see the double-bind here. Why, for example, are you unable to respond to the questions I'm posing? It's not clear to me why you are unable to 'do justice' to questions I might pose to you.

Because, I think, every question poses the impossible. But at the same time, the question is the birth of responsibility, calling for a response. 'No question, no response, no responsibility'.[236] Here is where I locate the double-bind: if I respond, then I run all sorts of risks of injustice. For instance, I would run the risk of endorsing a situation or line of questioning which I think is fundamentally mistaken or even violent. This is especially true for interviews governed by what we have called the axiomatics of the interview – governed by a metaphysics of presence. If I respond to such a line of questioning, do I not end up endorsing these assumptions? Or if I am questioned about my texts and simply respond, then 'I put myself in the situation of someone who felt *capable of responding*', as if I have 'a total and intact memory' and could recall every condition of production of a text – as if I was even aware of this *when I wrote*. But this would contradict in practice what my work has persistently claimed: that the author is not a master of her or his texts.[237] In these ways, to actually respond to the questions posed in the ritual of the interview would be doing an injustice. And so it would seem that justice would require *not* responding.

However – and here the double-bind arrives on the scene – 'if, still believing that this nonresponse was the best response, I decided not to respond, then I would run even worse risks'.[238] By not responding, it would seem that I am not taking seriously the interviewer *as* other. You are interrogating me, and asking me, most of the time, questions that I think are important. To not respond to them would signal a lack of respect – for you, and for the matters at hand, for 'what matters'. Moreover, my nonresponse, though perhaps cloaked in concerns about 'doing justice', could be another way of shirking my responsibility. So on the pretext of 'needing more time', I could perpetually defer a response; but such a postponed nonresponse 'can always shelter one comfortable, safe from all objection. And on the pretext of feeling incapable of responding *to* the other, and answering *for* oneself, does one not undermine, both theoretically and practically, the concept of responsibility, which is actually the very essence of the *socius*?'[239]

It is impossible to respond and impossible not to respond. That is just another way of saying that the interview is a situation of responsibility.

So the way you deal with this is by employing some of the 'oblique' strategies we've noted?

I would not say 'oblique'. I grant that this is a term I have often used in the past.[240] But 'on reflection, the oblique does not seem to me to offer the best figure for all the moves that I have tried to describe in that way'.[241] I was too reticent and uncomfortable with a 'head-on' approach, as you say in English. This description of my strategy as 'oblique' is a bit too crude, still too geometric, and thus too calculating, suggesting that a response could be reduced to a formula or a calculus. But of course, that is precisely what *undoes* the situation of responsibility: if knowing what to do is a matter of calculation, of proceeding by means of an algorithm, then what I do will in fact be *ir*responsible.

Instead of an 'oblique' response, I would say that my strategy of response tries to proceed head-on, directly, in direct response, but from *within* the aporia of responsibility we have sketched. I have sometimes described this as a mode of 'testimony' or 'bearing witness' [*témoignage*]. As with any ethical situation, it is a matter of finding the least unjust way of responding; but even then, the response proceeds on the basis of faith, not knowledge. This is also why I have rejected a simple apophatics which, in a way, gives in to knowledge and thus remains silent. In response to the questioning of the other, I respond by testifying, which, we might say, is a way of telling the secret *without* telling the secret. What we might call a 'disclosure without disclosure'.

This formulation of a 'disclosure without disclosure' would seem to parallel other, shall we say, 'formulas' in your more recent works, such as 'religion without religion'.

I would immediately resist your suggestion that these are 'formulas'.

OK, fair enough. Let's leave them uncategorized. But it seems that there is a common way that you deal with questions of religion, the gift, hospitality, justice and democracy, either with a certain logic of sans *[without] or in terms of the* à venir, *the 'to come'. So you speak of a 'justice to come', a 'democracy to come', a 'hospitality to come', etc. Are these quasi-logics of the* sans *and the* à venir *convertible in some way?*

I always worry that convertibility is reductionistic, but I suppose that, yes, in an important sense, what is at stake in the formulations that employ 'without' is the same matter at issue when I speak of the 'to come'. It is a matter of that which haunts our current institutions and norms, which is both 'without' them, in the sense of being beyond or outside of them, but also 'to come' – something for which we await.

In your earlier work, you persistently criticize any notion of a 'teleology' or 'eschatology',[242] yet your later work is very much taken up with the thematic of the 'to come', and seems to have a deeply eschatological *element to it. How could we put together your earlier critique with your later affirmations? Have you changed your mind?*

No, I don't feel that I have changed anything on this score. 'It is true that I interrogate the idea of an *eschaton* or *telos* in the absolute formulations of classical philosophy. But that does not mean I dismiss all forms of Messianic or prophetic eschatology. I think that all genuine questioning is summoned by a certain type of eschatology, though it is impossible to define this eschatology in philosophical terms.'[243]

Would it not have to be an eschatology without parousia – *an eschatology without arrival? An eschaton perpetually deferred and thus* always *to come?*

Yes, an eschatology without eschaton, perhaps. Where the Messiah never shows up, for if that were the case – if the Messiah actually arrived – that would be the end of the story.

Isn't it somewhat equivocal, then, to describe that as an 'eschatology'? One might wonder if it isn't more of a utopia, *as Rorty suggested.*[244]

But as I protested then, I reiterate now: the democracy to come is not a utopia. Utopian logic, it seems to me, remains constrained by a chronological thinking of time, whereas I am trying to think of time differently. So when I say that we are looking for a justice to come, this should not be understood as a justice or democracy that is chronologically future – something that we are getting 'closer' to, day by day, under the banner of progress. But 'the messianic experience of which I spoke takes place here and now; that is, the fact of promising and speaking is an event that takes place here and now and is not utopian. This happens in the singular event of engagement, and when I speak of democracy to come this does not mean that tomorrow democracy will be realized, and it does not refer to a future democracy.'[245]

Then is the 'to come' a regulative Idea in the Kantian sense? I know that you often protest against such suggestions. But at the same time, methinks thou might protest too much. Saying that this is not a regulative Idea of course doesn't make it so. Could you explain how and why you see a difference?

Granted, when I speak of, for instance, 'the democracy to come', almost every time reference is made to the regulative Idea in the Kantian sense. But I do not want the idea of a democracy to come to be reduced to this, mainly because 'the regulative Idea remains on the order of the *possible*, an ideal possible, of course, that is infinitely deferred'. In other words, the regulative Idea remains a chronological notion. But the democracy to come is heterogeneous to chronology and thus cannot be understood on the register of the possible. This is why I have suggested that it must be thought under the rubric of the 'im-possible'. 'This im-possible is not a (regulative) *idea* or *ideal*. It is what is most undeniably *real*. And sensible.

Like the other. Like the irreducible and non-appropriable differance of the other.' This is why 'democracy will never exist, in the sense of a present existence: not because it will be deferred but because it will always remain aporetic in its structure'.[246]

Yet, it must be said, 'the regulative Idea remains, for lack of anything better, if we can say "lack of anything better" with regard to a regulative Idea, a last resort. Though such a last resort or final recourse risks becoming an alibi, it retains a certain dignity. I cannot swear that I will not one day give in to it.'[247]

In several places, particularly in the late 1990s, when discussing the notions of 'the messianic' and a 'religion without religion', you were faced with questions how this relates to determinate, concrete religions (e.g. religions of the book). During the Villanova roundtable, for instance, you seem to be undecided as to whether to take a Levinasian or Heideggerian way out of this aporia.[248] Would you formulate the problem and a response any differently now? Would you be comfortable with the suggestion that your 'messianic' is another messianism?

I continue to resist the suggestion that what I call 'the messianic' is simply another, albeit minimal messianism, because that would compromise the universality which I think is essential to the messianic as I describe it. I would prefer to say, as I suggest in *Adieu*, that there can be a recognition of the Torah *before* Sinai. But for this reason, I can no longer oppose the Levinasian and Heideggerian 'solutions' as I suggested earlier. In that schema, I tended to link Levinas to a strategy that posited a historical, determinate revelation as the condition for thinking the messianic, and then I described the 'Heideggerian gesture' as the positing of an originary and formal messianic which was the condition of possibility for particular, determinate revelations. But I would now say that both of these readings need to be revised. On the one hand, as I pointed out in *Adieu* (119), it is Levinas who points to the possibility of a Torah *before* the particularity of Sinai. And on the other hand, it seems that it is Heidegger, or at least the young Heidegger, who was interested in recovering a deeper but still determinate, even 'Lutheran', revelation. 'I have recalled in several different places that the theme and word *Destruktion* [of which *deconstruction* is a certain analogue] designated in Luther a desedimentation of instituted theology (one could also say onto-theology) in the service of a more originary truth of Scripture. Heidegger was obviously a great reader of Luther. But despite my enormous respect for this great tradition, the deconstruction that concerns me does not belong, in any way, and this is more than obvious, to the same filiation.'[249]

It is interesting to me that when you have recently painted a more textured picture of this 'messianic', it has often been in connection with anti-globalization movements, especially those opposed to the regimes of the International Monetary Fund, the G8, etc. What hath Jerusalem to do with Geneva (or Seattle)?

I would suggest that from the beginning, my work has been interested in contesting received notions of *sovereignty*. One could say that the deconstruction of the metaphysics of presence, and the attendant deconstruction of received understanding of the author, and the authority of the author, were all aimed at calling into question the notion of the author as *sovereign*, even the sovereignty of the subject as such. And that would be 'in the name of the other', we might say: the other too often excluded by this sovereign autonomous subject. So also, as I have turned my attention to institutions such as international law, foreign policy, immigration, etc., I have the same interests: to contest given notions of sovereignty, particularly the sovereignty of this modern institution, the nation-state, 'along with the undeniable onto-theology that founds it, even in what are called democratic regimes'.[250] In the name of nationalist sovereignty we find the most unjust systems of exclusion and repression. So, one of the features of the democracy to come will be a rejection of this received understanding of sovereignty (as exclusive power-over). And in the name of this democracy to come 'I would naturally plead for a radical transformation – I don't know whether this will come about in the short run – which would call into question even the Charter [of the United Nations], that is to say, the respect for the sovereignties of the nation-states and the non-divisibility of sovereignties'.[251]

However, to oppose this received understanding and onto-theology of sovereignty is not to reject sovereignty as such – not even the sovereignty of the State. For it is certainly the case that, in a world governed by transnational corporations, it might be in the interest of justice to take the side of the State, to shore up the sovereignty of the State against the hegemonic impositions of international economic powers.[252] So, though 'I believe it is necessary, by way of a philosophical, historical analysis, to deconstruct the political theology of sovereignty, at the same time you shouldn't think that you must fight for the dissolution pure and simple of all sovereignty: that is neither realistic nor desirable.'[253] (And since we drew the analogy earlier, this same point holds with respect to the deconstruction of authorship or the sovereignty of the author: this is not to advocate the simple dissolution of the author, which would be neither possible nor desirable.)

In your most recent work, such as Voyous, *one gets the sense that there is beginning to be a more concrete community associated with what you've been describing as 'the messianic'. Would you risk citing an example where you see this 'weak force' at work?*

'I would say that today, one of the incarnations, one of the implementations of this messianicity, of this messianism without religion, may be found in the alter-globalization movements. Movements that are still heterogeneous, still somewhat unformed, full of contradictions, but that gather together the weak of the earth, all those who feel themselves crushed by the economic hegemonies, by the liberal market, etc.'[254]

This sounds similar to what Michael Hardt and Antonio Negri describe as 'the multitude': a 'set of singularities' based 'not on identity or unity [but] on what it has in common', namely, a shared resistance to the hegemonies of Empire.[255]

Yes, perhaps; I would be sympathetic to such an account. 'I believe it is the weak who will prove to be strongest in the end and who represent the future. Even though I am not a militant involved in these movements, I place my bet on the weak force of these alter-globalization movements, who will have to explain themselves, to unravel their contradictions, but who march against all the hegemonic organizations of the world. Not just the United States, but also the International Monetary Fund, the G8, all those organized hegemonies of the rich countries, the strong and powerful countries of which Europe is a part. It is these alter-globalization movements that offer one of the best figures of what I would call messianicity without messianism.'[256]

It has been noted that you were not manning the barriers in the events of May '68. Are you now advocating a more engaged activism? Is deconstruction finally hitting the streets, not in Paris, but in Seattle and Genoa?

I reject the simplistic notion of what counts as 'activism', which seems to retain a problematic distinction between theory and practice – as if the labours of research might not be political *in themselves*. Not just in service of a politics, or something to be 'applied' to politics, but political activities as such. Indeed, 'deconstruction (and I am not at all embarrassed to say so and even to claim) has its privileged place in the university and in the Humanities as the place of irredentist resistance or even, analogically, as a sort of principle of civil disobedience, even of dissidence in the name of a superior law and a justice of thought'.[257] In that sense, I hope that deconstruction is a kind of activism beyond the simplistic binary politics that so often informs what we call 'activism'.

I would suspect that many who are part of this 'weak force' would be surprised to hear that they are part of a 'messianic' movement, given that many would be atheists and have nothing to do with 'religion'. What do you think they would make of you signing them up for a messianic mission?

As I have persistently emphasized, this is a messianicity *without* messiah, a religion *without* religion, that has nothing to do with the dogmas or institutions of particular, determinate religions. It doesn't even really privilege the Abrahamic religions (Judaism, Christianity, Islam). It is a messianicity without content that is beyond the particularities of contingent revelations, which are too often linked to the continuing wars of religion. 'I believe we must seek today, very cautiously, to give force and form to this messianicity, without giving in to the old concepts of politics (sovereignism, territorialized nation-state) – and without giving in to the churches or to the religious powers, theologico-political or theocratic orders, whether they be the theocracies of the Islamic Middle East, or whether they be the disguised theocracies of the West.'[258]

What, then, is the relationship between the spread of this messianicity and the expansion of secularity? Political theorists described as 'agonists' (Connolly, Mouffe, et al.) advocate a more agonistic, pluralistic public sphere and reject the feigned commonality of 'the secular'. But it seems to me that your religion without religion must support some programme of secularization.

I am not advocating a false secularity which is, in reality, the imposition of a particular ideology. So I would advocate a radical pluralism. However, the question of secularity is more complex. On the one hand, I have tried to show that the modern political notion of sovereignty, particularly the sovereignty of the nation-state, is a secularization of a distinct theological heritage.[259] But on the other hand, I think that many of our political concepts and institutions are insufficiently secularized. In this respect, I would unapologetically advance the project of secularization inaugurated with the Enlightenment, specifically concerning 'the relationship between the political and the theological'; more specifically, I think the experience of the Enlightenment unique to Europe has left a distinct mark on political space with regard to religious *doctrine* – not religion or faith as such, but 'with regard to the authority of religious doctrine over the political'.[260] If by secular we mean a space which grants an independence from religious doctrine, dogma, authority and institutions, then what I have called the 'messianicity without messianism' entails (or requires) secularity.

In conclusion, perhaps we could consider a specific theme I have addressed in the book. In particular, I try to make the case for the continuity between your earliest work in phenomenology and the philosophy of language and your later work which explicitly deals with questions of ethics, politics and religion. I try to do this by demonstrating the political import of différance. And your suggestion a moment ago, concerning the analogy between the sovereignty of states and the sovereignty of authors (and the deconstruction of both), helps to clarify this sense of a continuity that is deeply political. This is against some of your critics, and even some of your admirers, who think that your turn to ethical and political concerns was in some way a break with your earlier work. How would you characterize the relationship between your early and later work? Should we speak of Derrida I and II?

Not at all, and I have persistently criticized those who have suggested such a shift or *Kehre* in my work (including Rorty). I would not even want to articulate this in terms of a movement from implicit to explicit, because I think that the ethical and political themes – the concern for justice – are *explicitly* present from 1962 onwards. So we need a different category to account for this. (Of course, I'm conceding here to your question. If we had more time, I would protest your assumptions about my *oeuvre*, about the very possibility of an *oeuvre* [see *Taste*, 14–15]. But let us, for the sake of time, forego such a complication.)

'Speaking figuratively, the seism is a better image for what I mean: the moment of a seism has been prepared for a very long time by invisible micro-displacements in the earth. And then at a certain point, from our point of view, there is what we call an earthquake; but the earthquake, from the point of view *of the earth*, is nothing. If anyone found it amusing to follow this game or this necessity, they would discover that there is not a single text of mine that was not precisely, literally and explicitly announced ten or twenty years beforehand. In everything I've published there are always touchstones announcing what I would like to write about later on – even ten or twenty years later on, as I said. So, for instance, it is true that in my more recent work I pose the question of the institution more and more. But everything that links deconstruction to the question of the apparatus of the institution is already present in *Of Grammatology*. Or when, to take another example, I stated in the address at Cardozo Law School that there is an indeconstructible, that deconstruction *is* justice, it somehow shocked and surprised those who took themselves to be allies of deconstruction. But it could be shown that there was nothing I said on that occasion that wasn't included in my earlier texts' (*Taste*, 46, 49, 56). So I would contend that there is a fundamental consistency in the diverse texts you mention. Indeed, 'I would be presumptuous enough to say that you couldn't find any discontinuity in my theoretical discourse. There are lots of changes in terms of emphasis, or displacements, but there is no systemic discontinuity.'[261]

But surely it is the case that your works in the late 1960s and 1970s have a different 'feel' than your most recent works. For instance, it seems that Nietzsche is much more prominent in your early work, whereas a Levinasian voice seems to predominate in your work since the 1990s. Can it be that one can be both Nietzschean and Levinasian? I wouldn't have thought so; and I suspect that Levinas would not think so, insofar as the first line of Totality and Infinity *[about being 'duped' by morality] seems aimed at Nietzsche. So does one of those influences trump the other in your work?*

'If Nietzsche has always been such an important point of reference for me – I still remember the first time I read him, in Algeria – this is first of all because he is a thinker who practises a *psychology of philosophers*' (*Taste*, 35). In other words, what I learned from Nietzsche was a genealogical orientation of philosophy and the history of philosophy. And in this respect, I think a Levinasian orientation overlaps with this Nietzschean theme: is there a more scrupulous genealogist of western metaphysics than Levinas? Both Nietzsche and Levinas, we might suggest (to put it a bit simply), are interested in what the philosophical tradition has repressed. In that sense, there is no need for one to 'trump' the other, as you suggest.

After Derrida

What now, after Derrida? I hope, through the course of our analyses here, that we have put to rest 'Derrida' – the myth of Derrida. But since I began this project, we have also laid to rest Jacques Derrida. Only his corpus remains. Can Derrida's remain a 'live' theory?

For several years critics of deconstruction have commonly dismissed Derrida by pronouncing that deconstruction is *passé* and past its prime. By the time we got to the late 1990s, some were already documenting the 'end' of deconstruction. But such claims were usually based on a glance at Modern Language Association conference programmes (where, certainly, Derrida is no longer the 'fad' of assistant professors of English or Cultural Studies) and were invoked as a way of dispensing with taking Derrida seriously. But the silliness of such claims is akin to someone noting the demise of existentialism in Left Bank cafés and thus concluding that we needn't really bother reading Heidegger or Sartre anymore. Granted, another generation's distance will open up for us new avenues of encountering Derrida's corpus and assessing his influence not only on philosophy but on a host of disciplines. But even now, in Derrida's wake, his work provokes much thought and his corpus has left many tracks to follow.

To take seriously one of the key figures of twentieth-century philosophy will require a patient interrogation of the texts that remain, and remain to come. Derrida will continue to be engaged as a privileged interpreter of the philosophical tradition, and an indispensable figure in phenomenology and literary theory. This will not be the place to launch a 'critique', though one could perhaps suggest an agenda for further research: questions that Derrida has left for us to answer. On the one hand, there are questions internal to what we might call, looking for a shorthand, 'Derrida studies'. What remains of Derrida is a corpus that will continue to unfold (as lectures are published, archives are explored, correspondence comes to light, etc.). Questions remain to be asked concerning Derrida's relation to modernity and the Enlightenment, how to 'reconcile' the competing voices of Nietzsche and Levinas, the shape of his 'politics', the viability of his account of religion, and much more. On the other hand, more broadly, Derrida bequeaths to us a productive theoretical framework that engenders real illumination and insight into structures and their operation – which is precisely why his work was received so widely. As such, there remains much to be done, picking up on hints from Derrida, or finishing trails he began to explore, or even inventing fields he couldn't have imagined. In his wake there must continue to be, for example, a radical critique of institutions; a continued confrontation of philosophy and literature, extended also to film and other media; and a more nuanced understanding of 'the public' and its relation to international networks of telecommunication. After Derrida we do well to continue to read closely and productively the forces at work in texts that expose them to their other, and in that deconstruction, open us up to the Other. After Derrida there remains this responsibility to the Other.

Bibliography

The extent of Derrida's corpus makes the composition of a bibliography a daunting task for a finite being. And the secondary literature, in proper proportion, is nearly overwhelming.[262] As such, this bibliography aims to include a *representative* and *comprehensive*, but not exhaustive, account of Derrida's corpus, focused on book-length works. These are drawn from across the range of his career as well as a disciplinary and thematic range. In addition, I have included a selection of 101 key secondary works, drawn from across the period of Derrida's reception in the UK and United States (from the mid-1970s to the present) that represent a range of disciplines from literature, architecture, politics, philosophy, theology and religious studies. With this selection of 101 key works, I don't mean to assert a defined 'canon', but do want to include what have come to be seen as landmark texts – what, before Derrida, we might have called 'classics' – which have generated further discussion. While secondary sources are arranged alphabetically by author, the reader is encouraged to consider dates of publication in order to trace the history of 'Derrida reception' in English-speaking theory.

Works by Jacques Derrida

Books (listed by date of first publication)

1962 'Introduction' to *L'Origine de la géométrie* by Edmund Husserl, trans. Jacques Derrida (Paris: Presses Universitaires de France) / *Edmund Husserl's 'Origin of Geometry': An Introduction*, trans. John P. Leavey (Lincoln: University of Nebraska Press, 1978; 1989 2nd edition).

1967 *De la grammatologie* (Paris: Editions de Minuit) / *Of Grammatology*, trans. Gayatri Chakravorty Spivak (Baltimore: Johns Hopkins University Press, 1974, 1976, 1997 [corrected edition]).

—— *L'écriture et la différence* (Paris: Editions du Seuil) / *Writing and Difference*, trans. Alan Bass (Chicago: University of Chicago Press, 1978).

—— *La voix et le phénomène* (Paris: Presses Universitaires de France) / *Speech and*

Phenomena, trans. David B. Allison (Evanston: Northwestern University Press, 1973).

1972 *La Dissémination* (Paris: Editions du Seuil) / *Dissemination*, trans. Barbara Johnson (Chicago: University of Chicago Press, 1981).

——— *Marges de la philosophie* (Paris: Editions du Minuit) / *Margins of Philosophy*, trans. Alan Bass (Chicago: University of Chicago Press, 1982).

1974 *Glas* (Paris: Galilée) / *Glas*, trans. John P. Leavey and R. Rand (Lincoln: University of Nebraska Press, 1986).

1975 *L'Archéologie du frivole: Lire Condillac* (Paris: Gonthier-Denoël) / *The Archeology of the Frivolous: Reading Condillac*, trans. John P. Leavey, Jr. (Pittsburgh: Duquesne University Press, 1980).

1978 *Epérons: les styles de Nietzsche* (Paris: Aubier-Flammarion) / *Spurs: Nietzsche's Styles*, trans. Barbara Harlow (Chicago: University of Chicago Press, 1979).

——— *La vérité en peinture* (Paris: Aubier-Flammarion) / *The Truth in Painting*, trans. Geoffrey Bennington and Ian McLeod (Chicago: University of Chicago Press, 1987).

1980 *La carte postale: de Socrate à Freud et au-delà* (Paris: Aubier-Flammarion) / *The Post Card: From Socrates to Freud and Beyond*, trans. Alan Bass (Chicago: University of Chicago Press, 1987).

1982 *L'oreille de l'autre: otobiographies, transferts, traductions: texts et débats avec Jacques Derrida*, C. Lévesque and C. V. McDonald (eds) (Montreal: VLB Editions) / *The Ear of the Other: Otobiography, Transference, Translation: Texts and Discussions with Jacques Derrida* (Lincoln: University of Nebraska Press, 1988).

1983 *D'un ton apocalyptique adopté naguère en philosophie* (Paris: Galilée) / trans. by John P. Leavey, Jr., in *Raising the Tone of Philosophy: Late Essays by Immanuel Kant, Transformative Critique by Jacques Derrida*, Peter Fenves (ed.) (Baltimore: Johns Hopkins University Press, 1993).

——— *Signéponge*, with parallel English translation by Richard Rand (Chicago: University of Chicago Press).

1984 '*Bonnes volontés de puissance (Une réponse à Hans-Georg Gadamer)* ["Good Will to Power (A Response to Hans-Georg Gadamer)"]', in *Text und Interpretation*, Philippe Forget (ed.) (Munich: Wilhelm Fink Verlag) / translated by Diane Michelfelder and Richard Palmer as 'Three Questions to Hans-Georg Gadamer', in *Dialogue and Deconstruction: The Gadamer–Derrida Encounter*, Michelfelder and Palmer (eds) (Albany: SUNY Press, 1989): pp. 52–4.

1986 *Mémoires for Paul de Man*, trans. Cecile Lindsay, Jonathan Culler, Eduardo Cadava, and Peggy Kamuf (New York: Columbia University Press; revised and augmented edition, 1989) / later published in French as *Mémoires pour Paul de Man* (Paris: Galilée, 1988).

——— *Schibboleth*, pour Paul Celan (Paris: Galilée) / 'Shibboleth', trans. Joshua Wilner in *Midrash and Literature*, Geoffrey Hartmann and Sanford Budick (eds) (New Haven: Yale University Press, 1986): pp. 307–47.

——— *Parages* (Paris: Galilée; rev. ed., 2003).

1987 *Psyché: inventions de l'autre* (Paris: Galilée; rev. ed., 2003).

—— *Feu la Cendre* (Paris: Editions des Femmes).

—— *Ulysses gramophone: deux mots pour Joyce* (Paris: Galilée) / 'Two words for Joyce', trans. Geoffrey Bennington in *Post-Structuralist Joyce: Essays from the French*, Derek Attridge and D. Ferrer (eds) (Cambridge: Cambridge University Press, 1984), pp. 145–58; and 'Ulysses Gramophone: Hear Say Yes in Joyce', trans. Tina Kendall and Shari Benstock in *James Joyce: The Augmented Ninth*, Bernard Benstock (ed.) (Syracuse: Syracuse University Press, 1988), pp. 27–75.

—— *De l'esprit: Heidegger et la question* (Paris: Galilée) / *Of Spirit: Heidegger and the Question*, trans. Geoffrey Bennington and Rachel Bowlby (Chicago: University of Chicago Press, 1989).

1988 *Limited Inc.*, G. Graff (ed.), trans. Samuel Weber (Evanston: Northwestern University Press) / *Limited Inc.*, Elisabeth Weber (ed.) (Paris: Galilée, 1990).

1990 [1954] *Le problème de la genese dans la philosophie de Husserl* [Derrida's Master's thesis] (Paris: Presses Universitaires de France) / *The Problem of Genesis in Husserl's Philosophy*, trans. Marian Hobson (Chicago: University of Chicago Press, 2003).

—— *Du droit à la philosophie* (Paris: Galilée) / *Who's Afraid of Philosophy?: Right to Philosophy 1*, trans. Jan Plug (Stanford: Stanford University Press, 2002) and *Eyes of the University: Right to Philosophy 2*, trans. Jan Plug *et al.* (Stanford: Stanford University Press, 2004).

—— *Mémoires d'aveugle: L'autoportrait et autres ruines* (Paris: Editions de la Réunion des musées nationaux) / *Memoirs of the Blind: The Self-Portrait and Other Ruins*, trans. Pascale-Anne Brault and Michael Naas, (Chicago: University of Chicago Press, 1993).

—— 'Force of Law: The "Mystical Foundation of Authority" ', *Cardozo Law Review*, reprinted in *Deconstruction and the Possibility of Justice*, Drucilla Cornell, Michael Rosenfeld, and David Gray Carlson (eds), (New York: Routledge, 1992) / *Force de loi* (Paris: Galilée, 1994).

1991 'Circonfession', in *Jacques Derrida*, with Geoffrey Bennington, (Paris: Seuil) / 'Circumfession', in *Jacques Derrida*, with Geoffrey Bennington, (Chicago: University of Chicago Press, 1993).

—— *Donner le Temps: 1. La Fausse Monnaie* (Paris: Galiliée) / *Given Time: I. Counterfeit Money*, trans. Peggy Kamuf (Chicago: University of Chicago Press, 1992).

—— *L'autre cap: suivi de la democratie ajournée* (Paris: Minuit) / *The Other Heading: Reflections on Today's Europe*, trans. Pascale-Anne Brault and Michael B. Naas (Bloomington, IN: Indiana University Press, 1992).

1992 *Donner la mort* in *L'éthique du don, Jacques Derrida et la Pensée du Don*, (Paris: Transition) / *The Gift of Death*, trans. David Wills (Chicago: University of Chicago Press, 1995).

1993 *Spectres de Marx* (Paris: Galilée) / *Specters of Marx: The State of the Debt, the Work of Mourning, and the New International*, trans. Peggy Kamuf, (New York: Routledge, 1994).

1993 *Apories: Mourir-s'attendre aux limites de la vérité* in *Le Passage des Frontières: Autour de Travail de Jacques Derrida*, (Paris: Galilée) / *Aporias*, trans. Thomas Dutoit, (Stanford: Stanford University Press, 1993).

—— *Passions* (Paris: Galilée) / Included in *On the Name*, trans. David Wood, John P. Leavey and Ian McLeod (Stanford: Stanford University Press, 1995).

—— *Sauf le nom* (Paris: Galilée) / Included in *On the Name*, trans. David Wood, John P. Leavey and Ian McLeod (Stanford: Stanford University Press, 1995).

—— *Khôra* (Paris: Galilée) / Included in *On the Name*, trans. David Wood, John P. Leavey, and Ian McLeod (Stanford: Stanford University Press, 1995).

1994 *Politiques de l'amitié*, (Paris: Galilée) / *Politics of Friendship*, trans. George Collins (London: Verso, 1997).

1995 *Mal d'archive: Une impression freudienne* (Paris: Galilée) / *Archive Fever: A Freudian Impression* (Chicago: University of Chicago Press, 1996).

1996 *Echographies: de la télévision* (Paris: Galilée) / *Echographies of Television*, trans. Jennifer Bajorek (Cambridge: Polity).

—— *La Religion: Seminaire de Capri*, with Gianni Vattimo (Paris: Editions de Seuil et Editions de Laterza) / *Religion*, Jacques Derrida and Gianni Vattimo (eds) (Stanford: Stanford University Press, 1998).

—— *Le Monoliguisme de l'autre: ou la prothése d'origine* (Paris: Galilée) / *Monoligualism of the Other or The Prosthesis of Origin*, trans. Patrick Mensah (Stanford: Stanford University Press, 1998).

—— *Résistances à la psychanalyse* (Paris: Galilée) / *Resistances of Psychoanalysis*, trans. Peggy Kamuf, Pascale-Anne Brault and Michael Naas, (Stanford: Stanford University Press, 1998).

1997 *De l'hospitalité* (Paris: Calmann-Lévy) / *Of Hospitality*, with Anne Dufourmantelle, trans. Rachel Bowlby (Stanford: Stanford University Press, 2000).

—— *Adieu – à Emmanuel Lévinas* (Paris: Galilée) / *Adieu to Emmanuel Levinas*, trans. Pascale-Anne Brault and Michael Naas (Stanford: Stanford University Press, 1999).

—— *Cosmopolites de tous les pays, encore un effort!* (Paris: Galilée)

—— *Du droit à la philosophie du point du vue cosmopolitique* (Paris: Verdier).

—— *Il Gusto del Segreto* (Roma: Gius) / *A Taste for the Secret*, Giocomo Donis and David Webb (eds), trans. Giocomo Donis (Cambridge: Polity, 2001).

1998 *Demeure*, with Maurice Blanchot (Paris: Galilée) / *The Instant of my Death: Demeure: Fiction and Testimony*, trans. Elizabeth Rottenberg, (Stanford: Stanford University Press, 2000).

—— *Le rapport bleu. Les sources historiques et théoriques de Collége international de Philosophie*, with F. Châtelet, J.-P. Faye, and D. Lecourt, (Paris: PUF).

—— *Voiles*, with Hélène Cixous (Paris: Galilée) / *Veils*, trans. Geoffrey Bennington (Stanford: Stanford University Press, 2001).

1999 *L'animal autobiographique* (Paris: Galilée).

2000 *Le toucher, Jean-Luc Nancy* (Paris: Galilée).

2000 *Etats d'âme de la psychanalyse: Adresse aux Etats Généraux de la Psychanalyse* (Paris: Galilée) / translated by Peggy Kamuf as 'Psychoanalysis Searches the States of Its Soul: The Impossible Beyond of a Sovereign Cruelty', in Jacques Derrida, *Without Alibi* (Stanford: Stanford University Press, 2002), pp. 238–80.

—— *Tourner le mots. Au bord d'un film*, with Safaa Fathy (Paris: Galilée).

2001 *Deconstruction Engaged: The Sydney Seminars*, Paul Patton and Terry Smith (eds) (Sydney: Power Publications).

—— *On Cosmopolitanism and Forgiveness*, trans. Mark Dooley (London: Routledge, 2001).

—— *L'Université sans condition* (Paris: Galilée) / 'The University Without Condition', trans. Peggy Kamuf in Jacques Derrida, *Without Alibi* (Stanford: Stanford University Press, 2002), pp. 202–37.

—— *The Work of Mourning*, Pascale-Anne Brault and Michael Naas (eds) (Chicago: University of Chicago Press) / *Chaque Fois Unique, La Fin du Monde* (Paris: Galilée, 2003).

—— *Atlan* (Paris: Gallimard).

—— *Limited Inc II* (Paris: Galilée).

—— *La Connaissance des Textes*, with Simon Hantai and Jean-Luc Nancy (Paris: Galilée).

—— *Foi et Savoir / Le Siècle et le Pardon*, with Michel Wievorka (Paris: Le Seuil).

—— *Dire L'événement, est-ce possible?: Séminaire de Montreal pour Jacques Derrida*, with Alexis Nouss and Gad Soussana (Paris: L'Harmattan).

—— *Papier Machine* (Paris: Gallimard).

2002 *Without Alibi*, ed. and trans. Peggy Kamuf (Stanford: Stanford University Press).

—— *Marx et Sons* (Paris: PUF/Galilée).

—— *Artaud le Moma* (Paris: Galilée).

—— *Fichus* (Paris: Galilée).

2003 *Béliers. Le dialogue ininterrompu : entre deux infinis, le poème* (Paris: Galilée) / 'Uninterrupted Dialogue: Between Two Infinities, the Poem [abridged]', trans. Thomas Dutoit and Philippe Romanski, *Research in Phenomenology* 34 (2004), pp. 3–19.

—— *Genèses, Généalogies, Genres: les secrets de l'archive* (Paris: Galilée).

—— *H.C. pour la vie, c'est à dire . . .* (Paris: Galilée).

—— *Voyous: Deux essays sur la raison* (Paris: Galilée) / *Rogues: Two Essays on Reason*, trans. Pascale-Anne Brault and Michael Naas (Stanford: Stanford University Press, 2005).

2005 *A la vie à la mort* (Paris: Galilée).

Readers

1991 *A Derrida Reader: Between the Blinds*, Peggy Kamuf (ed.) (New York: Columbia University Press).

1992 *Acts of Literature*, Derek Attridge (ed.) (New York: Routledge).
1998 *The Derrida Reader: Writing Performances*, Julian Wolfreys (ed.) (Lincoln: University of Nebraska Press).
2002 *Acts of Religion*, Gil Anidjar (ed.) (New York: Routledge)

Interview Collections

A helpful bibliography of interviews will be found in Elisabeth Weber's translation of *Points . . .*, pp. 495–9.

1972 *Positions* (Paris: Editions de Minuit) / *Positions*, trans. Alan Bass (Chicago: University of Chicago Press, 1981).
1992 *Points de suspension: entretiens*, Elisabeth Weber (ed.) (Paris: Galilée) / *Points . . . : Interviews, 1974–1994* (Stanford: Stanford University Press, 1995).
1999 *Sur Parole: Instantanés Philosophiques* (Éditions de l'aube).
2001 *De quoi demain . . .: Dialogue*, with Elisabeth Roudinesco (Paris: Fayard/ Galilée) / *For What Tomorrow . . .: A Dialogue*, trans. Jeff Fort (Stanford: Stanford University Press, 2004).
2002 *Negotiations: Interventions and Interviews, 1971–2001*, Elizabeth G. Rottenberg (ed.) (Stanford University Press).
2003 *Philosophy in a Time of Terror: Dialogues with Jürgen Habermas and Jacques Derrida*, ed. Giovanna Borradori (Chicago: University of Chicago Press).
2004 *Counterpath: Traveling with Jacques Derrida*, interviews with Catherine Malabou (Stanford: Stanford University Press).

Select Books and Articles on Jacques Derrida in English

In what follows, I have confined the bibliography to works in English, and mainly to monographs and edited collections. I have also sought to include a representation from across the period of Derrida's reception in English-speaking scholarship as well as works across the disciplines where Derrida has made an impact: mainly in philosophy and literary theory, but also in architecture, education, psychoanalysis, law, political theory, theology, and religious studies.

Atkins, G. Douglas, *Reading Destruction, Deconstructive Reading* (Lexington: University of Kentucky Press, 1983).
Battaglia, Rosemarie Angela, *Presence and Absence in Joyce, Heidegger, Derrida, Freud* (Albany: SUNY Press, 1985).
Beardsworth, Richard, *Derrida and the Political* (London: Routledge, 1996).
Bennington, Geoffrey, *Derridabase* in Geoffrey Bennington and Jacques Derrida,

Jacques Derrida, trans. Geoffrey Bennington (Chicago: University of Chicago Press, 1993).

—— *Legislations: The Politics of Deconstruction* (New York: Verso, 1994).

—— *Interrupting Derrida* (New York: Routledge, 2000).

Brunette, Peter and David Wills, *Screen/Play: Derrida and Film Theory* (Princeton: Princeton University Press, 1989).

Burke, Seán, *The Death and Return of the Author: Criticism and Subjectivity in Barthes, Foucault, and Derrida*, 2nd edn (Edinburgh: Edinburgh University Press, 1998).

Caputo, John D., (ed.) *Deconstruction in a Nutshell: A Conversation with Jacques Derrida* (New York: Fordham University Press, 1997).

—— *Radical Hermeneutics: Repetition, Hermeneutics, Deconstruction* (Bloomington: Indiana University Press, 1987).

—— *The Prayers and Tears of Jacques Derrida: Religion Without Religion* (Bloomington: Indiana University Press, 1997).

Carroll, David, *Paraesthetics: Foucault, Lyotard, Derrida* (New York: Routledge, 1989).

Cixous, Hélène, *Portrait of Jacques Derrida as a Young Jewish Saint*, trans. Beverley Bie Brahic (New York: Columbia University Press, 2004).

Clark, Timothy, *Derrida, Heidegger, Blanchot: Sources of Derrida's Notion and Practice of Literature* (Cambridge: Cambridge University Press, 1992).

Corlett, William, *Community Without Unity: A Politics of Derridian Extravagance* (Durham, NC: Duke University Press, 1993).

Cornell, Drucilla, *The Philosophy of the Limit* (New York: Routledge, 1992).

Cornell, Drucilla, Michael Rosenfeld, and David Gray Carlson, (eds), *Deconstruction and the Possibility of Justice* (New York: Routledge, 2002).

Coward, Harold, *Derrida and Indian Philosophy* (Albany: SUNY Press, 1990).

Coward, Harold and Toby Foshay, (eds), *Derrida and Negative Theology* (New York: State University of New York Press, 1992).

Critchley, Simon, *The Ethics of Deconstruction: Derrida and Levinas* (Oxford: Blackwell Publishers, 1992; 2nd edn, Edinburgh: Edinburgh University Press, 1999).

Culler, Jonathan, *On Deconstruction: Theory and Criticism after Structuralism* (Ithaca: Cornell University Press, 1982).

Dasenbrock, Reed Way, (ed.), *Redrawing the Lines: Analytic Philosophy, Deconstruction, and Literary Theory* (Minneapolis: University of Minnesota Press, 1989).

Descombes, Vincent, *Modern French Philosophy*, trans. L. Scott-Fox and J.M. Harding (Cambridge: Cambridge University Press, 1981).

Dews, Peter, *Logics of Disintegration: Poststructuralist Thought and the Claims for Critical Theory* (London and New York: Verso, 1987).

Dillon, M.C., *Semiological Reductionism: A Critique of the Deconstructionist Movement in Postmodern Thought* (Albany, NY: SUNY Press, 1995).

—— *Ecart and différance: Merleau-Ponty and Derrida on Seeing and Writing* (Atlantic Highlands, NJ: Humanities Press, 1997).

Edmundson, Mark, *Literature against Philosophy, Plato to Derrida: A Defence of Poetry* (Cambridge: Cambridge University Press, 1995).

Eagleton, Terry, *Literary Theory: An Introduction* (Minneapolis: University of Minnesota Press, 1983).

Evans, J. Claude, *Strategies of Deconstruction: Derrida and the Myth of the Voice* (Minneapolis: University of Minnesota Press, 1991).

Feder, Ellen K., Mary C. Rawlinson, and Emily Zakin, (eds), *Derrida and Feminism: Recasting the Question of Woman* (New York: Routledge, 1997).

Fish, Stanley E., 'With Compliments of the Author: Reflections on Austin and Derrida', *Critical Inquiry* (8, 1981–2), pp. 693–721.

Forrester, John, *The Seductions of Psychoanalysis: Freud, Lacan, Derrida* (Cambridge: Cambridge University Press, 1990).

Gasché, R., *The Tain of the Mirror* (Cambridge, MA: Harvard University Press, 1986).

Glendinning, Simon, *On Being With Others: Heidegger, Wittgenstein, Derrida* (London: Routledge, 1998).

Glendinning, Simon, (ed.), *Arguing with Derrida* (Oxford: Blackwell Publishers, 2002).

Gutting, Gary, *French Philosophy in the Twentieth Century* (Cambridge: Cambridge University Press, 2001).

Handelman, Susan, *The Slayers of Moses : The Emergence of Rabbinic Interpretation in Modern Literary Theory* (Albany, NY: SUNY Press, 1982).

Hart, Kevin, *The Tresspass of the Sign: Deconstruction, Theology, and Philosophy* (Cambridge: Cambridge University Press, 1989).

Hartman, Geoffrey, *Saving the Text: Literature / Derrida / Philosophy* (Baltimore, MD: Johns Hopkins University Press, 1981).

Harvey, Irene E., *Derrida and the Economy of* différance (Bloomington: Indiana University Press, 1986).

Hobson, Marian, *Jacques Derrida: Opening Lines* (London: Routledge, 1998).

Holland, Nancy J., *Feminist Interpretations of Jacques Derrida* (University Park, PA: Pennsylvania State University Press, 1997).

Jencks, Charles, *What is Postmodernism?*, 4th edn (West Sussex: John Wiley & Sons, 1996).

Johnson, C. M., *System and Writing in the Philosophy of Jacques Derrida* (Cambridge, Cambridge University Press, 1993).

—— *Derrida: The Scene of Writing* (London: Phoenix, 1997).

Kamuf, Peggy, *The Division of Literature, or the University in Deconstruction* (Chicago: University of Chicago Press, 1997).

Krell, David Farrell, *The Purest of Bastards: Works of Mourning, Art, and Affirmation in the Thought of Jacques Derrida* (University Park, PA: Pennsylvania State University Press, 2000).

Krupnick, Mark, *Displacement: Derrida and After* (Bloomington: Indiana University Press, 1983).

Leavey, John P., Jr., *Glassary* (Lincoln: University of Nebraska Press, 1986).

Leitch, Vincent B., *Deconstructive Criticism: An Advanced Introduction* (New York: Columbia University Press, 1983).

Llewelyn, John, *Derrida on the Threshold of Sense* (Basingstoke: Macmillan, 1986).

Lucy, Niall, *Debating Derrida* (Melbourne: Melbourne University Press, 1995).

—— *A Derrida Dictionary* (Oxford: Blackwell Publishers, 2004).

Maclachlan, Ian, (ed.), *Jacques Derrida: Critical Thought* (Aldershot: Ashgate, 2004).

Madison, Gary B., *Working Through Derrida* (Evanston, IL: Northwestern University Press, 1993).

Magliola, Robert R., *Derrida on the Mend* (West Lafayette: Purdue University Press, 1984).

Marion, Jean-Luc, *Reduction and Givenness: Investigations of Husserl Heidegger, and Phenomenology* trans. Thomas A. Carlson (Evanston: Northwestern University Press, 1998).

—— *Being Given: Toward a Phenomenology of Givenness*, trans. Jeffrey L. Kosky (Stanford: Stanford University Press, 2002).

Martin, Bill, *Matrix and Line: Derrida and the Possibilities of Postmodern Social Theory* (Albany, NY: SUNY Press, 1992).

May, Todd, *Reconsidering Difference: Nancy, Derrida, Levinas, and Deleuze* (University Park, PA: Pennsylvania University Press, 1997).

Megill, Allan, *Prophets of Extremity: Nietzsche, Heidegger, Foucault, Derrida* (Berkeley: University of California Press, 1985).

Meyer, Michael, (ed.), *Questioning Derrida: With His Replies on Philosophy* (Aldershot: Ashgate, 2001).

Michelfelder, Diane P., and Richard E. Palmer, (eds), *Dialogue & Deconstruction: The Gadamer-Derrida Encounter* (New York: State University of New York Press, 1989).

Moore, Stephen D., *Poststructuralism and the New Testament: Derrida and Foucault at the Foot of the Cross* (Minneapolis: Fortress Press, 1994).

Muller, John P. and William J. Richardson, (eds), *The Purloined Poe: Lacan, Derrida, and Psychoanalytic Reading* (Baltimore, MD: Johns Hopkins University Press, 1988).

Naas, Michael, *Taking on the Tradition: Jacques Derrida and the Legacies of Deconstruction* (Stanford: Stanford University Press, 2003).

Norris, Christopher, *Deconstruction: Theory and Practice* (London: Methuen, 1982).

—— *Deconstruction and the Unfinished Project of Modernity* (London: Routledge, 2000).

—— *Derrida* (Cambridge, MA: Harvard University Press, 1987).

—— *The Truth about Postmodernism* (Oxford: Blackwell Publishers, 1993).

—— *What's Wrong With Postmodernism: Critical Theory and the Ends of Philosophy* (Baltimore: Johns Hopkins University Press, 1990).

Patrick, Morag, *Derrida, Responsibility, and Politics* (Aldershot: Ashgate, 1997).

Rapaport, Herman, *Heidegger and Derrida: Reflections on Time and Language* (Lincoln: University of Nebraska Press, 1989).

—— *Later Derrida: Reading the Recent Work* (New York: Routlege, 2003).

Ray, William, *Literary Meaning: From Phenomenology to Deconstruction* (Oxford: Blackwell, 1984).

Rorty, Richard, 'From Ironist Theory to Private Allusions: Derrida', *Contingency, Irony, and Solidarity* (Cambridge: Cambridge University Press, 1989), pp. 122–37.

—— 'Philosophy as a Kind of Writing: An Essay on Derrida', *Consequences of Pragmatism* (Minneapolis: University of Minnesota Press, 1982), 89–109.

Rothfield, Philip, (ed.), *Kant after Derrida* (Manchester: Clinamen Press, 2003).

Royle, Nicholas, (ed.), *Deconstructions: A User's Guide* (New York: Palgrave, 2000).

Rutledge, David, *Reading Marginally: Feminism, Deconstruction and the Bible* (Leiden: E.J. Brill, 1996).

Ryan, Michael, *Marxism and Deconstruction: A Critical Articulation* (Baltimore, MD: Johns Hopkins University Press, 1982).

Sallis, John, (ed.), *Deconstruction and Philosophy: The Texts of Jacques Derrida* (Chicago: University of Chicago Press, 1987).

Silverman, Hugh J., (ed.), *Derrida and Deconstruction* (London: Routledge, 1989).

Silverman, Hugh J. and Don Ihde, (eds), *Hermeneutics and Deconstruction* (Albany, NY: SUNY Press, 1985).

Searle, John, 'Reiterating the Differences: A Reply to Derrida', *Glyph 1* (1977), 198–208.

Sim, Stuart, *Derrida and the End of History* (New York: Totem Books, 1999).

Smith, James K.A., *The Fall of Interpretation: Philosophical Foundations for a Creational Hermeneutic* (Downers Grove: InterVarsity Press, 2000).

Smith, Joseph and William Kerrigan, (eds), *Taking Chances: Derrida, Psychoanalysis, and Literature* (Baltimore: Johns Hopkins University Press, 1984).

Smith, Robert, *Derrida and Autobiography* (Cambridge: Cambridge University Press, 1995).

Spivak, Gayatri Chakravorty, 'Translator's Preface' to Jacques Derrida, *Of Grammatology* (Baltimore: Johns Hopkins University Press, 1976), ix–lxxxvii.

Sprinkler, Michael, (ed.), *Ghostly Demarcations: A Symposium on Jacques Derrida's 'Specters of Marx'* (New York: Verso, 1999).

Staten, H., *Wittgenstein and Derrida* (Oxford: Blackwell Publishers, 1985).

Sychrava, Juliet, *Schiller to Derrida: Idealism in Aesthetics* (Cambridge: Cambridge University Press, 1990).

Taylor, Mark C., *Erring: A Postmodern A/theology* (Chicago: University of Chicago Press, 1984).

Todd, Jane Marie, *Autobiographics in Freud and Derrida* (New York: Garland, 1990).

Ulmer, Gregory L., *Applied Grammatology: Post(e)-Pedagogy from Jacques Derrida to Joseph Beuys* (Baltimore: Johns Hopkins University Press, 1985).

Ward, Graham, *Barth, Derrida and the Language of Theology* (Cambridge: Cambridge University Press, 1995).

Weber, Samuel, *Institution and Interpretation* (Minneapolis: University of Minnesota Press, 1987).

Wheeler, Samuel C., III, *Deconstruction as Analytic Philosophy* (Stanford: Stanford University Press, 2000).

Wigley, Mark, *The Architecture of Deconstruction: Derrida's Haunt* (MIT Press, 1993).

Wood, David, *Derrida: A Critical Reader* (Oxford: Blackwell Publishers, 1992).

Wood, David and Robert Bernasconi, (eds), *Derrida and Différance* (Coventry: Parousia Press, 1985).

Notes

Introduction

1. See, for example, the compilation CD *Deconstructing Beck* (Seeland Records, 1998) or the Pygmy Children album, *Deconstruct* (Cleopatra, 1995).
2. A cover story for the October 2001 issue of *Food Product Design* spoke of 'deconstructing pies and turnovers'. As an exercise to get some sense of the ubiquity of deconstruction, I invite the reader to perform a Google search with the following formula: search for 'deconstruct' or 'deconstructing' + [any food item]. For example, search: deconstruct + key lime pie. The curious collections of results will tell us something both about the range across which the language of deconstruction has been appropriated, as well as the polysemic nature of the Internet.
3. See, for example, Allan Bloom, *The Closing of the American Mind* (Simon & Schuster, 1988), p. 379 *passim*.
4. Derrida suggests that reading is a political activity, or better, apolitical *responsibility*. 'I would assume that political, ethical, and juridical responsibility requires a task of infinite close reading. I believe this to be the condition of political responsibility: politicians should read. . . . Reading, in the broad sense which I attribute to this word, is an ethical and political responsibility.' See 'Hospitality, Justice, and Responsibility: A Dialogue with Jacques Derrida', in *Questioning Ethics*, Richard Kearney and Mark Dooley, (eds) (London: Routledge, 199), pp. 67, 78. Elsewhere he almost chastises academics and journalists for propagating stereotypes which are the products of a mode of 'scholarly practice', we might say, that is 'careless about respecting and patiently reading through work that actually requires time, discipline, and patience, work that requires several readings, new types of reading, too, in a variety of different fields' (*Points*, 401).
5. There is, then, a deep alterity to monsters, which means that there can also be a certain slippage, so that what 'shows itelf' (*se montre*) could be a monster – or a god. That is why the very strangeness that would lead some to name a Derrida-monster could also lead others to almost erect a Derrida-god. For a careful account of this slippage of constitution, see Richard Kearney, *Strangers, Gods, and Monsters* (London: Routledge, 2002).

6. Belle's retort to Gaston might repay some analysis: 'He's not the monster, Gaston. You are!'

7. I will generally use the term 'Derrida', in scare quotes, to indicate the mythic or 'received' Derrida.

8. In seeking to oppose the common myths and caricatures of Derrida and deconstruction – as enemy of all that is good and true – one is often tempted to then simply paint a picture of Derrida as the most classical and traditional defender of the Good or the voice of Tradition. But that would be precisely a domestication of Derrida. If deconstruction isn't something *radical*, then we might as well retreat to the comforts of Arnoldian criticism, T. S. Eliot, or Gadamerian hermeneutics. But deconstruction *is* monstrous in a sense; it *is* disruptive and critical, but not in the way that it is commonly assumed.

9. The obituaries in major international newspapers (*Le monde, New York Times*) resurrected these Derrida-monsters (often by recalling associations with Heidegger and de Man, taken to be anti-Semitic monsters). As such, after his death, the globe was once again swept by the 'Derrida' myth.

10. The flysheets are reproduced in the primary communications organ of the university, *The Cambridge Reporter* (20 May 1992), pp. 685–8.

11. *Non placet* flysheet, signed by W. S. Allen, *et al.*, reprinted in the *Cambridge University Reporter* (20 May 1992), p. 687.

12. *Ibid.*

13. *Ibid.*

14. Derrida comments on the externality of these critics, as well as their utilization of the media for what was properly an academic debate, in *Points*, pp. 400–05.

15. As if one could judge an *oeuvre* by randomly opening a page and judging its style!

16. After the dust had settled, post-vote reflections were gathered from both sides and published as 'Symposium: Reflections on "The Derrida Affair" ', *The Cambridge Review* 113 (No. 2318), October 1992, pp. 99–127, with contributions from Marian Jeanneret, Nicholas Denyer, Christopher Predergast, Brian Hebblethwaite, Susannah Thomas, and Christopher Norris; an 'Interview' with Derrida followed on pp. 131–9 (reprinted in *Points*, 399–419).

17. Brian Hebblethwaite in 'Symposium', *Cambridge Review*, p. 109. Predergast notes that there was dissension *within* the Philosophy Faculty, some signing *placet*, some *non-placet* (p. 107).

18. Derrida does not 'attack' the university *as such*, though admittedly the university *as currently configured*. Hebblethwaite ontologizes or essentializes the current organization of the university as 'natural' or identifies the current form of the university with the university 'as such'. For further discussion, see 3.1.4.

19. It seems a bit telling that, though he cites others, Hebblethwaite's article does not include a single citation of Derrida. As University Information

Officer, Susannah Thomas's contribution to the post-affair 'Symposium' is of interest. 'If we look at the way that the press was able to communicate the ideas first of all, I think a comparison with the communication of scientific ideas is interesting [a parallel that Derrida himself invokes; see *Points*, 115–17]. I will start from the basic premise that both the issues covered here and in the reporting of science are not understood by the non-specialist. The onus therefore is on the writer to explain the issues and their importance. This debate, in terms of public understanding, already had one big difference – there is not a philosophy page in national papers [in Britain]. Although allocation of space to science guarantees its inclusion on a regular basis that philosophy does not get, it also means that this debate was carried on in the news and features pages of the press which the layman may be more likely to read. Despite starting with this advantage of location within a newspaper, the debate of ideas was not very well served' (*Points*, 113). However, I am puzzled by how she could claim that 'unlike a crisis situation where accurate information is vital, the debate was, to a large extent, unaffected by the factual inaccuracies' (*Points*, 114). It was precisely basic factual inaccuracies of the *non-placet* charges that stemmed from failing to actually *read* Derrida's text. Christopher Norris's contribution to the 'Symposium', 'Of an Apopletic Tone Recently Adopted in Philosophy', patiently undoes the *non-placet* charges on the basis of simple textual clarification.

20. René Wellek, 'Destroying Literary Studies', in *The New Criterion Reader*, Hilton Kramer, (ed.) (New York: The Free Press, 1988), pp. 29–36.

21. *Ibid.*, p. 30.

22. *Ibid.*, p. 31.

23. Which, of course, just repeats what might be the founding scene of philosophy: the charges against Socrates for 'corrupting the youth'.

24. *Ibid.*

25. Though, as Derrida notes, 'Concerning the majority of the "facts", I have yet to find anything in this investigation that was not already known, and for a long time, by those who take a serious interest in Heidegger' (*Points*, 181). Derrida's more expansive engagement of these questions is found in *Of Spirit*. For further considerations of Heidegger, Nazism, and the next generation's relationship to Heidegger's work, see John D. Caputo, *Demythologizing Heidegger* (Bloomington, IN: Indiana University Press, 1993) and Hugo Ott, *Martin Heidegger: A Political Life*, trans. Allan Blunden (New York: Basic Books, 1993).

26. Richard Wolin, (ed.), *The Heidegger Controversy: A Critical Reader* (1st edn, New York: Columbia University Press, 1991; 2nd edn, Cambridge, MA: MIT Press, 1993).

27. Much of the subsequent exchange between Derrida, Thomas Sheehan, Richard Wolin, and others, revolved around legal questions of just *who* had the 'right' to give permission for the text to be translated and published in English. Wolin had contacted *Le Nouvel Observateur* and secured

permission, but Derrida maintained that '*Le Nouvel Observateur* does not have the right to authorize without my accord the republication of my text in translation. Any competent lawyer will confirm this to be the case' (*Points*, 452, reprinting one of Derrida's letters to *NYRB*). But in the end, Derrida emphasizes what is at issue is not primarily a matter of legal right but common academic courtesy. 'Even supposing, *concesso non dato*, that my legal agreement were not necessary, how can one justify that Mr. Wolin "forgot", for months and months, to ask me, at least out of courtesy, for my authorization to include a long text of mine in his book? Did he think I was dead?' (*Points* 452–3). We will return to this final question.

28. Richard Wolin, Letter to the Editor, *NYRB*, 11 Feb 1993.
29. Ever since 'Différance' (1968), Derrida's work has evoked parallels – with important differences – with 'negative theology'. For later discussions, see Derrida, 'How to Avoid Speaking' and *Sauf le nom* in *On the Name*. The definitive discussions of deconstruction and negative theology are Kevin Hart, *The Trespass of the Sign* (Cambridge: Cambridge University Press, 1989) and John D. Caputo, *The Prayers and Tears of Jacques Derrida* (Bloomington, IN: Indiana University Press, 1997), pp. 1–56.
30. Derrida notes in particular that such a notion was common on the American scene. 'It is true that in certain circles (university or cultural, especially in the United States) the technical and methodological "metaphor" that seems necessarily attached to the very word "deconstruction" has been able to seduce or lead astray'. See Jacques Derrida, 'Letter to a Japanese Friend', in *The Derrida Reader*, Peggy Kamuf, (ed.) (New York: Columbia University Press, 1991), p. 273.
31. *Ibid.*, p. 273.
32. *Ibid.*
33. Perhaps what's really at stake in deconstruction is a question of *how to read* (see *OG*, lxxxix, 157–9). In this respect, one can find a crystallization of Derrida's deconstructive reading practice in the example of his reading of Rousseau: 'One could make him say quite a different thing. And Rousseau's text must constantly be considered as a complex and many-leveled structure; in it, certain propositions may be read as interpretations of other propositions that we are, up to a certain point and with certain precautions, free to read otherwise. Rousseau says A, then for reasons that we must determine, he interprets A into B. A, which was already an interpretation, is reinterpreted into B. After taking cognizance of it, we may, without leaving Rousseau's text, isolate A from its interpretation into B, and discover possibilities and resources there that indeed belong to Rousseau's text, but were not produced or exploited by him' (*OG*, 307).
34. Derrida, 'Letter to a Japanese Friend', p. 272.
35. *Ibid.*, p. 270.
36. *Ibid.*, p. 272.
37. *Ibid.*, p. 275.
38. Derrida, 'Deconstruction and the Other', p. 124.

39. *Ibid.*
40. There is, however, a more nuanced charge of nihilism made against Derrida by John Milbank, Catherine Pickstock and Connor Cunningham. Readily conceding that Derrida's thought is not a-moral or apolitical, they argue that Derrida nevertheless works from an *ontology* that is nihilistic in a more technical sense. See 4.2.3.
41. Derrida, 'Hospitality, Justice, and Responsibility', p. 78.
42. For a discussion, see the interview, 'Of a Certain Collège International de Philosophie to Come' (*Points*, 109–14) and more fully and thematically, *Du droit à la philosophie.*
43. Derrida, 'Deconstruction and the Other', p. 125.
44. *Ibid.*, p. 118.
45. Thus, despite Derrida's persistent critique of 'teleological' or 'eschatological' thinking, there is a *kind* of eschatology that animates deconstruction (as is also the case with Marxism). 'I think that all genuine questioning', Derrida remarks, 'is summoned by a certain type of eschatology, though it is impossible to define this eschatology in philosophical terms' (*Ibid.*, p. 119). We will return to these concerns in 3.1 below.
46. *Ibid.* As we'll see in 3.2.1, Derrida's language here is deeply Levinasian.
47. After adopting this strategy and outline for the book, I was happy to find confirmation of such a hermeneutic lens in J. Hillis Miller, 'Derrida's Others', in *Applying: To Derrida*, John Brannigan, Ruth Robbins and Julian Wolfreys, (eds) (London: Macmillan, 1996), pp. 153–70. However, I hope that this strategy avoids and counters what Derrida rightly recognizes as an increasingly facile reference to Levinas. As he notes, 'the word "other", "respect for the other", "opening to the other", etc., has become a bit tedious. There is something mechanical in this moralizing usage of the word "other", and sometimes there is also something a bit mechanical in references to Levinas in recent years – something artificial and facile.' See Jacques Derrida, *Sur Parole: Instantanés philosophiques* (Paris: Aube, 1999), p. 63.
48. Derrida, 'Deconstruction and the Other', p. 123.
49. Derrida hints at this in *Archive Fever*, trans. Eric Prenowitz (Chicago: University of Chicago Press, 1996).
50. Derrida, 'Deconstruction and the Other', in Kearney, (ed.), p. 108. Derrida goes on to note in this 1981 interview that 'the Judaic dimension remained at that stage a discrete rather than a decisive reference' (p. 108). Later he would come to recognize that Levinas's *philosophical* interest in alterity was generated by the *non-philosophical* sources of Judaism – mirroring Derrida's own concern to 'disturb' philosophy with the *non*-philosophical, what is otherwise-than-philosophy. '[T]o discover the non-place or *non-lieu* would be the "other" of philosophy. This is the task of deconstruction' (p. 112). We will return to the question of philosophy's 'other' in Chapter 2 below.
51. With this suggestion, I don't mean to 'biographize' Derrida's theoretical

work, but only to recognize what he himself persistently notes, *viz.*, the way in which his work has been 'marked' by his experiences. For an illuminating methodological account of the non-reductionistic relation between biography and philosophy, see Martin Beck Matustik, *Jürgen Habermas: A Philosophical–Political Profile* (Lanham, MD: Rowman & Littlefield, 2001).

52. In *Glas*, speaking about Genet, Derrida remarks: 'Yesterday he let me know that he was in Beirut, among the Palestinians at war, encircled outcasts. I know that what interests me always takes (its/his) place over there, but how to show that?' (Derrida, *Glas*, trans. John P. Leavey, Jr. and Richard Rand (Lincoln: University of Nebraska Press, 1986 [French, 1974]).

53. Ivan Kalmar, *The Trostkys, Freuds, and Woody Allens: Portrait of a Culture* (Toronto: Penguin, 1994), pp. 141–2.

54. Jacques Derrida, 'Deconstruction and the Other', an interview in Richard Kearney, (ed.), *Dialogues with Contemporary Continental Thinkers* (Manchester: Manchester University Press, 1984), p. 107, emphasis added.

55. Derrida later remarked (in 1983) that his experience of anti-Semitic exclusion produced 'a paradoxical effect': 'a desire for integration in the non-Jewish community, a fascinated but painful and suspicious desire' while at the same time maintaining 'an impatient distance with regard to the Jewish communities' (*Points*, 121).

56. I'm alluding here to Terry Eagleton's critical assessment of the state of theory in *After Theory* (New York: Basic Books, 2003).

57. If we spend a disproportionate amount of time on Derrida's phenomenological beginnings, this is because I am convinced that it is the piece of Derrida that has been most ignored by those who have appropriated his work (especially in the States). But it is precisely because this phenomenological horizon has been ignored that such appropriations have been largely *mis*appropriations.

Chapter 1

58. Jacques Derrida, 'Autoimmunity: Real and Symbolic Suicides, A Dialogue with Jacques Derrida', in Giovanna Borradori, *Philosophy in a Time of Terror: Dialogues with Jürgen Habermas and Jacques Derrida* (Chicago: University of Chicago Press, 2003), p. 87, first emphasis added.

59. Martin Heidegger, *Being and Time*, trans. J. Macquarrie and J. Edwards (San Francisco: Harper & Row, 1962), §§1–2. For a helpful discussion of parallels between Wittgenstein and Derrida, see Newton Garver's lucid 'Preface' to *SP*, pp. ix–xxix. On the 'linguistic turn' more generally, see Richard Rorty, (ed.), *The Linguistic Turn* (Chicago: University of Chicago Press, 1967) and *Philosophy and the Mirror of Nature* (Princeton: Princeton University Press, 1979).

60. Not in the sense of the narrow 'philosophical anthropology' Heidegger rejects (i.e., a 'humanistic' philosophical anthropology *as* fundamental ontology), but rather in a broader, descriptive sense: philosophical anthropology as an account of the conditions of human identity, community, and being-in-relation. Derrida himself is not allergic to the term (see *MP*, 113). What he rejects, following Husserl and Heidegger, is anthropolog*ism*, or the notion of deducing an ontology from an existential analytic of the *anthropos* (*MP*, 116).

61. For instance, as we'll see below, once one appreciates the *originary* status of language, it follows that there is an 'irreducible otherness that divides the self-identity of the living present' ('The Time of a Thesis', p. 40); that is, the relationship to others is a fundamental aspect of identity, introducing an alterity at the core of identity.

62. Derrida, 'The Time of a Thesis', p. 40.

63. Derrida, 'The Time of a Thesis', pp. 37, 39.

64. We're invoking here two Nietzschean epigraphs: first, Nietzsche's account in *Twilight of the Idols*, and second, his notation: 'Socrates, he who does not write', cited as the epigraph to Chapter 1 of Derrida's *Of Grammatology* (p. 6).

65. For a representative account, see Plato's *Republic*, Books VI and VII.

66. In 4.1.1 we will consider the way in which Derrida's reading of Husserl parallels his reading of Plato.

67. Husserl's text 'The Origin of Geometry' is included as an appendix to the English translation of Derrida's *Edmund Husserl's* Origin of Geometry: *An Introduction* (*IHOG*) and I will cite the pagination in this edition.

68. Perhaps another way into the issue would be to ask the question: Is Euclidean geometry 'invented' by Euclid, or 'discovered' by Euclid?

69. Husserl remarks that the community of persons – which is the 'site' of communication – is primarily a *linguistic community*, 'a community of those who can reciprocally express themselves . . . as men with a common language' (162). One should note the homogeneity of Husserl's ('normal') 'world' and 'community', where everyone speaks the same language. This preference for univocity will be discussed further below.

70. Husserl seems unattentive to the slippage that occurs between this 'inside' and 'outside'. Matters of slippage in communication are taken up extensively by Derrida in *The Post Card* (see 2.2.2).

71. *Being and Time*, §35.

72. We should note, I think, that one is not contesting the *distinction* as much as the *relationship* between these two (what we also called the signifier and the signified): there is, of course, a sense in which the 'meaning' *exceeds* and therefore is not identical to the empirical word, whether phonetic or graphic. But to concede that distinction does not entail *a relation of non-dependence*. It is the latter which is at stake in Husserl: though conceding the distinction, Derrida wants to maintain that the signified 'remains essentially *tied* . . . to a real spatiotemporality' (70, emphasis added). (Or, in

other words, all 'idealities' are *bound* idealities [71–2,76].) The question is the nature of this *knot*.

73. Edmund Husserl, *Experience and Judgment*, trans. James S. Churchill and Karl Ameriks (Evanston, IL: Northwestern University Press, 1973), p. 267.

74. *Ibid.*

75. One might also say that corporeality goes all the way down. See *IHOG*, 89n.92.

76. The occasion for this analysis here is Husserl's account of *writing*, but the burden of Derrida's *Of Grammatology* is to demonstrate that this is an essential trait of *language* – hence his designation of language as *arche-writing* (see 1.4.3).

77. It is interesting to note that in *Of Grammatology*, Derrida remarked that, in contrast to Husserl, 'Peirce goes very far in the direction that I have called the de-construction of the transcendental signified' (*OG*, 49).

78. For an account of an Augustinian semiotics (and references to the relevant literature), see James K. A. Smith, *Speech and Theology: Language and the Logic of Incarnation*, Radical Orthodoxy Series (London: Routledge, 2002), Ch. 4.

79. Edmund Husserl, *Logical Investigations*, trans. J. N. Findlay (New York: Humanities Press, 1970 [1900; 2nd edn, 1913], Volume 1, henceforth abbreviated in the text as *LI*.

80. 'The two notions of sign do not therefore really stand in the relation of more extensive genus to narrower species' (*LI*, 269).

81. It should be noted that Husserl has no sense of an 'unconscious' or 'sub-conscious' which we almost assume in a post-Freudian, psycho-analytic climate. For Husserl, the 'Freudian slip' or body language are meaningless (whereas for Freud they are oblique access to what one *really* means).

82. Husserl does grant that one could, very loosely, speak of 'talking to onself', but this would only be metaphorical and by analogy (*LI*, 279–80).

83. This claim parallels the claim in *IHOG* that idealities are inherently 'bound' or 'intertwined' with the materiality of language (*IHOG*, 89n.92).

84. For Levinas's critique of ontology, see *Totality and Infinity*, trans. Alphonso Lingis (Pittsburgh: Duquesne University Press, 1969). For an introduction to Levinas's thought, see Adriaan Peperzak, *To the Other: An Introduction to the Philosophy of Emmanuel Levinas* (Lafayette, IN: Purdue University Press, 1993).

85. The 'voice' then is closely linked to the disembodied soul (see earlier). This link is explored in more detail in 'Plato's Pharmacy' (see 4.1.1).

86. Husserl unpacks this key analysis in the Fifth Meditation in his *Cartesian Meditations*. For Derrida's analysis, see 'Violence and Metaphysics' in *WD*.

87. There is also a psychoanalytic aspect to this part of Derrida's project, maintaining that the self, particularly the author or speaker, cannot be 'master' of his or her intentions precisely because the self is not master of consciousness: there is an *un*conscious which eludes mastery.

88. See further discussion of this point in 'Differance' in *SP*, pp. 146–8.
89. Derrida notes an irony here: 'ethnocentrism will apparently be avoided at the very moment when it will have already profoundly operated, silently imposing its standard concepts of speech and writing' (*OG*, 121).
90. I have suggested a critique along these lines in my *The Fall of Interpretation: Philosophical Foundations for a Creational Hermeneutic* (Downers Grove, IL: InterVarsity Press, 2000), pp. 121–9.
91. Derrida notes that he continues to call this arche-*writing* 'only because it essentially communicates with the vulgar concept of writing' in the tradition he seeks to deconstruct (*OG*, 56). This illustrates the way in which deconstruction 'inhabits' structures from the inside (*OG*, 24).
92. It is only a 'provisional name' (*SP*, 129).
93. The metaphysics of presence privileges the 'present' in terms of both space and time – the 'here' and the 'now'. The 'here' and the 'now' are taken to be the site and moment that are undisturbed by any alterity, exteriority or other. Derrida shows the way in which both the not-here (and not-me) and the not-now (the past and future) are *constitutive* of the ego's here and now.
94. 'One could call *play* the absence of the transcendental signified as limitlessness of play, that is to say as the destruction of onto-theology and the metaphysics of presence' (*OG*, 50). This play cannot *in principle* be halted, or cannot be stopped *as such*. But as we'll see in Chapter 2 below, that does not mean that there are not legitimate *curbings* of this play nor does it mean that there is an absence of criteria in interpretation.
95. This parallels Levinas's account of subjectivity in *Otherwise Than Being, or Beyond Essence*, and also bears analogy to Jean-Luc Marion's account of the subject as 'the gifted' or 'the interlocuted' in *Being Given*, trans. Jeffrey Kosky (Stanford: Stanford University Press, 2003). I have discussed both of these models in my 'The Call as Gift: The Subject's Donation in Marion and Levinas', in *The Hermeneutics of Charity*, James K. A. Smith and Henry Venema, (eds) (Grand Rapids: Brazos, 2004), pp. 217–27.

Chapter 2

96. See Jacques Derrida, 'The Time of a Thesis: Punctuations', trans. Kathleen McLaughlin in *Philosophy in France Today*, Alan Montefiore, (ed.) (Cambridge: Cambridge University Press, 1983), p. 36.
97. *Ibid.*, p. 37.
98. 'The Time of a Thesis', pp. 37–8.
99. 'Deconstruction and the Other', p. 108.
100. This 'methodological' strategy – invigorating philosophy by exposing it to what is otherwise-than-philosophical – has important precedents. First, we could compare the project of the young Heidegger, for whom the 'facticity' of Greek ethical life (as distilled in Aristotle) and Christian

religious experience (as unpacked by St Paul) were catalysts for retooling the task of philosophy. See Martin Heidegger, *The Phenomenology of Religious Life*, trans. Jennifer Gossetti and Matthias Fritsch (Bloomington, IN: Indiana University Press, 2004). I have unpacked this project in my *Speech and Theology: Language and the Logic of Incarnation* (London: Routledge, 2002), Ch. 3. Second, this strategy finds a parallel in Levinas's work, where Judaism confronts ontology in order to deconstruct Western philosophical categories. On this point, see Jill Robbins, *Prodigal Son/Elder Brother: Interpretation and Alterity in Augustine, Petrarch, Kafka, Levinas* (Chicago: University of Chicago Press, 1991), pp. 100–32.

101. This is one of the meanings of the title 'Tympan': 'We know that the membrane of the tympanum, a thin and transparent partition separating the auditory canal from the middle ear (the *cavity*), is stretched obliquely' (*MP*, xii–xiii). This is one of the meanings of the opening line: 'To tympanize – philosophy' (*MP*, x).

102. In Plato's context, there was an intrinsic link between poetry and religion, so poetry had a kind of double-alterity with respect to philosophy – both aesthetic and religious (paralleling two non-philosophical sites of interest to Derrida: literature and religion).

103. See Rorty, 'Remarks on Deconstruction and Pragmatism', in *Deconstruction and Pragmatism*, Chantal Mouffe, (ed.) (London: New York, 1996), pp. 13–17. One of the funnier moments of Kirby Dick and Amy Ziering Kofman's documentary *Derrida* is when an eager sophomore approaches Derrida after a lecture in New York and tells him that she read one of his 'novels' last summer and liked it very much. Derrida kindly smiled and thanked her.

104. Derrida, 'Remarks on Deconstruction and Pragmatism', in *ibid.*, p. 79. So also Derrida emphasizes that he is not interested in *reducing* concepts to metaphors. While he rejects the 'classical opposition' between the two, his 'new articulation' of the distinction is not a collapsing of concepts into metaphor (*MP*, 262–3).

105. 'Remarks', p. 79.

106. Derrida, 'Des Tours de Babel', trans. Joseph F. Graham in *The Derrida Reader*, Peggy Kamuf, (ed.) (New York: Columbia University Press, 1991), p. 253.

107. To appreciate the political import of this, it would be instructive to contrast deconstruction's interest in multiplying languages with Samuel Huntington's (basically racist) critique of the 'Hispanicization' of (Protestant) American culture as a threat to 'American identity' – especially because Hispanic immigrants won't learn English. See Samuel Huntington, *Who Are We?: The Challenges to America's National Identity* (New York: Simon & Schuster, 2004), pp. 158–70. Interestingly, this discussion appears in a chapter entitled 'Deconstructing America' in a section of the book entitled 'Challenges to American Identity'. In a section on 'the deconstructionist movement' (pp. 141–5), Derrida's name does not

appear. For a critique of Huntington, see Michael Hardt & Antonio Negri, *Multitude: War and Democracy in the Age of Empire* (New York: Penguin, 2004), pp. 33–5.

108. Jacques Derrida, *The Gift of Death*, trans. David Wills (Chicago: University of Chicago Press, 1995), pp. 100–01, 109. See 3.2.2 below.

109. This interest in memoirs and autobiography also translates into Derrida's interest in self-portraiture, as unpacked in *Memoirs of the Blind*.

110. Derrida, 'Remarks on Deconstruction and Pragmatism', p. 80.

111. *Ibid.*, p. 80.

112. *Ibid.*

113. *Ibid.*

114. *Ibid.*

115. *Exergue* derives from the Greek and means 'outside the work'; the term was used to describe the space on a coin or medal reserved for inscriptions. See *MP*, 209n.1.

116. Nietzsche, 'On Truth and Falsity in their Ultramoral Sense', cited at *MP*, 217.

117. Derrida cites the query of Gaston Bachelard: 'who knows whether, in consciously borrowing from the beehive the term cell in order to designate the element of the living organism, the human mind has not also borrowed from the hive, almost unconsciously, the notion of the cooperative work of which the honeycomb is the product' (cited at *MP*, 261)?

118. Actually, as Derrida notes, once one gives up the sense of an original 'literal' sense, one might also have to give up the sense of even originary 'metaphor' – since 'metaphor generally implies a relation to an original "property" of meaning, a "proper" sense to which it indirectly or equivocally refers'. Thus, more properly, what Derrida is pointing to is 'catachresis': 'a violent production of meaning, an abuse which refers to no anterior or proper norm' ('Deconstruction and the Other', p. 123).

119. The psychoanalytic metaphor is common in Derrida. He examines the same 'return' in psychoanalysis in 'Freud and the Scene of Writing' in *WD*. In particular, he considers the impact of Freud's shift (in 1896) from 'natural' metaphors to writing metaphors, particularly the notion of a 'writing pad' or 'writing machine' as the basic metaphor to account for the working of the psyche (*WD*, 199–200). Dreams are seen as a kind of 'writing' that demand *interpretation* (*WD*, 207–08). Thus, psychoanalysis is fundamentally a kind of hermeneutics, and the analyst the master hermeneut (see 'Le facteur de la vérité' in *PC*, pp. 411–96).

120. *Positions* was also somewhat non-traditional in that it was a collection of interviews that came to be regarded as an integral 'work'. We will consider the genre of the interview in more detail in Chapter 5.

121. In the 'Villanova Roundtable', Derrida confesses: 'The way I refer to St. Augustine is really not very orthodox; it is rather – a sin!' See John D. Caputo, *Deconstruction in a Nutshell* (Bronx, NY: Fordham University Press, 1997), p. 20.

122. Jacques Derrida, 'Circumfession', in Geoffrey Bennington and Jacques Derrida, *Jacques Derrida* (Chicago: University of Chicago Press, 1993), p. 248.

123. This lack is supplemented by John P. Leavey, Jr.'s *Glassary* (Lincoln, NB: University of Nebraska Press, 1986).

124. Derrida, 'Deconstruction and the Other', p. 122.

125. I would argue that there is a significant difference between the 'possibility' of going astray and the 'fatal necessity' of such. For a critique of Derrida on this score, see James K. A. Smith, 'How to Avoid Not Speaking: Attestations', in *Knowing* Other-*wise: Philosophy on the Threshold of Spirituality*, James H. Olthuis, (ed.) (Bronx, NY: Fordham University Press, 1997), pp. 217–34 and *idem.*, 'Limited Inc/arnation: Revisiting the Derrida/Searle Debate', in *Hermeneutics at the Crossroads*, Kevin Vanhoozer, James K. A. Smith and Bruce Ellis Benson, (eds) (Bloomington, IN: Indiana University Press, forthcoming).

126. Rorty's observation is insightful: '[Derrida's] Anglophone fans typically use Derrida for the same purposes as Marx and Freud have long been used by literary critics. . . . These fans . . . think that there is a method called "deconstruction" which one can apply to texts and teach to students. I have never been able to figure out what this method is, nor what was being taught to students except some such maxim like "Find something that can be made to look self-contradictory, claim that that contradiction is the central message of the text, and ring some changes upon it." Application of this maxim produced, in the 1970s and 1980s, tens of thousand of "deconstructive readings" of texts by American and British professors – readings which were as formulaic and boring as the tens of thousands of readings which resulted from dutifully applying the maxim, "Find something that can be made to sound like a symptom of an unresolved Oedipus complex" ' ('Remarks on Deconstruction and Pragmatism', pp. 14–15).

127. Derrida, 'Deconstruction and the Other,' p. 123.

128. Derrida, 'Following Theory', p. 27.

Chapter 3

129. This repays further analysis that we cannot undertake here. The issue is what one means by an eschatology. Derrida rejects notions of the eschatological which posit the future arrival of an *eschaton* that can be *identified* as just. For Derrida, this could never be the case because finitude itself entails a certain injustice. But on the other hand, there is a deeply *futural*, even *hopeful* looking to the future that drives deconstruction. I have discussed this further in my 'Determined Hope: A Phenomenology of Christian Expectation', in Miroslav Volf and William Katerberg, (eds),

The Future of Hope: Essays on Christian Tradition Amid Modernity and Postmodernity (Grand Rapids, MI: Eerdmans, 2004), pp. 200–27.

130. 'Deconstruction and the Other', p. 119.

131. Or *religious* reconciliation, as in the 'transformation of the sinner' (*OCF*, 35), or giving forgiveness 'meaning' by effecting a reconciliation between God and the sinner (*OCF*, 36).

132. As noted above with respect to hospitality, I think there are good reasons to question Derrida's analysis here but will bracket such a critique in this context.

133. Cf. 'signals', p. 53. The relation is somehow semiotic, but as such, would be governed by the semiotics we sketched in Chapter 1, such that what signals is both presence and absence.

134. Jacques Derrida, *The Other Heading: Reflections on Today's Europe*, trans. Pascale-Anne Brault and Michael B. Naas (Bloomington, IN: Indiana University Press, 1992), p. 17.

135. *Ibid.*, p. 15, cf. p. 30.

136. *Ibid.*, p. 29.

137. *Ibid.*, p. 77.

138. Derrida, 'The Time of a Thesis', p. 42.

139. See Derrida's helpful discussion of this in 'The Villanova Roundtable', pp. 5–8; and in 'Of a Certain Collège International de Philosophie Still to Come' in *Points*, pp. 109–14.

140. Derrida helpfully complicates the picture by suggesting that we cannot be simply *either* Jewish *or* Greek, but rather 'Jewgreek' (*WD*, 153).

141. Levinas, *The Infinite Conversation* cited by Derrida in *Adieu*, p. 132n.35.

142. For the classic treatment of Derrida and religion, see John D. Caputo, *The Prayers and Tears of Jacques Derrida* (Bloomington, IN: Indiana University Press, 1997). Also consult the bibliography for work by Kevin Hart and Mark C. Taylor.

143. Many of Derrida's key texts on religious themes and texts have been collected in Jacques Derrida, *Acts of Religion*, Gil Anidjar, (ed.) (London: Routledge, 2002).

144. As Derrida notes, his entire generation was introduced to Husserl and Heidegger by Levinas's groundbreaking work, particularly *The Theory of Intuition in Husserl's Phenomenology*, still a classic exposition (see *Ad* 10–11).

145. For a helpful account of Levinas's project as an 'ethics of ethics', see Jeffrey Dudiak, *The Intrigue of the Other* (Bronx, NY: Fordham University Press, 2001).

146. Levinas and Derrida both emphasize that chronological terms don't work here: the third is always already present in the face of the Other. But in the phenomenological description, one almost pedagogically begins with the account *as if* it were dyadic.

147. It should be noted that Levinas opposes 'metaphysics' to 'ontology': the latter is a discourse that legitimates and reifies the sphere of the same; the former begins from the fundamental relation to the Other. So

'metaphysics' here is fundamentally different from 'the metaphysics of presence' that Derrida has sought to deconstruct. In Levinas's terms, it would be an 'ontology of presence'.

148. See Levinas's reading of Descartes's key argument regarding the presence of the idea of the infinite *in* the finite ego in Descartes's Third Meditation in *Totality and Infinity*, pp. 210ff.

149. There are two problems here which I will simply note but not develop: (1) it does not seem self-evident that the sense of an *unconditional* welcome follows from the welcome of the infinite. I think Derrida confuses the genitive here; (2) It is not at all clear what an unconditional welcome could possibly mean for finite creatures or finite institutions. I develop these criticisms in more detail in my *Holy Wars and Democratic Crusades: Deconstructing Myths of Religious Violence and Secular Peace* (forthcoming).

150. Derrida notes this early in 'Violence and Metaphysics': 'this being-together as separation precedes or exceeds society, collectivity, community. Levinas calls it *religion*. It opens ethics. The ethical relation is a religious relation' (*WD*, 95–6).

151. Derrida, 'Hospitality, Justice, and Responsibility', p. 73.

152. Derrida, 'Following Theory', pp. 31–2.

153. Derrida, 'Hospitality, Justice, and Responsibility', p. 66.

154. *Ibid.*

155. This theme, which we cannot develop here, is explored in more detail in *Memoirs of the Blind*.

156. Derrida, 'Hospitality, Justice, and Responsibility', p. 66.

157. For further discussion, see Derrida, 'Faith and Knowledge: The Two Sources of "Religion" at the Limits of Reason Alone'. I have criticized this Kantian paradigm in 'Re-Kanting Postmodernism?: Derrida's Religion Within the Limits of Reason Alone', *Faith and Philosophy* 17 (2000): 558–71; and 'Is Deconstruction an Augustinian Science?: Augustine, Derrida, and Caputo on the Commitments of Philosophy', in James H. Olthuis, (ed.), *Religion With/out Religion: The Prayers and Tears of John D. Caputo* (London: Routledge, 2001), pp. 50–61.

158. This mad faith stands in contrast to the comfortable religiosity that secures middle class existence. 'If you want to experience faith as something reassuring and wise', Derrida comments, 'something reliable or probable, it's not faith. Faith must be mad, or absurd, as they say sometimes. That's the condition of faith – the distinction between faith and knowledge, for instance' ('Following Theory', p. 36).

159. There is a Levinasian correlate of this 'translation' in 'God and Philosophy' (for a discussion see *GD*, 82–4).

160. Derrida alludes to this in his reading of Marx, recounting 'what was for me, and for those of my *generation* who shared it during a whole lifetime, the experience of Marxism, the quasi-paternal figure of Marx, the way it fought in us with other filiations' (*SM*, 13–14). See *Work of Mourning* (pp. 192–5, 214–15) for a discussion of this 'generation'.

161. For an interesting philosophical 'snapshot' of this period, see Derrida's essay 'The Ends of Man' (in *MP*), a report on French philosophy composed during May 1968.
162. Derrida, *Other Heading*, p. 57.
163. See Jacques Derrida, *Positions*, trans. Alan Bass (Chicago: University of Chicago Press, 1981), pp. 61–8.
164. Derrida, *Positions*, p. 63.
165. *Ibid.*, p. 62.
166. '[D]econstruction has never been Marxist, no more than it has ever been non-Marxist, although it has remained faithful to a certain spirit of marxism, to at least one of its spirits for, and this can never be repeated too often, there is *more than one* of them and they are heterogeneous' (*SM*, 75). One of the 'other' Marxist spirits, which deconstruction *does* renounce, is Marx's confident philosophy of history (*SM*, 74) and what Lyotard called the 'metanarrative' of Marx's pretension to be offering a rationally legitimated 'science' of history and economics.
167. Derrida is alluding here to a point he makes in *Of Spirit*: critique, which is essentially negative and questioning, is always already preceded by a mode of affirmation and 'promise' which is its condition of possibility. Thus, before the question of critique is the affirmation that is inherent to language (see 4.2.2). In the same way Derrida contends that even 'the lie' lives off of a more originary promise (see *Without Alibi*, pp. 28–70).
168. The notion of the 'messianic' was broached earlier in *FL*; it seems to have made its way into Derrida's discourse via an engagement with Walter Benjamin, specifically his 'Theses on the Philosophy of History' in *Illuminations*.
169. Derrida, *Other Heading*, p. 56.
170. I have critically examined these themes in much more detail in my 'Determined Violence: Derrida's Structural Religion', *Journal of Religion* 78 (1998), pp. 197–212. This logic is subjected to more sustained critique in my *Holy Wars and Democratic Crusades*.
171. Jacques Derrida, 'The Principle of Reason: The University in the Eyes of its Pupils', trans. Catherine Porter and Edward P. Morris, *Diacritics* 13 (1983), p. 5. This essay might be read as Derrida's 'What is Enlightenment?', or in the spirit of *The Conflict of the Faculties*. Derrida engages the latter at pp. 19–20.
172. See Jacques Derrida, *Voyous* (Paris: Galilée, 2003), p. 211.
173. Jacques Derrida, 'The "World" of the Enlightenment to Come (Exception, Calculation, Sovereignty)', trans. Pascale-Anne Brault and Michael Naas, *Research in Phenomenology* 33 (2003), p. 10.
174. Such a critique of given conceptions of reason is presaged in Heidegger's *Discourse on Thinking* (San Francisco: Harper & Row, 1959).
175. Derrida, 'The "World" of the Enlightenment to Come', p. 25.
176. *Ibid.*, p. 27, all emphases original.
177. *Ibid.*, p. 31.

178. *Ibid.*, pp. 33–4.
179. *Ibid.*, p. 35.
180. *Ibid.*
181. Jacques Derrida, 'Faith and Knowledge', p. 18.
182. Derrida, 'The "World" of the Enlightenment to Come', p. 39.
183. *Ibid.*, p. 40.
184. *Ibid.*, pp. 46–7.
185. Jacques Derrida, 'The Last of the Rogue States: The "Democracy to Come", Opening in Two Turns', trans. Pascale-Anne Brault and Michael Naas, *South Atlantic Quarterly* 103 (2004), 329.
186. 'The "to come," ' Derrida comments, 'suggests not only the promise, but also the fact that democracy will never exist, in the sense of a present existence: not because it will be deferred but because it will always remain aporetic in its structure' (*ibid.*, p. 331).
187. Derrida, 'Autoimmunity: Real and Symbolic Suicides', in *Philosophy in a Time of Terror*, p. 91.

Chapter 4

188. For appropriations of Derrida within particular disciplines, such as literary theory, architecture, and theology, consult the secondary bibliography.
189. We might compare Gilles Deleuze's corpus: one cannot easily distinguish his 'systematic' works (*Difference and Repetition, Logic of Sense*, and the works with Guattari) from his landmark historical studies of Kant, Hume, Leibniz and Bergson.
190. See Jacques Derrida, *Le problème de la genèse dans la philosophie de Husserl* (Paris: Presses Universitaires de France, 1990), pp. 1–2. We might suggest that it was Husserl, as much as Nietzsche, who taught Derrida the practice of genealogy.
191. This way of putting it pays homage to the influence of one of his teachers that Derrida regularly notes: Tran-Duc-Thao, *Phénomenologie et matérialisme dialectique* (Paris, 1951).
192. Derrida, 'Deconstruction and the Other', in R. Kearney, (ed.), p. 113.
193. *Ibid.*, pp. 113–14.
194. Derrida in '*As if* I were Dead', p. 220.
195. As Rorty once put it, 'Derrida throws himself into the arms of the texts he writes about' (Rorty, 'Remarks on Deconstruction and Pragmatism', p. 14).
196. Jacques Derrida, 'Following Theory', p. 9.
197. *Ibid.*, p. 7. This double relation of following and departing is often poignantly expressed in the works gathered together in Derrida, *The Work of Morning*, Pascale-Anne Brault and Michael Naas, (eds) (Chicago: University of Chicago Press, 2001).
198. Derrida, 'Deconstruction and the Other', p. 117.

199. See the discussion of 'truth as a woman' in *Spurs: Nietzsche's Styles*, trans. Barbara Harlow (Chicago: University of Chicago Press, 1979); of sexual difference in '*Geschlecht*: Sexual Difference, Ontological Difference', trans. Ruben Berezdivin, *Research in Phenomenology* 13 (1983), pp. 65–83 and '*Geschlecht* 2: Heidegger's Hand', trans. John P. Leavey Jr. in *Deconstruction and Philosophy*, John Sallis, (ed.) (Chicago: University of Chicago Press, 1987). On the 'feminine' in Levinas, see 'At This Very Moment in This Work Here I Am', trans. Ruben Berezdivin, in *Re-Reading Levinas*, Robert Bernasconi and Simon Critchley, (eds) (Bloomington, IN: Indiana University Press, 1991), pp. 11–48. See also discussions in interviews, including 'Deconstruction and the Other', p. 121, and 'Women in the Beehive: A Seminar with Jacques Derrida', in *Men in Feminism*, Alice Jardine and Paul Smith, (eds) (New York: Methuen, 1987), pp. 189–203.

200. In preceding chapters, we have already considered Derrida's relation to Husserl (1.2–1.3), Levinas (3.2.1), Kierkegaard (3.2.2), and Marx (3.3.1). Space will not permit us to consider the importance of other philosophical figures such as Hegel and Augustine, nor literary figures such as Joyce, Genet and Baudelaire. Resources in the Bibliography will point to further reading along these lines.

201. See Jacques Derrida, 'Plato's Pharmacy', in *Dissemination*, pp. 61–171.

202. See Jacques Derrida, 'How to Avoid Speaking: Denials', trans. Ken Frieden, in *Languages of the Unsayable: The Play of Negativity in Literature and Literary Theory*, Sanford Budick and Wolfgang Iser, (eds) (New York: Columbia University Press, 1989), pp. 3–70 and 'Khôra', trans. Ian McLeod in *On the Name*, pp. 89–127.

203. For further discussion of negative theology and the via negativa in this respect, see James K. A. Smith, *Speech and Theology*, Chs. 1 and 5.

204. See Derrida, 'Khôra', pp. 90–1.

205. While *Speech and Phenomena* was Derrida's first book to appear in English (in 1973), its rigorous focus on Husserl and high-level questions in phenomenology restricted its readership mainly to those working in phenomenology. More influential to Derrida's reception by literary theory was the 1976 publication of *Of Grammatology*; Spivak's massive introductory essay shaped a generation of readers of Derrida's work.

206. Indeed, the notion of a 'weak force' in his last works, especially *Voyous* (pp. 105–13), suggests something quite different. For a discussion of Derrida's invocation of the 'will to power', see 4.2.2 below.

207. Derrida, *Positions*, pp. 9–10; cf. pp. 54–5.

208. See the very helpful questions put to Derrida by Stephen Mulhall in 'Wittgenstein and Deconstruction', *Ratio* (new series) 13.4 (2000), pp. 407–14, and Derrida's 'Response to Mulhall' (pp. 415–18).

209. For more on Derrida's relation to the Yale School, see the works by Atkins, Culler and Leitch in the secondary bibliography.

210. Jacques Derrida, 'Three Questions to Hans-Georg Gadamer', trans. Diane Michelfelder and Richard Palmer, in *Dialogue & Deconstruction: The*

Gadamer-Derrida Encounter, Michelfelder and Palmer, (eds) (Albany, NY: SUNY Press, 1989), p. 53. The original title of Derrida's talk in French was 'Bonnes volontés de puissance' = 'The Good Will to Power'.

211. See Gadamer, 'Reply to Jacques Derrida', in *ibid.*, pp. 55–7. 'Even immoral beings try to understand one another', Gadamer replied in exasperation. 'I cannot believe that Derrida would actually disagree with me about this. Whoever opens his mouth wants to be understood; otherwise, one would neither speak nor write. And finally, I have an exceptionally good piece of evidence for this: Derrida directs questions to me and therefore he must assume that I am willing to understand them' (p. 55).

212. Jacques Derrida, 'Uninterrupted Dialogue: Between Two Infinities, the Poem', trans. Thomas Dutoit and Philippe Romanski in *Research in Phenomenology* 34 (2004), pp. 3–19 (pp. 3–4).

213. Derrida, *Of Spirit: Heidegger and the Question*, trans. Geoffrey Bennington and Rachel Bowlby (Chicago: University of Chicago Press, 1989), p. 94.

214. *Ibid.*, p. 129.

215. *Ibid.*, p. 130.

216. *Ibid.* This theme is also developed in 'The History of the Lie: Prolegomena', in *Without Alibi*.

217. See Jürgen Habermas, *The Philosophical Discourse of Modernity*, trans. Fredrick Lawrence (Cambridge, MA: MIT Press, 1984).

218. Habermas notes this as something of a turning point. 'When he received the Adorno prize, Derrida, for his part, gave a highly sensible speech in the Paulskirche in Frankfurt, in which the spiritual affinity of these two minds was impressively manifested. This kind of thing leaves no one unmoved.' See 'America and the World: A Conversation with Jürgen Habermas', *Logos* 3.3 (Summer 2004), available at http://www.logosjournal.com/habermas_america.htm.

219. See Jacques Derrida and Jürgen Habermas, 'Unsere Erneuerung. Nach dem Krieg: Die Widergeburt Europas', *Frankfurter Allgemeine Zeitung*, May 31, 2003, p. 33 (available in English as 'Europe: Plea for a Common Foreign Policy' at http://watch.windsofchange.net/themes_63.htm).

220. Recall the discussion of the exchange with John Searle above (2.3). And all of the signatories of *The Times* letter around the 'Cambridge affair' are associated with the analytic tradition (see 0.1.1).

221. See especially Rorty, 'From Ironist Theory to Private Allusions: Derrida', in *Contingency, Irony, and Solidarity* (Cambridge: Cambridge University Press, 1989), pp. 122–37.

222. Geoffrey Bennington offers a helpful proviso to such a project, worrying that in order for the 'real' (i.e. Oxbridge) philosophers to take Derrida seriously, they will need to be convinced that one can find 'arguments' in Derrida. But this would miss Derrida's trenchant critique of just what constitutes 'argument'; thus, what we would get, under the guise of Derrida as a 'real' philosopher would be a domesticated Derrida. 'This process of transcription might then be taken to produce an "improved"

Derrida – perhaps in the sense in which polite society in the Morningside district of Edinburgh used to talk of cats being taken to the vet to be "improved".' See Bennington, 'For the Sake of Argument (Up to a Point)', *Ratio* (new series) 13.4 (2000), pp. 332–45 (p. 336).

223. See the special issue of *Ratio* (new series) 13.4 (2000), with contributions from Glendinning, Bennington, A. W. Moore, Stephen Mulhall, Thomas Baldwin and Darren Sheppard, with responses from Derrida.

224. Derrida in *ibid.*, pp. 351, 381.

225. Alain Badiou, *Infinite Thought: Truth and the Return to Philosophy*, trans. and eds Oliver Feltham and Justin Clemens (London: Continuum, 2003), pp. 45–6.

226. *Ibid.*, p. 48.

227. *Ibid.*, p. 56.

228. See, for instance, Slavoj Žižek, *The Sublime Object of Ideology* (London: Verso, 1989), pp. 153–200; and *Did Somebody Say Totalitarianism? Five Interventions in the (Mis)Use of a Notion* (London: Verso, 2002), pp. 141–189. For a critique of Derrida's 'religion without religion', see Žižek, *The Puppet and the Dwarf: The Perverse Core of Christianity* (Cambridge, MA: MIT Press, 2003), pp. 5–6, 139–43.

229. Terry Eagleton, *After Theory* (Cambridge, MA: Basic Books, 2003), pp. 46, 153–62.

230. *Ibid.*, p. 165.

231. *Ibid.*, p. 160. For Eagleton, this also points to the need for a certain reassertion of *theology* and the concrete practices of religious communities. As such, he echoes the critique of Derrida offered by 'Radical Orthodoxy' in the work of Graham Ward and John Milbank. See especially Ward, *True Religion* (Oxford: Blackwell, 2003) and John Milbank, *The Word Made Strange* (Oxford: Blackwell, 1997), pp. 219–32 and *Being Reconciled* (London: Routledge, 2003), pp. 138–61. I have discussed this further in *Introducing Radical Orthodoxy* (Grand Rapids, MI: Baker Academic, 2004), pp. 240–3.

Chapter 5

232. Even the imposition of the word 'theory' in the title is a bit of an injustice. As Derrida once noted, 'I never use the word "theory" in the way that you do here; I don't use the word "theory" after you, after the Americans and English speakers.' So if one talks about working 'after theory', Derrida remarks that he 'would translate this into French as "life after philosophy", after deconstruction, after literature' ('Following Theory', p. 8).

233. Derrida once remarked: 'In certain cases, the interviews may orient someone toward a reading of the books. For the greatest majority, however, they "take the place of"; an image is constructed that gets along very well without texts, without books. And I find that worrisome' (*Points*, 154).

234. 'Between Brackets', in *Points*, 5–29, conducted in September 1975. A

follow-up interview was conducted in late October 1975 and is republished as '*Ja*, or the *faux-bond*' in *Points*, 30–77. Both employ a similar strategy.

235. Or consider the case of Derrida's *faux*-dialogue with *Le Monde*, in which he cites a Latin phrase (again in brackets), to which his interlocutor responds: 'So now you're speaking Latin over the telephone?' (*Points*, 178).
236. Jacques Derrida, 'Passions: "An Oblique Offering",' in *On the Name*, Thomas Dutoit, (ed.) (Stanford: Stanford University Press, 1995), p. 23.
237. These risks of response are discussed in *ibid.*, pp. 18–21.
238. *Ibid.*, p. 21.
239. The risks of nonresponse are outlined in *ibid.*, pp. 21–2.
240. See, for instance, *MP*, pp. xiii–xvi.
241. *Ibid.*, p. 13.
242. See *IHOG* 45n.37, 72n.70; *MP* 121.
243. 'Deconstruction and the Other', p. 119.
244. 'Derrida seems to me as good a humanist as Mill or Dewey. When Derrida talks about deconstruction as prophetic of "the democracy that is to come", he seems to me to be expressing the same utopian social hope as was felt by these earlier dreamers' (Rorty, 'Remarks on Deconstruction and Pragmatism', p. 14).
245. Derrida, 'Remarks on Deconstruction and Pragmatism', p. 83.
246. Jacques Derrida, 'The Last of the Rogue States: The "Democracy to Come", Opening in Two Turns', trans. Pascale-Anne Brault and Michael Naas, in *South Altantic Quarterly* 103 (2004), 329, 331.
247. *Ibid.*, p. 333.
248. See 'The Villanova Roundtable: A Conversation with Jacques Derrida', in *Deconstruction in a Nutshell*, John D. Caputo, (ed.) (Bronx, NY: Fordham University Press, 1997), pp. 23–4. The same hesitation is seen in 'Foi et savoir'.
249. Derrida, 'The "World" of the Enlightenment to Come', p. 52.
250. *Ibid.*, p. 48.
251. 'For a Justice to Come: An Interview with Jacques Derrida', first published in *De Standaard Letteren*, March 18, 2004, available (in French, English, and Dutch) at http://www.brusselstribunal.org/derrida.htm.
252. Derrida, *Sur parole*, p. 45.
253. 'For a Justice to Come', *op. cit.*
254. 'For a Justice to Come'.
255. See Michael Hardt and Antonio Negri, *Multitude: War and Democracy in the Age of Empire* (New York: Penguin, 2004), pp. 99–100.
256. 'For a Justice to Come'.
257. Jacques Derrida, 'The University Without Condition', in *Without Alibi*, and trans. Peggy Kamuf, (ed.) (Stanford: Stanford University Press, 2002), p. 208.
258. 'For a Justice to Come'.
259. Derrida, 'The "World" of the Enlightenment to Come', p. 45.
260. Derrida, 'Autoimmunity: Real and Symbolic Suicides', pp. 116–17.
261. Derrida, 'Following Theory', p. 26.

Bibliography

262. For other bibliographic efforts, see Joan Nordquist, *Jacques Derrida: A Bibliography*, Social Theory: A Bibliographic Series, No. 2 (Research and Reference Services, 1986); James Hulbert, *Jacques Derrida: An Annotated Bibliography*, Garland Reference Library of the Humanities, No. 534 (London: Taylor & Francis, 1988); William R. Schultz and Lewis L. B. Fried, *Jacques Derrida: An Annotated Primary and Secondary Bibliography*, Garland Bibliographies of Modern Critics and Critical Schools, Vol. 19 (London: Taylor & Francis, 1993) – a work of 882 pages; and Joan Nordquist, *Jacques Derrida II: A Bibliography*, Social Theory: A Bibliographic Series, No. 37 (Research & Reference Services, 1995). Geoffrey Bennington provides an almost exhaustive bibliography of Derrida's works up to 1990 in Bennington and Derrida, *Jacques Derrida*, pp. 356–73. See also the bibliography complied by Peter Krapp at http://www.hydra.umn.edu/derrida/jdyr.html.

Name Index

Allen, W. S. 131n.11
Alighieri, Dante 50
Aristotle 16, 39, 56, 98, 138n.100
Augustine 27, 58, 98, 140n.121,
    146n.200
Austin, J. L. 63

Bachelard, Gaston 140n.117
Badiou, Alain 103, 148n.225
Baldwin, Thomas 148n.223
Barthes, Roland 7
Baudelaire, Charles 98, 146n.200
Benjamin, Walter 101, 144n.168
Benson, Bruce Ellis 141n.25
Bennington, Geoffrey 147n.222,
    148n.223, 150n.262
Bergson, Henri 145n.189
Bernasconi, Robert 146n.199
Blanchot, Maurice 98
Bloom, Alan 6, 96, 130n.3
Bloom, Harold 99
Blunden, Allan 132n.25

Caputo, John D. 132n.25, 133n.29,
    140n.121, 142n.142, 149n.248
Celan, Paul 94
Cohen, Hermann 98
Critchley, Simon 65, 146n.199
Cunningham, Connor 134n.40

Davidson, Donald 102
Deleuze, Gilles 84, 145n.189

de Man, Paul 99
Denyer, Nicholas 131n.16
Descartes, René 98
Dewey, John 149n.244
Dick, Kirby 139n.103
Dooley, Mark 130n.4
Dudiak, Jeffrey 142n.145

Eagleton, Terry 103, 135n.56,
    148n.231
Eliot, T. S. 131n.8
Engels, Frederick 67
Eribon, Didier 7
Euclid 21, 136n.68

Farias, Victor 7
Faye, Jean-Pierre 85
Foucault, Michel 7, 84, 101
France, Anatole 54
Freud, Sigmund 85, 93, 96, 98,
    137n.81, 140n.119, 141n.126
Fried, Lewis L. B. 150n.262
Fukuyama, Francis 85

Gadamer, Hans Georg 4, 99, 100,
    101, 131n.8, 147n.211
Garver, Newton 102, 135n.59
Gasché, Rudolph 102
Genet, Jean 58, 98, 135n.52,
    146n.200
Glenndinning, Simon 102,
    148n.223

Graff, Gerald 63
Guattari, Felix 145n.189

Habermas, Jürgen 88, 100, 101,
    147n.217, 147n.218,
    147n.219
Hart, Kevin 133n.29, 142n.142
Hartmann, Geoffrey 99
Hardt, Michael 114, 129n.107,
    149n.255
Hebblethewaite, Brian 5, 131n.16,
    131n.17, 131n.18, 131n.19
Hegel, G. W. F. 17, 38, 50, 58, 93, 96,
    98, 146n.200
Heidegger, Martin 7, 10, 16, 22, 38,
    75, 85, 93, 96, 97, 99, 100, 102,
    112, 118, 131n.9, 132n.25,
    135n.59, 136n.60, 138n.100,
    142n.144, 144n.174
Heine, Heinrich 14
Hulbert, James 150n.262
Hume, David 145n.189
Huntington, Samuel 139n.107
Husserl, Edmund 13, 18, 19–38, 39,
    43, 46, 51, 89, 94, 95, 98, 99,
    106, 136n.60, 136n.66, 136n.67,
    136n.69, 136n.70, 136n.72,
    137n.76, 137n.77, 137n.81,
    137n.82, 142n.144, 145n.190,
    146n.200, 146n.205
Hyppolite, Jean 46

Jabés, Edmond 94
Jeanneret, Marian 131n.16
Joyce, James 94, 98, 102, 146n.200

Kalmar, Ivan 14
Kant, Immanuel 89, 93, 98,
    145n.189
Katerberg, William 141n.129
Kearney, Richard 130 n.4, 130 n.5
Kierkegaard, Søren 48, 52, 66, 75,
    80–84, 146n.200
Krapp, Peter 150n.262

Leavey Jr., John P. 141n.123
Leibniz 145n.189
Le Pen, Jean-Marie 68
Levinas, Emmanuel 14, 31, 36, 47,
    52, 66, 75, 76–80, 95, 97, 105,
    112, 117, 119, 134n.47, 134n.50,
    137n.84, 138n.95, 138n.100,
    142n.141, 142n.144, 142n.146,
    142n.147, 143n.148, 143n.150,
    146n.199, 146n.200
Lévi-Strauss, Claude 18, 38, 39,
    40–41, 42, 43, 51
Luther, Martin 112
Lyotard, Jean-François 84, 101,
    144n.166

Mallarmé, Stephane 93, 98
Marion, Jean-Luc 138n.95
Marx, Karl 67, 84–88, 141n.126,
    143n.160, 144n.166, 146n.200
Matustik, Martin Beck 134n.51
Mill, John Stewart 149n.244
Millbank, John 134n.40, 148n.231
Miller, J. Hillis 99, 134n.47
Moore, A. W. 102, 148n.223
Mulhall, Stephen 146n.208,
    148n.223

Negri, Antonio 114, 139n.107,
    149n.255
Nietzsche, Friedrich 56, 85, 93, 96,
    97, 117, 119, 136n.64, 145n.190
Norris, Christopher 5, 102, 131n.16,
    131n.19
Nordquist, Joan 150n.262

Olthuis, James H. 141n.125,
    143n.157
Ott, Hugo 132n.25

Parmenides 93
Pascal, Blaise 98
Peirce, C. S. 27, 137n.77
Pickstock, Catherine 134n.40

Plato 17–19, 23, 38, 39, 43, 49, 55,
    57, 69, 75, 89, 93–6, 136n.65,
    136n.66, 139n.102
Predergast, Christopher 131n.16,
    131n.17

Rapaport, Herman 65
Robbins, Jill 138n.100
Rorty, Richard 50–1, 65, 102, 111,
    116, 135n.59, 139n.103,
    141n.126, 145n.195, 147n.221,
    149n.244
Rosenzweig, Franz 98
Rousseau, Jean-Jacques 38, 39, 40,
    42–4, 51, 57, 106, 133n.33

Sartre, Jean-Paul 98, 118
Saussure, Ferdinand de 27, 39
Scholem, Gershom 98
Schultz, William R. 150n.262
Searle, John 6, 62, 63, 147n.220
Sheehan, Thomas 7, 132n.27
Sheppard, Darren 148n.223
Smith, Barry 5
Smith, James K. A. 137n.78, 138n.90,
    138n.95, 138n.100, 141n.125,

143n.157, 144n.170, 146n.203,
    148n.231
Spivak, Gayatri Chakravorty 96, 97,
    146n.205

Taylor, Mark C. 142n.142
Thao, Tran-Duc 145n.191
Thomas, Susannah 131n.16,
    131n.19

Van Gogh, Vincent 94
Vanhoozer, Kevin 141n.125
Venema, Henry 138n.95
Volf, Miroslav 141n.129
Voltaire, François-Marie Arouet de
    88

Ward, Graham 12, 148n.231
Wellek, René 6, 131n.20
Wheeler, Samuel 102
Wittgenstein, Ludwig 16, 25, 59, 98,
    102, 135n.59, 146n.208
Wolin, Richard 7, 8, 132n.27

Ziering, Amy 139n.103
Žižek, Slavoj 103, 148n.228

Subject Index

absence 25, 27, 28, 29–31, 35
  as transcendence 27
  subject constituted by 37
activism 114–15
Algeria 14
analogy 50
aporia 80–1, 108, 109
arche-writing 42, 43–5, 56–7, 98
asylum 68–69
author, authorship 8, 106, 109
  death of 4, 7, 22, 25
  rights of 7
  sovereignty of 113
authorial intent 4, 7, 64, 98, 104,
  105–6
autobiography 52, 57–8

Babel 51
Beauty and the Beast 2–3

Cambridge 4–5, 8, 74
capitalism 85, 89, 103
Christianity 115
cities of refuge 70
Collège International de Philosophie
  11, 74
communism 67, 85
  Soviet 85
Communist Party 85, 87
community 21–3, 27, 34, 45, 51, 63,
  79
context 44, 62–4

cosmopolitanism 69, 88
Critical Inquiry 4
critical theory 101
criticism 61

'death of the author' *see* author,
  death of
deconstruction 3, 6, 9–13, 47, 50–1,
  55, 70, 80, 86, 90, 114
  as justice 66–7, 70, 90, 107, 116
  as political project 12–13
  defined 12
  in popular culture 1, 130n.2
  misappropriations of 1–2, 10
  misunderstandings of 3, 6, 61
decontextualization 64
democracy 12, 53, 66, 84, 86, 87, 88,
  110, 111
Destruktion (Heidegger) 10, 112
différance 10, 43–5, 60, 76, 94
double-bind 108–109

embodiment 17, 18, 21; *see also*
  incarnation
empire 114
Enlightenment, the 88–9
epistemology 15, 45, 51
equivocity 50
eschatology 67–8, 74, 86–7, 110,
  141n.129
essences 19
ethics 15, 27, 34, 45, 52, 69, 76, 82, 83

ethnocentrism 38, 39, 41, 45, 65, 91
Europe 67, 68, 72–4, 101, 114
event 46, 58, 90–1, 103

faith 83, 84, 143n.158
forgiveness 71–2
Forms (Plato) 18–19, 23, 95; *see also* essences
Frankfurt School 101–2

globalization 91, 114
Groupe de recherché sur l'enseignement de la philosophie (GREPH) 11, 74

hermeneutics 99–102
    of suspicion 100
hospitality 15, 65, 66, 69–71, 76–80

immigration 68–9
incarnation 21, 23–7, 32; *see also* embodiment
institutions 10, 67, 84
interpretive police 63–4
intersubjectivity 34, 40, 71; *see also* community
iterability 60, 64
International Monetary Fund 113, 114
International Parliament of Writers 68–9
Islam 115

Jewishness 14–15
Judaism 15, 78, 115, 134n.50
justice 65–8, 80–84, 86, 87; *see also* law

khôra 95–6

language 14, 16–45, 59
    private 25
    see also arche-writing, writing
law 66–67, 77, 79–80, 80–81
    international 68–69, 79, 113
    see also justice

linguistic turn 16
literary theory 99
literature 18, 19, 45, 46–64, 75
    theory of 18, 46
logocentrism 38–39, 41, 42, 43, 50, 65

margin 49
Marxism 84–8
    spirit of 86
media 5, 131n.19
messianic, the 68, 86, 112–4
messianicity 79, 114
messianism 86, 90, 112
metaphor 54–7, 59
    in the sciences 56
metaphysics 15, 17, 54, 60, 78, 95–6, 103, 142n.147
    of presence 31–2, 38
    see also ontology
monster 2–3, 59, 88
    Derrida as 2, 3, 5, 8–9
Mount Moriah 84

Nazism 7, 85
negative theology 75, 133n.29
New Criterion 4, 6
New York Review of Books 7–8
nihilism 11, 27, 67

objectivity 20–2
    depends on language 24
ontology 17, 45, 51, 142n.147; *see also* metaphysics

perspectivalism 97
pharmakon 10, 25, 94–95
phenomenology 13, 14, 16–45, 46
philosophy 11–12, 18, 75
    analytic 102–3
    constructive 92
    and literature 47–51, 58, 59
    history of 92–4, 117
    professional 57, 58
phonocentrism 31, 33–4, 36, 43

Platonism 19, 23, 32, 33
pluralism 51
politics 51, 77, 79–80, 84
postmodernism 103
power 89
proper name 40–1
psychoanalysis 98, 137n.87,
    140n.119
public 53, 59, 60, 65, 72
Pythagorean theorem 19
    as a phenomenon 20

rationality 88–91
reading 130n.4, 133n.33
reason *see* rationality
reference 13–14, 28, 61–2
regulative idea 111–12
relativism 11, 67, 90
religion 65–6, 75–80, 110–11,
    112–113
    without religion 78, 110, 112,
    115

secret 52–3, 110
secularity 115–116
semiotics 27
signs 27–30
singularity 52
soul 23, 32
    see also embodiment, incarnation
sovereignty 89–90, 113
speech 29, 32, 33, 36–7, 39, 94–5;
    see also language, voice, writing
state, the 79, 89–90

structuralism 10, 38, 40–1
supplement 10, 42

Tel Quel 85
testimony 110
theory 103, 104, 148n.232
'there is nothing outside of the text'
    44–5, 56, 61
third, the 77
time 36, 37–8, 111
Torah 78–9, 112
trace 76
tradition 19, 74
transcendence 27, 30, 33, 38
truth 26, 38, 54–5, 58
Truth and Reconciliation
    Commission (South Africa) 71

undecidability 80–1, 82
university 11–12, 67, 73–4, 88
univocity 50, 52, 55

violence 40–1, 51, 52, 77–8, 105
    original 41, 78
voice 39, 94–95; *see also*
    phonocentrism, speech

writing 16, 17–18, 22, 25, 39, 46,
    94–5; *see also* arche-writing,
    language

xenophobia 31

Yale School 99

Index of Derrida's Works

More sustained expositions of core themes are indicated in **bold**.

Adieu to Emmanuel Levinas **76–80**

Dissemination 57, **94–5**

'Force of Law' **80–2**

Glas 51, 57, **58–9**
Gift of Death 52, **82–4**, 97

Introduction to Husserl's Origin of Geometry **18–27**, 32

Margins of Philosophy **48–9**, **54–6**, 57, 62–3

Limited Inc **63–4**

Of Grammatology 18, 34, **38–45**, 56–67, 76, 106, 116
Of Spirit 100–1, 144n.167
On Cosmopolitanism and Forgiveness **68–72**

The Other Heading 67, **72–3**

Positions 57, 85
Post Card 51, 57, **59–60**, 61, 98

Specters of Marx 67, **85–8**
Speech and Phenomena 18, 20, **27–38**

'Violence and Metaphysics' (*Writing and Difference*) 47, 52, 76, 80